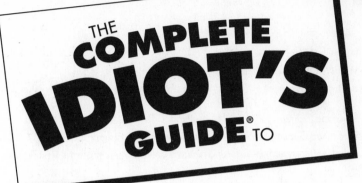

THE

COMPLETE IDIOT'S GUIDE® TO

Amateur Theatricals

by John Kenrick

ALPHA

A member of Penguin Group (USA) Inc.

This book is dedicated to Mary Pinizzotto Marotta and Frank L. Crosio, whose patience and unfailing support made every page possible.

ALPHA BOOKS

Published by the Penguin Group

Penguin Group (USA) Inc., 375 Hudson Street, New York, New York 10014, U.S.A.

Penguin Group (Canada), 10 Alcorn Avenue, Toronto, Ontario, Canada M4V 3B2 (a division of Pearson Penguin Canada Inc.)

Penguin Books Ltd, 80 Strand, London WC2R 0RL, England

Penguin Ireland, 25 St Stephen's Green, Dublin 2, Ireland (a division of Penguin Books Ltd)

Penguin Group (Australia), 250 Camberwell Road, Camberwell, Victoria 3124, Australia (a division of Pearson Australia Group Pty Ltd)

Penguin Books India Pvt Ltd, 11 Community Centre, Panchsheel Park, New Delhi—10 017, India

Penguin Group (NZ), cnr Airborne and Rosedale Roads, Albany, Auckland 1310, New Zealand (a division of Pearson New Zealand Ltd)

Penguin Books (South Africa) (Pty) Ltd, 24 Sturdee Avenue, Rosebank, Johannesburg 2196, South Africa

Penguin Books Ltd, Registered Offices: 80 Strand, London WC2R 0RL, England

Publisher: *Marie Butler-Knight*
Editorial Director: *Mike Sanders*
Managing Editor: *Billy Fields*
Senior Acquisitions Editor: *Paul Dinas*
Development Editor: *Michael Thomas*
Production Editor: *Megan Douglass*
Copy Editor: *Nancy Wagner*

Cartoonist: *Shannon Wheeler*
Book Designers: *Trina Wurst/Kurt Owens*
Cover Designer: *Kurt Owens*
Indexer: *Angie Bess*
Layout: *Brian Massey*

Contents at a Glance

Contents

Foreword

When I was asked to write a foreword to this book, my first reaction was "Why me?" True, I've been taking part in amateur theatricals nearly all my life, but our troupe isn't like any other community theatre—it marches so much to its own drummer that I wasn't sure I'd know what to make of a volume of general advice. How wrong I was! This book is a must read for anyone interested in "putting on a show."

As I read through this thorough, wide-ranging volume, it quickly became clear that there is no such thing as a "typical" amateur theatre effort, and that even the most idiosyncratic troupe stands to gain from the wisdom and experience presented in *The Complete Idiot's Guide to Amateur Theatricals*. The author offers simple, practical, and wonderfully human ways to deal with the run-of-the-mill challenges that confront every amateur presenter, as well as some others you might never expect to face. In addition to a clear-eyed look at the hard facts about financing, publicity, and getting through the recruiting and audition process, Kenrick deals sensitively with issues ranging from handicapped casting to handling backstage ego problems to appreciating and acknowledging the least of your volunteers.

One of this book's most admirable features is its willingness to state the obvious. In hindsight, much of the advice offered will seem like a no-brainer, but as every amateur theatre veteran can tell you, it's amazing how much can get missed or misconstrued in the whirlwind of putting on a show. Having the basics set down in the early planning stages can save no end of headaches and wasted effort later on.

The key to a smooth production is leaving as little as possible to chance, and this book is well worth the price just for the detailed production calendar offered in Chapter 11— a resource no first-time producer should be without. The entire executive team will find tremendous comfort in having this straightforward guide.

In the end, amateur theatre is all about community. I know of no other social activity, no other area of endeavor, professional or otherwise, in which friendships can spring up so quickly and take root so deeply. John Kenrick shows you how to smooth a great many of the bumps on your journey through the theatrical experience and allow you to enjoy the ride.

Louise T. Guinther

Louise T. Guinther is a lifelong member of the Gingerbread Players of Saint Luke's Church, Forest Hills, New York. She began her decades-long association with the company at the age of seven and has since performed nearly every imaginable function, onstage and backstage, from actress to usher to techie to playwright to cheerleader. After many years in the safety of the ensemble, she directed and produced her first show for the company in 2001. She is still getting over the shock.

Introduction

Amateur theatre is not just an American phenomenon. It is one of the most popular art forms in the world today. Every year, thousands of performances take place in churches, school auditoriums, community centers, libraries, banquet halls, parks, storefronts, backyards, living rooms—almost any kind of space in almost every community on Earth.

Limits? Amateurs defy and conquer them. The range of material presented by amateurs covers all forms of theatrical entertainment—Broadway plays and musicals, experimental works, Shakespeare, Kabuki, Gilbert and Sullivan, cabaret, restoration comedy, concerts, grand opera, recent hits, historic pageants, and vintage folktales—you name it, volunteer casts and crews are out there somewhere performing it. Hundreds of thousands take part in amateur stage performances, tapping into reservoirs of commitment, talent, and creativity they never knew they had. Millions more attend these shows, cheering as their relatives, friends, and neighbors shine onstage.

All of this is exciting, and yes, you *can* make it happen right where you live. But don't kid yourself! Putting on a show involves lots of hard work, particularly for those in charge. No book is going to turn putting on a show into an easy, no-sweat process. But by working with the ideas in these pages, you can make your amateur production more manageable and even enjoyable.

Some so-called professionals maintain a rather condescending attitude toward amateur entertainment, which always strikes me as the height of hypocrisy. Practically every showbiz pro got his or her start in some kind of school or community production. That is where people are first "bitten by the bug." While many schools and other organizations have long-standing theatre programs, new people are always entering the field. Some put on a show to build community spirit or raise money for a good cause. Others want to start a new local tradition or perhaps revive one interrupted by budget cuts. Still others find that their job or community position requires them to put some kind of entertainment together.

Whichever of these groups you may fall into, you've come to the right place for help. *The Complete Idiot's Guide to Amateur Theatricals* is designed for first-timers, providing a thorough look at what it will take to make your production a reality. Experienced amateur producers can also find useful ideas in these pages. If you've put on shows with limited success in the past, this book shows you how to take your efforts to the next level. From picking the right project to building a stronger team to creating a socko publicity campaign—it is all outlined here, set out in clear terms by someone who has been involved in both amateur and professional theatre for decades.

And why would someone who has worked on Broadway productions still take part in amateur theatre? Simple—there is nothing like the energy and sheer love of performance found in amateur theatre. Audience expectations are now such that even school and community performances must meet high technical and creative standards. And even if there are professionally trained people lending a hand, these shows are primarily created by and for volunteers, people who do theatre for the love of it. It is my hope that this book helps you connect with your passion and helps you put on a show that you, your team, and your entire community can take pride in.

Where to Find What You Need in This Book

Much like any good stage production, this book follows a clear plan:

Part 1, "Making the Decision—'Reviewing the Situation'," shows you how to assess the facilities and human resources you need to make this theatrical dream become a reality. Who and what do you need, and what will you have to expect from yourself in the process?

Part 2, "Picking Your Project—'The Play's the Thing'," discusses some of the best plays, book musicals, and revues for first-timers, explaining how to make the best selection for your group—and even showing you how to create your own original shows.

Part 3, "Building Your Team—'Side by Side by Side'," takes a detailed look at each of the important positions on your production team. Having the right people in key jobs will save time and effort.

Part 4, "Going into Production—'Putting It Together'," leads you through the actual process of getting your show on its feet. Auditions, rehearsals, and the assembly of tech elements, sets, costumes, and props will make weeks seem like a matter of days … if you're lucky!

Part 5, "Marketing—'Sing Out, Louise!'" explains the important process of letting the world know about your efforts.

Part 6, "Showtime and Afterward—'Another Opening, Another Show'," walks you through those final tense days of rehearsal, the excitement of opening night, and the challenge of moving on to your next project.

Extras

In addition, you'll find the following useful information presented in sidebar format:

Backstage Whispers

These sidebars provide interesting quotes and useful insider tips.

Gremlins

Gremlins sidebars give you helpful warnings designed to help you steer clear of potential problems.

On Stage

Here you'll find stories of real-life amateur and professional theatrical experiences.

def•i•ni•tion

These sidebars contain definitions of theatrical terms you may be unfamiliar with.

Acknowledgments

For photos and more, my thanks to Louise Guinther and the Gingerbread Players of Forest Hills, New York. For photos and more, my thanks to Mr. Curt Ebersole and the music department of Northern Valley Old Tappan High School, New Jersey. Please note that photographer Tim Dingham took all of the NVOT photos used in this book. For permission to use their lighting unit photos, my sincere thanks to the folks at the Altman Lighting Company. For wisdom of all kinds, my deepest thanks to Carolyn Miller of Musical Theatre Works, San Francisco. For solid advice and a willing ear, thanks to Professor Richard Brown, theatre department of the University of Delaware. For unending moral support, thanks to Bruce Levy and Cory Rochester. Thanks to Vincent Kane, Rev. Harold Buckley, and the ongoing army of amateur directors, designers, and performers who have enriched my life over the years. Special thanks and hugs to Hilary Cohen for sifting through the text, proofing the howlers, and serving as head cheerleader.

Special Thanks to the Technical Reviewer

The Complete Idiot's Guide to Amateur Theatricals was reviewed by an expert who double-checked the accuracy of what you'll learn here, to help us ensure that this book gives you everything you need to know about organizing and staging amateur theatricals. Special thanks are extended to Louise T. Guinther.

Trademarks

All terms mentioned in this book that are known to be or are suspected of being trademarks or service marks have been appropriately capitalized. Alpha Books and Penguin Group (USA) Inc. cannot attest to the accuracy of this information. Use of a term in this book should not be regarded as affecting the validity of any trademark or service mark.

Part 1

Making the Decision—"Reviewing the Situation"

Putting on a show is a massive undertaking, so it demands serious forethought. Aside from being a tremendous personal commitment on your part, an amateur production affects the lives of many other people, requiring a communal outpouring of effort and talent. However enthusiastic you may be right now, I guarantee that there will be moments when you are going to wonder what ever possessed you to get involved in this project. So before you set a juggernaut in motion, it's important to have a clear idea of what you are about to do. So let's determine the real reasons why you want to put on a show and consider the people, resources, and options that are available to you.

Chapter 1

Doing a Show: "Let's Start at the Very Beginning"

In This Chapter

- ◆ Reasons people put on amateur shows
- ◆ A definition of amateur theatre
- ◆ The difference between "amateur" and "amateurish"
- ◆ Common disasters versus steps to success
- ◆ Why are *you* doing this show?

So you're going to put on a show. Before congratulating you, I have to ask one question: are you out of your mind? No, of course you're not! But this would be a good time to take a look at what amateur theatre is, consider the steps involved in putting on a successful production, and discuss the reasons people choose to get involved in amateur theatre. Some of those reasons are a lot better than others.

How Did You Get Into This?

Amateur productions are of many different kinds, ranging from *cabarets* and concerts to fully staged plays and musicals, and people put them together

def•i•ni•tion

Cabaret is a versatile form of entertainment that usually involves simple staging and a fluid combination of songs and/or comedy skits. Connective dialogue and/ or narration are optional.

for all kinds of reasons. Through my website (www. Musicals101.com), I often get messages from people in the midst of their first amateur production, as well as others sharing memories of past glories. Here are some favorites from the last 10 years:

◆ "My first show? We wanted to raise some money for the church, and I couldn't face the thought of running another bake sale, so I told the committee I would put together some kind of a show. Before I knew it, we were doing a full cast production of *Annie*. At least you can't say I'm afraid of taking on a challenge."

◆ "There were four teachers in our department, and each of us was expected to stage one play per semester. After appearing in so many shows as a student, I figured directing would be easy. I learned the hard way."

◆ "The boss is always saying we need to improve employee morale, so I suggested we put on a show as part of the annual holiday party. She said she loved the idea and that I should put together a cast and crew as soon as possible. I had no idea I was volunteering!"

◆ "We thought our songs were pretty good, but how are young songwriters supposed to get noticed? You can't just send your stuff to producers who've never heard of you, and there's no Tin Pan Alley anymore. We figured the one way to get our stuff heard was to put it on stage ourselves."

◆ "My commanding officer called me into his office and informed me that I was in charge of putting on shows that could both play in camp and travel right to the front. I was a trained musician, but I had no clue how to put on shows. We wound up performing off the back of a truck, and the men cheered the same as they would for Bob Hope."

◆ "I was fresh out of college. Landing a job at this school was a dream come true, but putting on a musical turned out to be one part of the job my music ed program had not prepared me for."

◆ "My girlfriend was directing for a community theatre and begged me to be her producer. I had no experience with this kind of thing, but she said it would be a snap. The amazing thing is that I still wound up marrying her and that we're still doing shows together."

Was putting on this show your idea, or was it something you were hornswoggled into? Either way, welcome to the insane, exhausting, and thrilling world of amateur theatre. You are becoming part of a tradition that stretches back thousands of years.

What Is Amateur Theatre?

Amateur theatre is any kind of theatrical performance staged by volunteers. And I want to take a few moments to defend a noble yet much maligned word. Thanks to years of misuse, many people today think *amateur* is some kind of an insult. All too often it is used to describe someone who is inexperienced or inept, a crass beginner.

def•i•ni•tion

The word **amateur** derives from the French–Latin term *amator*, which literally translates as "a lover" or "one who acts out of love."

An amateur does something for the love of it rather than for financial gain. This is a perfect description for those who pour countless hours and abundant talent into school and community theatre. We do it because we love it. Doing something purely for financial gain is a job. Doing something you love to do is the whole point of human existence. That isn't something to be ashamed of; it's something to celebrate!

In the dictionary, you'll find that *amateur* has an alternate definition: "one who dabbles." How could one word be saddled with such contradictory meanings? A "dabbler" and "one who does something for the love of it" are two very different creatures. By its very nature, amateur theatre requires dedication and perseverance—hardly the qualities of a dilettante.

Amateurs invented theatre. When the ancient Greeks turned choral odes into the first dramas in the fourth century B.C.E., the writers and actors were almost certainly unpaid volunteers. Centuries later, the first plays performed on Broadway in the early 1700s were staged by amateur groups. Today, amateurs present the overwhelming majority of dramatic performances in the United States and worldwide. Almost every professional in the performing arts got his or her first taste of show business through school or community productions.

Amateur Does Not Mean "Amateurish"

Many have confused the word *amateur* with *amateurish*—a spinoff of the original term that denotes "efforts that are not up to professional standards." That is not the same meaning! A professional is someone who does something for pay, but professionalism is an attitude—the ability to hold oneself and one's work to a high standard. Amateurs have delivered some of the most polished, professional-quality stage work I have ever seen. Conversely, some of the most amateurish efforts I have witnessed onstage were the work of paid professionals.

Backstage Whispers

Awaiting the start of a community theatre production, a woman of advanced years said to a companion, "I never know what to expect at these neighborhood shows. There are few things more unreliable than the efforts of inspired amateurs."

Gremlins

It is ridiculous to suggest professionals are inherently superior to amateurs. Remember, the *Titanic* was built by professionals; the Ark was built by amateurs.

Whenever family, friends, or neighbors give you any guff about being an amateur, remind them that our world relies on amateurs for its daily existence. Volunteer firemen, auxiliary police, Olympic athletes, hospital candy stripers, Scout troop leaders, campaign staffers, church choristers, and Little League coaches all do what they do for the love of it. Do these people somehow deserve less respect because they receive no pay for their efforts? And I hate to imagine where we would be without the countless individuals and community organizations that raise money for crucial causes.

Now, I'm not belittling professionals in any field, least of all in the theatre. But in the early twenty-first century, professional theatre is limited to a small number of communities. Amateurs keep theatre, music, and dance alive and thriving in almost every community on Earth, including towns and neighborhoods where professional theatre is unknown.

The time has long since come for those who look down on amateur theatre to get over themselves. We're talking about professional theatre's kissing cousin; shame on those who treat it like a poor relative! Amateur productions generate millions of dollars in rights income and entertain tens of millions of people every year. *Fiddler on the Roof* managed an impressive 3,242 performances during its original run on Broadway, but it has racked up hundreds of thousands more on amateur stages. I am proud of the work I've done in amateur theatre, and I applaud anyone who has the passion and the guts to do a show for the love of it.

When *Amateurs* Are "Amateurish"

Much as I hate to admit it, the negative connotations of *amateur* have been reinforced on too many occasions by unsuccessful amateur productions. We've all been to these sad fiascos, squirming in our seats and wondering when some merciful hand will close the curtain and let us leave. You find yourself wondering how so many well-intentioned people could put on such a terrible show. Well, the reasons are usually one or more of the following:

♦ Lack of common focus: the actors had one agenda; the designers had another; and the director a third.

♦ Somebody didn't say "no": there are times when designers, performers, and even directors have to be reined in.

♦ Too much or too little: if a hundred people audition when there are only five roles (or vice versa), you need a different show.

♦ The wrong material: if an amateur group in your area has just done *Les Misér-ables*, pick another show.

♦ The wrong staff: it is madness to do *West Side Story* if you don't have an experienced choreographer and a troupe of capable dancers in your likely talent pool.

♦ Messy finances: even in amateur theatre, sloppy accounting practices can sink a project.

♦ TMS (too much set): this is the most common disease ruining amateur performances today, followed closely by TML (too much lighting), TMC (too many costumes), and their costly cousin, TMSE (too much sound equipment).

♦ Wasted rehearsals: if you have people on hand and don't use them, you are wasting their time … and your own.

♦ Small audiences: if people don't know about your show, they won't come.

♦ Wasted success: "They had a hit a few years ago, but never followed up on it. What a shame."

On Stage

Lyricist-librettist Alan Jay Lerner (co-creator of *My Fair Lady* and *Camelot*) once asked veteran director-playwright Moss Hart if there was a secret to putting on a hit. Hart responded, "Each time I had a success, it was for a different reason. Each time I failed, it was for the same reason. I said yes when I meant no." Abiding by this advice will save you countless hours of frustration—in theatre, and in life!

First-time directors and producers are among the most likely perpetrators of these avoidable misdemeanors. However, you are another story! By working with the information in this book, you can sidestep some potential pitfalls and give your troupe and the public a theatrical experience worth savoring.

The Key Steps to Putting On a Successful Show

While there are many elements involved in any successful production, I have identified 11 basic steps that can set an amateur show on the road to applause and box-office profits:

1. Define your motivations and goals (Chapter 1).

2. Assess what you have (Chapters 2 and 3).

3. Assess what you don't have (Chapters 2 and 3).

4. Pick the right project (Chapters 4 and 5).

5. Create a budget and stick to it (Chapter 6).

6. Build a great production team (Chapters 7–10).

7. Create a workable production timetable (Chapter 11).

8. Make every audition and rehearsal count (Chapters 12–15).

9. Coordinate every element of your production (Chapters 16–20).

10. Get the word out (Chapters 21–23).

11. When it's over, start planning the next one (Chapter 26).

The first two steps are so important that I'll spend the rest of this chapter discussing them and then focus on the other steps in following chapters.

Defining Your Motivations and Goals

Have you asked yourself why you want to put on a show? I'm not talking about the surface reasons, like raising money or because it's a nice thing to do. Dig deeper. Why are you *really* doing this? Knowing the answer will help keep you focused in the weeks and months ahead. Not all reasons for putting on a show are created equal. Some are far better than others, and some are far worse.

The Worst Reasons

Lousy reasons for putting on a show would include the following:

◆ To fulfill a longtime showbiz fantasy

◆ To improve your standing in the community

◆ To prove you can be a hero

Because these reasons can pop into one's mind separately or all at once, let's consider each in brief detail.

Fulfilling a Showbiz Fantasy

Do you see yourself as the glamorous neighborhood impresario, presenting acclaimed hits, discovering fresh talent, and telling the chorus girl going on in place of your injured lead that she's "got to come back a star"? The theatre is nothing like that, especially at the amateur level. If you want to be the next Florenz Ziegfeld, go to Broadway and learn how to swim with the sharks. Amateur theatre is probably not the place for you.

Improving Your Standing in the Community

In amateur theatre, there are two things one should never expect—personal financial gain and widespread recognition. If you want your fellow citizens to look up to you and put your statue on a pedestal, get into politics or start a new religion. Odds are that amateur theatre is going to be a waste of your time.

Proving What Kind of a Hero You Can Be

Audiences smile when Peter Pan exclaims, "Oh, the wonderfulness of me!" but most people loathe anyone who exhibits that attitude in real life. As a producer or director, it's your job to shine the spotlight on others. No matter how completely you devote yourself to putting on a show, others will take most of the bows. If you want to be a star, appear in someone else's show. If you want to be a hero, become a volunteer fireman.

A Final Warning

As you contemplate putting on your first amateur show, I want you to appreciate just how gargantuan a task you're taking on. For the next few months, private time will fade away. Little things like reading, cooking, watching your favorite game, and spending time with loved ones will have to be put on hold. Whatever hobbies you have, kiss 'em good-bye for the duration. You will have to put your heart and soul into this project. Time and again you will have to compromise or sidetrack all your other life commitments.

Compared with you, professional producers and directors have it easy. Just like them, you are going to have to prove yourself simultaneously as an organizer, wheeler-dealer, inspirational speaker, psychologist, and arbiter of taste. However, in a professional production, the show is everyone's principal job. In amateur theatre, everyone in the company is trying to balance the needs of the show against the demands of work, classes, family—and sometimes (heaven help them) all three at once.

Some optimists will tell you that I'm overstating my case and that putting together a show is no big deal. As one person wrote in to my website: "It's true that putting on a show is tough, but I see no point in telling the truth if it is going to discourage people." Well, I couldn't disagree more. I believe certain people *should* be discouraged from putting on a show. Not everyone is up to this challenge! It requires hard work, and tons of it. Those high up on the production totem pole usually find the bulk of that hard work landing in their laps.

Spare yourself and others from an ill-considered decision. Once you launch this project, there will be no easy or graceful way to back out of it. If you're unsure about your commitment to putting on a show, don't do it.

On the other hand, if you think you can handle it, read on.

The Best Reasons

The world of amateur theatre has already had more than its share of fantasizers, do-gooders, and self-appointed heroes. There are far better reasons to put on a show:

Backstage Whispers

When songwriter Cole Porter was asked what motivated him to begin work on a new musical, his answer was simple: "A signed check."

- ◆ Because your job is on the line
- ◆ To teach
- ◆ To create joy
- ◆ To change lives
- ◆ To change your community
- ◆ Because something in you demands it

If only one or two of these are motivating you, you're in good shape. But take a few minutes to consider all of them, for they can provide you with useful motivation when the going gets rough.

Because Your Job Is on the Line

Think this one landed on the wrong list? Think again! Doing a show because your job requires it may not be the happiest reason, but it certainly is a valid one. I've known teachers, GIs, and office workers who landed in this predicament without the slightest clue as to what they should do next. If this describes your situation, take heart: this book is designed with you in mind.

To Teach

Every amateur theatre production is an adventure, regardless of the age group involved. To those experiencing theatre for the first time, it will all be new, and it is a special privilege to introduce such people to the techniques and traditions of the stage. For those who have done this sort of thing before, there will still be things to learn—new roles, new technical knowledge, and fresh problems to solve.

Of course, every teacher learns a great deal from the teaching process. Aside from the myriad tasks you must handle, you will learn the true meaning of teamwork. Theatre is a collaborative art form in which even the tiniest contribution plays a vital role. The kid running the *follow spot* is just as important as the stars basking in its glow. You will find yourself teaching and learning this lesson over and over again.

def•i•ni•tion

A **follow spot** is a large, high-powered lighting unit that can be directed (manually or electronically) to follow a performer onstage.

Schools have long recognized the academic value of putting on shows, but budget problems have forced an appalling number of school systems to cut or gut their music and theatre programs. This is tragic because the annual school play is far more than just a quaint tradition! It is a culturally enriching event that helps to link schools with families and the community at large. Theatre exposes children to other places, eras, and mind-sets. Talking about Victorian society is just another dull history lesson, but working on a production of *Oliver* can bring distant history to life. You can explain Nazi oppression till you're blue in the face, but performing *The Sound of Music* makes the nightmare of fascism tangible.

If you are affiliated with a school that has dropped the tradition of an annual play or musical, start making some noise. When the powers that be say there is no money for such a project, don't let that stop you. I discuss alternate sources of funding (and other financial concerns) in Chapter 6. If money is needed, there are all sorts of ways to find it. Amateur theatre belongs in every school, from kindergarten right up to the university level.

To Create Joy

No one is in amateur theatre for the money. Even those production experts who get paid earn far less than they would doing professional projects. Ultimately, people take time out of their busy lives to put on a show because they love the joy amateur theatre generates.

Some of that joy is generated in rehearsals, in the act of bringing together the many elements that make a show tick. Some of it comes from performances, when that crucial collaborator called the "audience" joins the mix. Some of it comes in the months and years that follow as people relish and take pride in the memory of a production. Few things you are part of will be remembered so lovingly or for so long. I have few clear memories of the classes I sat through in high school and college, but I recall every school show I worked on in vivid detail.

Creating joy is not limited to lighthearted entertainments. The heaviest of dramas can shed real light on human experience, and that light is what your audiences will delight in. A well-crafted production of *Death of a Salesman* or *Romeo and Juliet* generates joy as surely as any comedy or musical.

To Change Lives

Yes, amateur theatre changes lives. By the time a production ends, no one involved in it is the same person he or she was at the start. Aside from the tangibles that are learned, an intangible but undeniable growth comes from being part of a shared effort. Unlike competitive sports in which the shared effort ends with one team winning and another losing, everyone who is part of an amateur show is on a winning team. Getting a show on its feet and performing it for an audience is a victory, and we could all use more victories in our lives.

Almost everyone involved in an amateur production winds up redefining his personal boundaries and limitations. Even performers with the smallest of roles and crewmembers who are never seen onstage share in a deep and satisfying sense of accomplishment. And accomplishment breeds confidence! After facing and taming an audience, things like college applications, job interviews, and office presentations seem far less daunting.

To Change Your Community

The presence of live theatre can also redefine organizations, schools, neighborhoods, and even whole towns. Putting on a show can do as much for community spirit as a winning sports team. When audiences get the chance to applaud the accomplishments of family, friends, neighbors, classmates, and co-workers, a production's success becomes the entire community's success.

Don't just take my word on this. In 2002, The Performing Arts Research Coalition commissioned a study on the value of the performing arts in 10 American communities, including Austin, Boston, Minneapolis–St. Paul, Pittsburgh, and Seattle. It found that those who attended performing arts events believed that these performances enriched them as individuals. Furthermore,

> They believed strongly that the arts improve the quality of life and are a source of community pride, promote understanding of other people and different ways of life, help preserve and share cultural heritage, provide opportunities to socialize, and contribute to lifelong learning in adults. Above all, they believed that the arts contribute to the education and development of children.

So much for the rational reasons people have for putting on amateur productions. There is another reason, one that has nothing whatsoever to do with rational thought. In my opinion, it is the only reason that really matters ….

Because Something in You Demands It

Producing and directing an amateur show requires passion. If the best reason you can come up with for putting on a show is that it's part of your job and you have to do it, by all means go ahead. For many people, that is reason enough to do darn near anything. But if you're doing this voluntarily, you had better have a much deeper motivation. In my opinion, the only way you will be able to get through this mammoth task is if something in you demands it. You will need a fire within that spurs you on and sparks the involvement of others.

I'm talking about commitment here. Although rational reasons may be behind a commitment, the most powerful commitments reach down to the irrational level. If you know in the pit of your gut that you've just got to put on this show, then everything else will somehow fall into place.

I mentioned earlier that almost everyone involved in an amateur production winds up redefining personal boundaries. Well, that includes you. Putting on a show will force you to smash the barriers of your comfort zone and do things you've never done. Taking risks can be scary, but you may be amazed at what you can accomplish. Just don't waste time by waiting around for someone else to get the ball rolling. Mahatma Ghandi said, "Be the change you want to see in the world." As long as you have the good sense to stick within ethical and legal boundaries, you will find yourself with much to be proud of.

If you have gotten through all the arguments and warnings in this chapter and still want to put on a show, then I can finally say congratulations! I look on my work in amateur theatre as one of the most rewarding investments I have ever made. If you care enough to get involved, I am willing to bet that you will soon feel the same way.

From here on in, my goal is to help you build the best show you can. With all the hard work that lies ahead, don't forget to relish the many wonderful things that happen along the way, too.

The Least You Need to Know

- Amateurs invented theatre and have kept it alive and thriving for more than 2,000 years.

- An amateur does something for the love of it.

- There is no reason why amateurs should be "amateurish."

- Professionalism is defined by an attitude, not a paycheck.

- By putting on a show, you can teach, create joy, and enrich the lives of individuals and communities.

- The best reason for putting on a show is because your inner passion demands it.

People Power: "Getting to Know You"

In This Chapter

- ◆ Know your resources before you pick a project
- ◆ Look at the potential cast, crew, and creative people available to you
- ◆ Consider the administrative support you will need
- ◆ Take a detailed look at your talent and degree of commitment to the project
- ◆ Look at a theatre team as a family

Every situation has its good and bad points. By taking stock of what resources you have and don't have, you will be in a much better position to know what sort of show you can put on effectively. Begin by considering the people who will bring your vision to life, including your greatest human asset—yourself. Know what you bring to the process and what you will need others to bring.

Taking Stock

No matter how compassionate your nature, chances are you wouldn't feel much sympathy for a woman who packs her favorite ski sweaters for a trip to St. Thomas and even less for the young father of four who tries to convince his wife that a sporty two-seat roadster would make the perfect family car. When people let unimportant personal preferences blind them to obvious needs, they show a lack of common sense. From a distance, such decisions may seem comical, but when you are involved, they do not seem so funny.

Don't let personal preferences trick you into thinking that any group can perform any play. Here is an actual example of the kind of e-mails I get on an almost-weekly basis:

> We've just secured the rights to *West Side Story*, my all-time favorite musical. This is our school's first show in years, and my first time as a director. Could you give me a list of what this show requires—a cast breakdown, tech requirements, etc.?

Talk about putting the cart before the horse! It is madness to pick a show and *then* try to figure out if you have the resources to stage it. That's why we're going to spend the next two chapters assessing the people and facilities at your disposal.

When answering the questions posed in this chapter, take the time to write out your answers, and be absolutely fearless! Honesty now will strengthen every aspect of your production in the months to come. If what you lack seems to outweigh what you have, don't worry. There is a show to fit every need, and the only way to find the right one for your group is to have a clear picture of your needs. With a clear understanding of who and what you will be working with, as well as your personal strengths and weaknesses, you will be ready to pick the right material. Let's start by looking at the people power available to you.

Planning Production Staff: Basic Questions

A theatrical production is primarily about people. The talent and enthusiasm you bring to this project won't amount to much if no one else is on hand to make your show a reality. Even a small show with four or five performers onstage can require dozens of volunteers behind the scenes.

Begin with some preliminary questions:

- ◆ How many people can I realistically expect to audition for this show?
- ◆ What age groups and genders are in my probable talent pool?
- ◆ Do these performers have any degree of acting, musical, or dance experience?
- ◆ What design and technical talent is at my disposal? Any experience?
- ◆ How many people can I recruit for technical crews?
- ◆ If I'm doing a musical, do I have a musical director on hand?
- ◆ Can I recruit sufficient support staff?
- ◆ What kind of administrative talent can I rely on?
- ◆ Who will handle our printing needs?

If your answer to any of these questions is "I don't know," congratulations! You've passed the honesty test! Nobody really knows in advance how many people will want to get involved in an amateur production. You have to ask.

Putting Out a Feeler

If your school or organization has an established tradition of putting on shows, gathering a cast and crew should be fairly easy, but it can be a real challenge if you're starting from scratch. Although some people in your immediate circle may express interest in being part of a production, at some point you will have to reach out and see who else is willing to get involved. If your production is open to a relatively small group (a class, an office, etc.), a simple verbal poll or show of hands will give you an idea of how many people are interested.

To reach larger groups (an entire school or congregation, the general public, etc.), your best bet is to put out a *feeler* stating your plans and asking interested people to contact you. This can take the form of an oral announcement, a posted or published notice, a mailing—whatever best fits your situation. You have to give people an easy way to respond, such as speaking to you directly or sending an e-mail.

def•i•ni•tion

A **feeler** is a mailing, posting, or verbal announcement that literally tries to "feel out" any interest in the community, asking people who want to be part of your project to either contact you or attend a preliminary meeting.

Instead of giving out your private e-address, have your organization set up a web mailbox—or set up a separate e-address at a free service like yahoo.com or hotmail.com.

A mail feeler can be effort-intensive. You will have to obtain or assemble an address list (from local schools, community groups, etc.), create and collate the mailing, and pay for photocopying and postage. Be sure to include a return post card where respondents can list their name and contact information and check off areas of interest (acting, stage crew, publicity, etc.).

If you get a disappointing response to a feeler, you may have to drum up greater interest in this project or even consider setting it aside for a while. An encouraging response means it's time to call a preliminary meeting. Pick a time and place that will be convenient for as many people as possible. At the meeting, hold off discussing any show titles or other specific plans. Have forms asking for names, contact information, and what sorts of production jobs people are interested in.

> **Backstage Whispers**
>
> "I began by obtaining a mailing list and sending out a feeler, asking if people would be interested in a tuition-based theatre program for students in grades 2–12. We received a great response, and 4 months later we opened *Oliver* with a company of 80!"
>
> —Carolyn Miller of San Francisco's Musical Theatre Works

Potential Cast and Crew

After holding the preliminary meeting, look over your resulting lists and see what kind of volunteers you will be working with. What you see can help you pick the best show for your group to do. Pay special attention to the following issues:

- Overall numbers
- Level of experience
- Working with children
- Working with teens
- Working with adults
- All-male or all-female casts
- Race
- The potential for casting the physically challenged

Let's look at each of these concerns in detail.

Overall Numbers

The size of your talent pool is a key factor in planning a show. If only a dozen or so people express interest, you won't be able to put on a full-scale staging of *Les Misérables*. Conversely, when dozens sign up, staging a two-character drama like *Love Letters* would be a waste.

Level of Experience

You must also consider experience (or lack of it). If a large part of your talent pool has worked on shows before, they will have a better idea of what to expect. Nontheatrical experience also counts. For example, church choristers will have an easier time learning harmonies than people who have never looked at sheet music before, and they are well acquainted with the pressures of performing in public. Some shows require performers with special qualifications. It takes dance training to do justice to *A Chorus Line* or *Contact*, and the charms of *Amahl and the Night Visitors* will fade unless a cast has strong vocal skills. As I've mentioned before, absolute lack of experience is not necessarily a problem, especially for children and teens. Just be sure you keep their level of inexperience (and yours) in mind when planning your show.

Working with Children

Most young children are natural performers who love to be the center of approving attention, and most audiences dote on them. No wonder adult actors often warn, "Never share the stage with children or animals." When casting children, keep in mind that their youthful charm will do a lot to make up for any inexperience. As long as the little ones know where and when to come onstage, remember their lines, and deliver them clearly, they will steal most any scene they're in.

While performing is intuitive, acting is an abstract art, requiring the ability to step believably into a character's thoughts and emotions. Few children have the emotional or artistic resources required to do this. That's why it is unwise to cast kids age 12 or younger in roles written for adults. Most children can only portray adults from a child's point of view, offering parodies of adult behavior. This works well in plays written for juvenile performers but rarely with shows written for Broadway. The exceptions would be broad, family-friendly farces like *Once Upon a Mattress* or *Bye, Bye Birdie*.

Working with Teens

Junior high school productions of Broadway plays and musicals can work well, but you must choose them with discretion. Twelve-year-olds tend to shine in lighthearted material. Heavier emotions can seem strained or, worse yet, unintentionally funny.

High school involves a different set of guidelines. By age 16, most amateur actors can be expected to portray adult emotions, so most Broadway scripts are within their artistic range. When working with teens, it helps to remember what it felt like to be one. *A Chorus Line* describes their dilemma well: "Too young to take over, too old to ignore." Add the natural self-obsession of adolescence, and you have a passionate, volatile mix. In my experience, the best way to handle teens is by treating them as you would adults. Just try to remember that they aren't quite adults yet.

Working with Adults

Some directors and producers will tell you that actors of any age aren't quite adults yet. In a sense, this is true. Trained actors must learn how to strip away the layers of pretension that most adults protect themselves with. Although many amateurs are only beginning this process, even at the early stages they are often more vulnerable, more emotional, more insecure, more instinctive—in short, more childlike than the rest of us.

A good director or producer understands this and treats experienced actors with an attitude I have heard referred to as "informed respect." It takes nerve for anyone to get up onstage, and such courage deserves admiration. At the same time, an actor's insecurities can manifest in maddening ways. A well-balanced blend of encouragement, compassion, and discipline usually gets good results.

Of course, it can be a different story when dealing with inexperienced performers. Some will overact; others may be so subdued that they won't be audible beyond the first row of seats. (This understated, film-inspired approach is sometimes referred to as "I'm Ready for My Close-Up Syndrome.") Directors must be flexible with amateur actors, encouraging them to adjust their approach to a particular role, or even to acting in general. Aside from the basic suggestions in Chapters 13, 14, and 15, there are a number of good books on directing—see Appendix B for several suggested titles.

All-Male or All-Female Casts

A number of plays and musicals are designed for all-male or all-female casts, and there is a long-standing tradition of such casts doing Shakespeare or Gilbert and Sullivan.

However, teenage actors (and a surprising number of parents) can have problems with gender-blind casting, and some licensing firms discourage unisex casting, even at the amateur level. That is why many unisex institutions open up their casting to allow cast members of the opposite gender. My all-male high school had no trouble attracting girls from the local community to take part in stage productions.

Race

It's sad that race should still be a casting issue. Unless your play is one in which race is a factor in the plot (*Show Boat*, *Raisin in the Sun*, *Dreamgirls*), all actors deserve equal access to all roles. Professional theatre, television, and film have long since proven that skin color and ethnic origin have nothing to do with an actor's ability. Make your decisions accordingly. If racially mixed casting is likely to cause problems in your community, consider moving.

Casting the Physically Challenged

The physically challenged are part of the real world, so they should be part of your stage world, too. So-called "disabilities" are not barriers to participation in theatrical productions. Opening the stage to the physically challenged gives audiences access to talented performers who are often overlooked.

You can design any production to include the use of wheelchairs, braces, hearing aids, and more. Sure, it takes some effort, but it is well worth it. Think the deaf can't do musicals? When the National Theatre for the Deaf staged *Big River* with a creative mix of signing and singing, the results were so exhilarating that the production moved to Broadway, winning rave reviews and garnering several awards.

> **On Stage**
>
> The Lighthouse is an organization that serves the visually impaired. They have presented acclaimed stage productions with blind amateur actors for decades, building sets that can be navigated by touch.

If you aren't sure how to make rehearsals and performances accessible, there's no need to call in a pricey consultant. Talk to the performers in question, and let them tell you what they need. By casting the physically challenged, you won't just brighten the lives of disabled performers—you'll give audiences a richer, more enlightening experience.

Potential Production Staff and Crews

Take a look at the staff and crew positions outlined in Chapters 8 and 9. You will need to fill most, if not all of these jobs, finding qualified people to create sets, costumes, lighting, and sound. Be prepared to ask around and do some active recruiting. If you cannot find qualified people for every design position, decide who and what you can do without. A production without sets is feasible, but if you then deduct costumes, you may wind up with a bland stage picture. The only way to do without lighting is to stage a daytime performance outdoors. Whatever you do, be realistic in deciding how to apportion responsibilities. As I discuss in Part 3 of this book, you don't want to make the mistake of concentrating too many jobs on any individual, yourself included.

Gremlins

Be very careful about which jobs you define as non-essential. For example, if you don't have someone overseeing financial issues, you better have no bills to pay or ticket sales to keep track of!

Your Best Resource

You are always your own best resource. By putting on a show, you become a central resource to everyone else involved in the production. They will depend on you for leadership, inspiration, guidance, and strength. So it's crucial that you take a frank personal inventory before launching your production.

As with the nine questions that opened this chapter, you must be completely honest while answering the following lists. Have a friend go through the lists with you, someone who will be prepared to holler if you try to deceive yourself. Remember, there are no right or wrong answers. So long as you're honest, the results will help you plan a more effective production.

My Talents

Ask yourself these questions:

1. What experience do I have with theatrical production, if any?

2. What life talents do I bring to this process?

3. Am I more business-minded or creative/artistic? An organizer or a dreamer?

4. Do I get along well with other people?

5. Do I handle leadership positions well?

Although experience is not required, it's certainly useful. Even if your stage resumé is limited to appearances in a few school plays, that counts. It means you have some familiarity with the kind of environment you're looking to create.

The remaining questions involve your life talents, the core abilities you bring to any task. You may have little or no stage talent. Most professional producers have none, but they tend to be excellent organizers who know how to lead a team to a common goal. While many directors have been performers at some point, their success as directors is based on a strong creative sense and the ability to inspire and motivate.

By identifying your talents, you conversely define your weak points. Surround yourself with people whose abilities complement yours. If you are primarily business-minded, you may prefer serving as producer and finding someone else to be your director. On the other hand, if the creative aspects of production excite you most, find a producer to handle the business details. If you are a so-so organizer, you will need a strong stage manager to help keep you and your production on track.

My Time

Everyone today leads busy lives, and you are no exception. Now is the time to decide if you can afford to invest the time an amateur production requires. Ask yourself these questions:

1. Can I make time in my life for this project?
2. What other life commitments do I have?
3. How will putting on a show affect my job and my personal life?

Rehearsals will take up three to four hours a day on weekdays, and far more on weekends. Add in the meetings, side trips, errands, and emergencies any production involves, and you're facing the equivalent of taking on a second job. Even if you're getting a stipend for working on this show, trust me—no amount of money will fully compensate you for the number of hours involved.

All your other commitments will have to take a backseat for weeks, probably months. It's tough enough to put aside worthwhile community causes, but dealing with your job can be tougher. You will inevitably find yourself fielding production-related phone calls at work and investing a lot of mental energy in the show. Even the most supportive employer is not going to appreciate an amateur show having an adverse effect on your job performance. An advance discussion will give you some idea of your boss's attitude and expectations regarding your participation in such a project.

Your loved ones are an even bigger issue. Friends, parents, spouses, significant others, and children can place tremendous demands on your time. You need these people to support your involvement in a show. Can they handle your switching priorities for a prolonged period of time? Talk things over with them before making a commitment.

My Health and Temperament

Putting on a show is physically and emotionally demanding. You have to be healthy and stable to pull it off. Ask yourself these questions:

1. How is my overall health?

2. What tasks/situations tend to cause stress for me?

3. Do I work well with other people?

4. What are the best things people say about my personality? And the worst?

5. Do I have a temper? What gets my goat?

6. How do I respond to stress? How about massive stress?

7. How do I handle crises?

8. Do I know my physical and emotional limits?

If you have any serious or chronic medical condition, factor it into your decision to do a show. In particular, consider any time-consuming therapies or fatiguing medications that could affect your efforts.

People with hot tempers should stay away from amateur theatre, but they seem to be forever attracted to it. Drama belongs on the stage, not behind the scenes. That said, I guarantee there will be all sorts of offstage drama along the road to opening night. Plans will run amuck, personalities and schedules will clash, and Murphy's Law will kick in when you least expect it. At such times, no one would blame even the gentlest souls for howling with frustration. However, if you are the type who sees dilemmas as energizing challenges, welcome to the theatre! If unexpected problems tend to devastate you, please, please invest your time in less-stressful activities like macramé.

No matter how well adjusted you are, there are probably certain types of personalities and situations that tick you off. By recognizing your personal limits, you can avoid suffering a burnout that could leave your production team stumbling along toward opening night without you.

Commitment: Don't Kid Yourself

You must be clear about your level of personal commitment to this project. Of all the questions you have to ask yourself, none are more important than these:

1. Am I good at commitments?

2. Do I *have* to do this show?

It is not enough for a show to be something you *want* to do—it must be something you *have* to do. That means a total commitment. Nothing less will see you through. Do you get all fired up about projects, only to see your enthusiasm fade once the going gets tough? If so, let this cup pass.

You'll notice I haven't discussed what kind of commitment other people will make. At this stage, your commitment is the only one that matters because it will fuel everyone else's. Human beings instinctively want to please others, to tell stories and share pleasure—in short, to entertain. When you announce your plans to do a show, your passion will spark the passion of others, and nothing short of successful perform- ances will quench those passions. Along the way, there will be times when you will have to nudge those who fall short on their commitments and perhaps even pick up after them.

With all that in mind, ask yourself, do I *have* to do this show? If something in you says "yes," go for it.

Backstage Whispers

The musical *1776* quotes something John Adams actually wrote in a letter to his wife, Abigail: "There are only two creatures of value on the face of this earth: those with a commit- ment, and those who require the commitment of others."

A Kind of Family

Producing or directing a play means building a kind of family. While a workplace depends on monetary gain to provide motivation, volunteer efforts depend on people caring enough to take part. This is particularly true of amateur theatre where depict- ing and eliciting human emotions is the whole point of the project.

On Stage

Carolyn Miller of San Francisco's Musical Theatre Works explains the relationship between directors and cast members this way: "The students' self-discovery of the inner workings of a character is far more valuable than just acting the role, and it produces a much better, more believable, production. Our work with the students is based on an established trust and respect. With that trust and respect comes the ability to give direc- tion to a student, and they feel secure in taking the risk to try something new. Based on this trust and respect between student and director, the student learns that there is always a purpose in the director's request, and that it's going to be all right to try it. It's all part of the journey."

People working on a show share a powerful experience. Every performer takes a risk by getting up in front of an audience, and their success involves more than personal talent—it also depends on the efforts of the creative team and crews. The producer and director oversee and coordinate all these efforts, building an environment in which trust can grow. In effect, they become the heads of a temporary family, providing encouragement and admonishment as needed, balancing compassion with practicality.

The producer and director must make decisions based on the best interests of the production, even when those decisions are unpopular. Discipline, "tough love," demanding better efforts—all are required to make a theatrical family work. If you are up to this peculiar type of parenthood, the personal rewards are extraordinary. Former students tell me that the shows I did with them a decade or a quarter century ago changed their lives. I understand how they feel. Every amateur show I have ever worked on changed my life, too.

The Least You Need to Know

- Before deciding to put on a show, evaluate the people at your disposal.
- Different age groups have different needs, but all actors must be treated with a blend of compassion, respect, and discipline.
- Take a frank look at your personal assets.
- The decision to put on a show is also a commitment to build a temporary family—not something to be entered into lightly!

Chapter 3

Facilities: "What've We Got?"

In This Chapter

- ◆ Selecting the right rehearsal and performance space
- ◆ Anticipating your likely audience
- ◆ Considering the various options for setting up a performance space
- ◆ Dealing with insurance issues
- ◆ Evaluating lighting and sound equipment
- ◆ Looking on other performing groups as allies

A producer and director must know what facilities are available to him and how to make the most of them. The good news is that there is material appropriate for almost every facility. Think you have nothing to work with? Amazing things have been done with such "nothings." The Light Opera of Manhattan started its 20-plus-year existence with a performance in a living room, and I have seen audiences enchanted by children performing in school cafeterias beneath fluorescent lights. My hope is that this chapter will help you to identify some of the unexpected assets at your disposal.

Key Questions: Facilities, Equipment, and Other Resources

As in Chapter 2, you must answer the following questions with absolute honesty. Only clear, frank answers will help you plan a successful production.

- What kind of rehearsal space (as opposed to performance space) do I have access to?

- What will it cost?

- Will I need a formal lease or other written contract?

def•i•ni•tion

Cross space is hidden space on, behind, or beneath the stage allowing actors to cross unseen by the audience.

- What performance space am I planning to use? Is it a traditional stage? How often can I have access to it?

- Is there sufficient hidden space above or beside the playing area for sets, crew, etc.? Is there *cross space?*

- Are there sufficient backstage areas to serve as dressing rooms?

- Can the performance space accommodate my expected audience? How large are the stage and the backstage area?

- Are my rehearsal and performance spaces accessible to the physically challenged? Is public transportation or parking a concern?

- Are these spaces properly ventilated? Is heating or air-conditioning a concern?

- Do these spaces have sufficient emergency exits, fire extinguishers, and a sprinkler system? What do my local fire and safety codes require?

- Do these facilities include access to decent rest rooms, and will we have to maintain them?

- Are these facilities fully insured, or will our group have to provide its own coverage?

- Where will we construct and store sets, costumes, props, tools, and other production materials?

- What kind of lighting equipment do we have in hand? Can we borrow or purchase more?

- Do we need a sound system at all? If so, what is available on-site, and what can we afford to bring in?

- Who is our likely audience, and how large is it?

- What other amateur productions take place in our area? When are their performances scheduled?

Don't fret if you can't find the "perfect" space—such a thing rarely exists. There are ways to deal with certain flaws—you can hang drapes to kill an echo, and a fresh coat of paint can give dingy walls new life. If your performance area starts out as nothing more than a dark, empty room, don't despair. Great theatre can grow in unlikely spaces! As long as you can resolve important safety and technical concerns, you can make almost any space work.

Gremlins

There is often a great temptation to talk oneself into liking a rehearsal or performance space, especially if the terms are cheap or the location is convenient. Be realistic. You owe it to yourself, and to everyone who will work on or see your show, to provide a space that is clean, safe, and up to the demands of public use.

When it is time to make your decision about a potential space, ask yourself three final questions:

- Will it be safe to use?

- Can my group afford it?

- What could my group do with it?

If you're comfortable with the answers, you have a potential winner on your hands.

Rehearsal Space

If your production is affiliated with a school or church, odds are that you have access to classrooms and an auditorium. Many community theatres set up close relationships with such institutions to use their facilities at little or no cost. Your production may have to pay fees for electricity, custodial staff overtime, etc. If your performance space is small or only available for a limited time, you will have to arrange for separate rehearsal space.

The size of your production determines how much rehearsal space you need. For most plays, one room will be enough. Large-scale musicals can involve simultaneous music, dance, and dialogue rehearsals, in which case multiple rooms will be required.

Rent can be expensive. When selecting space, be sure that it is safe, well maintained, and large enough for your cast. Decent rest rooms are a must, as are proper ventilation and comfortable temperature control. Musical rehearsals usually require a piano, and you may also want electrical outlets for CD players and other equipment.

Some smaller productions can rehearse in private homes. If this option works for you, be sure you do it without abusing anyone's hospitality.

> **Gremlins** _____
>
> Beware of sharing space with other groups, such as sports teams. You cannot expect performers to rehearse on a stage while basketball practice is raging on the other side of the curtain. (Don't laugh, I've seen it happen.) Even if you get exclusive-use time slots, you may have to clear the space each day for the next users—which can be a real hassle.

Performance Space

It may be a formal auditorium with all the trappings, a school gymnasium with a stage at one end, a raised platform surrounded by seats in a basement room, or the back of a truck on a street corner. When a show is in progress, each of these spaces becomes a theatre and can contain as much magic as any of the hallowed auditoriums of Broadway. Certain constraints in the physical space can spark fresh creative solutions, obliging directors, and designers to focus on the essentials.

Whatever kind of performance space you find, remember not to become "married" to it. Over time, keep your eyes open to new possibilities, more attractive facilities that may become available. Let your group define its space, never the other way around!

Likely Audience

Your likely audience is a major factor in selecting a performance space. If you have a strictly predetermined audience, such as students and parents, co-workers, and so on, you probably have a space available to you and a reasonable idea of how many people will attend your performances. Those who open performances to the general public must guess at how many people to expect and then try to pick an appropriate performance space. When uncertain, it is best to err on the side of caution. Giving several "sold out" performances in a 200-seat space beats playing to a half-empty 500-seat theatre.

Accessibility is also an issue. Too often, people forego attending a performance because they are unable to make it up a flight of stairs. If your target audience includes people with physical challenges, pick a performance space that is either at ground level or reachable by elevator. You may also have to make special accommodations for wheelchairs. Sign language interpreters are now a regular part of many live events. Even if you do not expect a large number of deaf attendees, having one or more signed performances is an inclusive, community-building gesture. To find more information on audience accessibility, see Appendix B.

Types of Performance Space

Performance spaces come in a variety of formats:

- Proscenium
- Thrust
- Stadium
- Platform

- Arena/in the round
- Environmental staging
- Black box
- Found space

Each of these arrangements has its share of plusses and minuses.

Proscenium

This is the traditional setup used by most theatres and school auditoriums, with the entire audience facing a picture-framed stage. (*Proscenium* is the formal name for the frame surrounding a formal stage.) While a proscenium stage usually gives you such advantages as well-hidden *fly space* and accessible backstage areas, you have other options. Although most plays and musicals were conceived for such a stage, with a little imagination, you can perform them in any of the alternate arrangements listed here.

def•i•ni•tion

Also called "the flies," **fly space** is the space (if any) above a conventional stage where backdrops and other scenery may fly up out of the audience's sight. Many successful stages have no fly space at all.

A proscenium stage seating plan.

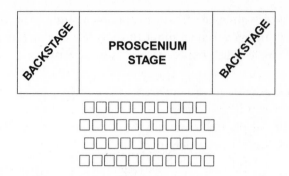

Thrust

In this arrangement, the stage thrusts out from the traditional proscenium, with spectators facing the stage from three sides. This puts the action right in the midst of the audience. Often used for intimate dramas and comedies, these stages can also accommodate musicals. Don't take my word for it. The legendary producer Florenz Ziegfeld produced a series of late-night revues on a thrust stage.

A thrust stage seating plan.

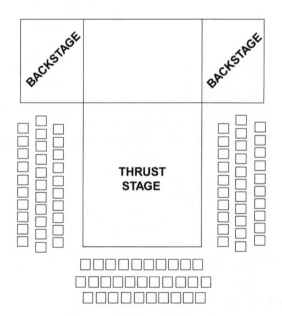

Stadium

This is the same seating arrangement used for basketball games in gymnasiums, with bleachers or banks of seats facing each other across a central performance area. This term can also refer to a performance area with seats or bleachers rising off to one side. Those sides of the performance area not devoted to seating can be draped to create wings. If using bleachers for seating, consider providing cushions for added comfort. You can adapt all kinds of shows to this format.

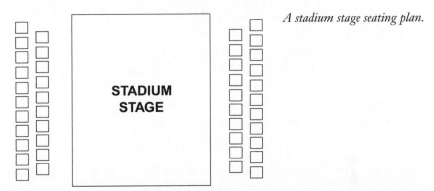

A stadium stage seating plan.

On Stage

The New York Youth Theatre staged *The Sound of Music* in a church basement, placing stadium-style seats to one side of a floor-level playing area. Maria made her entrance from the top of the audience, singing the title song as she walked down the aisle to the stage, as if descending a mountainside. What an inventive use of an unlikely space!

Platform

All this requires is a raised platform at one end of a room. It can also be the back of a truck or a platform built in the middle of a yard. While there are no hidden wings, this arrangement is ideal for concerts, as well as plays involving no more than a few simple set pieces.

A platform stage seating plan.

Arena/In the Round

Here, the audience is arranged on all sides of a central floor-level performance area. If that central area is square or rectangular, it is called an *arena stage;* when circular, it is *in the round.* This format can bring every seat into close proximity to the stage, and many actors find it exciting to perform with an audience surrounding them on all sides. However, there are negative aspects of this format. There are no wings, all entrances and exits must be made through the audience, and set elements must be designed to allow a clear view from every seat. With minimized decorative elements, these spaces put all the focus on the performers. Arena/in the round is a great choice for dramas, but by keeping sets down to a few low-lying pieces (tables, chairs, etc.), you can make this work for elaborate musicals.

An arena stage seating plan.

ARENA STAGE

Environmental Staging

The show takes place throughout the available space, whether it is a theatre, an old building, a street, or even a private home. The action moves from place to place or even room to room. If seated, the audience chooses where to look—if standing, they walk along, following the action. Environmental staging is used for street theatre and on-location murder mysteries, but it can be adapted for traditional shows. Hal Prince used this format for his long-running 1974 Broadway revival of *Candide.*

> **On Stage**
>
> Music education programs all across the United States have had extraordinary success using environmental staging in so-called *prism concerts*. Like light breaking into a prismatic rainbow, these events present a continuous series of selections performed by various groups of musicians in locations all around an auditorium.

Black Box

This is a plain room—often on the small side—with the entire interior painted black, from floor to ceiling. The blackness gives any space added flexibility and indicates that this is not just any room; it is a place where dreams can come to life. A black box can utilize any of the seating layouts listed here.

Found Space

This is any space designed for another purpose that you convert to theatrical use. It can be a storefront, abandoned church, band shell, or even the back of a truck. Some of these structures naturally lend themselves to theatrical use, but others require some imaginative renovation. If someone offers you such a space for little or no rental, remember that plumbing, electricity, and fire safety issues can turn a "gift" into a financial liability, so know what your legal safety standards are. In found space, you can install any of the stage arrangements described here.

Lease Agreements

Most facilities will insist on a formal lease or other written agreement. If for any reason your landlord fails to ask for one, insist on it yourself. Think of this contract as a friend, protecting both sides against misunderstandings and faulty memories. Any written agreement should clarify what you have to pay to the landlord (flat rent, percentage of the gate, a share of the concessions, etc.) and when. If a document includes any terms that you feel uneasy about, don't sign it. Always respect your inner warning light! Instead of being talked into something, confer with legal counsel before putting your name on the dotted line.

If the landlord is to provide anything more than space or if your group is expected to do anything besides pay rent, be sure the contract includes all the details. Many facilities require some payment in advance or at least security and cleaning deposits. To get those deposits returned, be sure to do whatever you're supposed to do (basic cleanup, repair of minor damages, and so on) and then follow up with the facility.

Insurance

Do not even think about skipping over this section—yes, I mean you! First-time producers and directors almost always overlook insurance issues until late in the game and then wind up in a panic.

Why do you need insurance? We live in a world where accidents happen and where costly lawsuits are a fact of life. No matter how careful your staff is or how well maintained the facilities are, people are going to slip, trip, and have other unlikely mishaps. Now and then someone is legitimately injured, and in a few sad cases, dishonest people are looking to make a quick buck. And there is always the chance that a member of the cast or crew will be accidentally injured in the course of rehearsals or performances. So, like it or not, liability coverage is a necessity for any amateur theatre group.

Schools, churches, and other public facilities now carry liability insurance as a matter of course, but most want to avoid claims against their policies. As a result, these facilities require groups using their space to carry separate liability coverage. There is no need to panic about this. Just speak to a local insurance broker about creating a package that covers all your rehearsals and performances. In fact, speak to several brokers and get the best deal you can. The cost will not be crippling; it will be far more affordable than a lawsuit. And such coverage will provide you real peace of mind in the months ahead. Just be sure to have all insurance questions settled before going into production.

Lights

Most auditoriums have some sort of stage lighting equipment installed, and this may be enough for a simple production. Check to see if your space already has sufficient *rigging* over the stage to permit the hanging of lights and scenery. Otherwise, you will need to bring in *light trees* to provide sufficient coverage. Is the wiring adequate for high-powered equipment? Consult your lighting designer to find out what you will need; then confer with the facility managers to see what can be worked out. A production must be visible, so be prepared to spend whatever it takes to provide sufficient lighting. You will find a detailed discussion of lighting equipment in Chapter 19.

def•i•ni•tion

Rigging is a system of ropes and cables around and above the performing area, used to hang lights and set elements.

Light trees are freestanding metal poles used to hold banks of lights.

Hidden Space and Equipment

If the performing area doesn't have fly space above the stage or the rigging necessary to hang sets and lighting, you will be limited to earthbound set pieces and will need *wings* to hide production elements that are not in use. Traditional stages usually have *masks* to further obscure the wings.

Be sure all backstage and auxiliary spaces are clean and safe to use. With all equipment, realize that it does not have to be "state of the art" to be useful. All it has to be is reliable. Whether something is operated by computer or by old-fashioned elbow grease, it must work every time you need it.

def•i•ni•tion

Masks are dark curtains used to hide production elements that are not in use.

Wings are offstage areas immediately next to the stage but hidden from the audience.

Sound

Many auditoriums come equipped with some sort of built-in sound system, even if it's nothing more than a microphone, amplifier, and two speakers. For simple productions, that can be enough. Otherwise, you will have to rent or purchase more, and sound equipment can be costly. If the performance space has decent acoustics and your expected audience is 300 or fewer, you may not need a sound system at all. See Chapter 20 for more on projection, the natural, no-cost option.

Your stage crew will probably require an intercom system to permit communication during performances. See Chapter 20 for further details.

On Stage

You are probably not planning an actual road tour, but some amateur productions offer performances at more than one location. The elementary school productions I directed gave special performances at a senior residence and a local nursing home. We used no sets or major equipment—only costumes, key props, and a tape recorder to provide prerecorded accompaniment. We performed with nothing more than room lighting, and the children improvised adjustments in the blocking. It was hard to tell whether the kids or the seniors enjoyed these performances more.

Local Theatre Groups

Know who your cultural neighbors are. Like that wonderful Sondheim lyric says, "No one is alone!" There are probably other amateur performing arts entities in your area—community groups, high schools, colleges, and so on. This includes theatre companies, orchestras, dance troupes … almost any organization that stages public performances. Instead of fearing or resenting these groups, think of them as your natural allies. Sure, a little rivalry might stir up from time to time, but it's usually trivial and encourages extra effort. The people running these groups already know what it takes to put on shows in your locality. They can be rich resources of talent and advice, as well as mailing lists and free or inexpensive loans of desperately needed equipment, materials, and contacts. Of course, in the future you must be ready to lend a helping hand to those who have helped you. Those who take had better be ready to give in return.

Are there any professional performing arts companies nearby? It's a good idea to form relationships with them, too. Learn about any special programs they may offer for students or amateur talent. Professional troupes may offer summer courses or internships that would interest members of your team, and many regional theatres now organize awards programs for local high school productions. These companies may also help you find the local professional talent you will need on your team.

Network with all these groups, and stay in frequent touch. I'm not talking about aimless schmoozing! Develop warm ties with these colleagues. At the very least, you can prevent competing performance schedules. Odds are that people from other theatre groups will make a point of catching your show. Take this as a compliment, and be sure to return that compliment when those groups have productions.

The Least You Need to Know

- Before deciding to put on a show, evaluate the facilities and equipment at your disposal.

- Many effective performance space formats exist. If a traditional proscenium space is not available, get creative.

- Don't feel that a particular stage format limits you. Shows can be physically adapted to fit most any kind of space.

- Leases and insurance are facts of theatrical life. Get comfortable with them.

- Develop cordial relationships with the other amateur and professional groups producing in your area.

Part 2

Picking Your Project—
"The Play's the Thing"

No matter what your facilities and level of ability, there is a play, musical, or other project that will be the perfect choice for your group to present. Now that you've gone through the grueling assessments in Part 1, you are equipped to consider the best available options. If one of the existing works does not strike your fancy, you can create an original show. Matching your group with the right material and producing it all with a sound financial plan will increase the odds that your production turns out to be success.

Chapter 4

Great Shows for Beginners: "We Can Do It!"

In This Chapter

- How to pick the right show for your group
- An extensive list of plays and musicals well suited to inexperienced amateur groups
- Some thoughts on live versus prerecorded accompaniment
- Guidance regarding performance rights

Running an amateur theatre program does not mean producing any play that strikes your fancy. You have to consider your facilities, your people power, and your likely audience. (If for any reason you skipped Chapters 2 and 3, please go back and read them before going any further.) After completing those thorough assessments of the talent and resources at your disposal, you will be far better prepared to pick the perfect show for your group.

Picking the Right Show

While seasoned amateurs can present almost any show, certain plays are more beginner-friendly than others. Why break your group in with a three-plus-hour marathon like *King Lear* or *My Fair Lady?* Just as mountain climbers start out by climbing smaller peaks, new theatre groups and inexperienced directors can learn by presenting simpler shows. This chapter offers an array of titles that are accessible and proven audience pleasers. Unless otherwise noted, all these shows are appropriate for general audiences.

Plays

Literally thousands of plays are available, ranging from Shakespeare's classics to recent Broadway hits. The good news is that royalties for plays tend to be far less expensive than for musicals. In all these listings, you will get:

- The title of the show

- The number of male (M) and female (F) actors required

- The need (if any) for a separate chorus

- The need (if any) to combine any smaller roles to accommodate a small cast, or to split any precombined casting to allow for a larger cast

- The number of sets required (Where one specific set is required, I call for *1 set;* when specific settings are not required, I call for a *unit set.*)

- The licensing company

> **On Stage**
>
> The function of the "chorus" or "ensemble" has changed over the last 50 years. Formerly on hand to provide singing and dancing support to the leads, the anonymous chorus has been replaced by myriad specifically named speaking and singing characters. In these listings, I specify whenever a show has a separate ensemble, as well as those shows that include nonsinging "extras."

> **def•i•ni•tion**
>
> A **unit set** is one basic set used for an entire production, to which furniture and props can be added or subtracted as needed to suggest shifting locales.

For musicals, I give the minimum number of actors required, "plus ensemble." This is because many larger shows have been designed with multiple casting options to allow greater flexibility when setting cast size.

In some cases, I have used the word *variable* to denote shows where the casting requirements are flexible. For example, some of Shakespeare's plays can be done with as few as half a dozen actors—or as many as three dozen, depending on the director's approach.

The licensing companies listed here are as follows:

♦ DPUB: Dramatic Publishing Company

♦ DPS: Dramatists Play Service

♦ MTI: Music Theatre International

♦ SF: Samuel French

♦ TAMS: Tams Witmark

Full contact information for these and other firms is available in Appendix B.

Dramas

Straight drama is a popular choice with amateur groups, but beginners should be cautious. Theatre is about illusion, and the heavier the material, the more seamless the illusion must be. While you may be itching to do *Hamlet* or *Death of a Salesman*, I urge beginners to aim for lighter works that are more amenable to amateur stagings. For example, contemporary audiences have tremendous interest in mysteries, so you will find several listed here.

♦ *And Then There Were None* (8 M, 3 F, 1 set): Eight guests marooned in an English country house are being murdered, one by one. Also known as *Ten Little Indians*, this Agatha Christie comic mystery is a major audience favorite. SF

♦ *Angel Street* (2 M, 3 F, 2 extras, 1 set): This delicious tale presents a man diabolically trying to drive his wife insane, until a Scotland Yard inspector offers her hope. The original British title was *Gaslight*. SF

♦ *Deathtrap* (3 M, 2 F, 1 set): Is a faltering playwright willing to kill to steal a young writer's work? A bit of gay subplot is thrown in as a smokescreen. DPS

♦ *Diary of Anne Frank* (5 M, 5 F, 1 set): This much-loved tale portrays a Jewish girl coming of age as her family hides from the Nazis. DPS

♦ *Little Women* (5 M, 7 F, 1 set): There are various dramatizations of Louisa May Alcott's classic novel about four sisters coming of age. Find one that best fits your taste; then let the beloved characters do the rest. SF

♦ *Our Town* (17 M, 7 W, bare stage with props): Thornton Wilder's touching masterpiece depicts small-town American life. SF

♦ *Sleuth* (2 M, 1 set): A mystery writer tricks his wife's lover into a deadly duel of wits. This is a crackling tour de force for two strong actors and one gifted set designer. SF

On Stage

Some groups avoid dramas because they are "too serious," but this is misguided thinking. Many so-called dramas include comic characters and situations. For example, mysteries like *Deathtrap* and *Sleuth* offset the suspense with hilarious comic material. So your group can make 'em laugh and gasp all in the same show!

♦ *To Kill a Mockingbird* (11 M, 6 W, plus ensemble, unit set): Christopher Sergel penned this fine stage adaptation of the powerful Harper Lee novel. DPUB

♦ *Twelve Angry Men/Women/Citizens* (15 M/F, 1 set): Originally all male, this surefire audience pleaser can be done with mixed or all-female casting, too. DPUB

♦ *Witness for the Prosecution* (17 M, 5 F, plus ensemble, 2 sets): A British murder trial has a triple-flip surprise ending. This is Agatha Christie's finest script, but the male and female leads must be outstanding to make this show work. SF

Comedies

Laughs sell tickets! That's why Neil Simon is the most renowned—and most frequently produced—contemporary playwright. You'll see a number of his plays listed here, along with other comedies that lend themselves well to amateur stagings.

♦ *Arsenic and Old Lace* (11 M, 3 F, 1 set): A young man discovers his two aging aunts are serial mercy killers. Great characters make this a comic feast for actors and audiences. SF

♦ *Brighton Beach Memoirs* (3 M, 4 F, 1 set): Neil Simon's semi-autobiographical hit has teenager Eugene Jerome coming of age in Depression-era Brooklyn. SF

♦ *Broadway Bound* (4 M, 2 F, 1 set): This wonderful sequel to *Brighton Beach Memoirs* (using the same set) has Eugene and his brother breaking into professional comedy writing as their family faces a series of domestic crises. SF

♦ *Come Blow Your Horn* (3 M, 4 F, 1 set): Neil Simon's first hit had a 33-year-old playboy contending with his naïve younger brother and exasperated parents. This script has lots of laughs and is relatively easy to stage. SF

♦ *Hay Fever* (4 M, 5 F, 1 set): An eccentric, temperamental theatrical family "entertains" weekend guests at their country house. The witty dialogue requires polished delivery, and the 1920s costuming must be superb, but with only one set, this Noel Coward gem is worth considering. SF

◆ *The Imaginary Invalid* (8 M, 4 F, 1 set): This Moliere classic is about a wealthy hypochondriac saved from financial ruin by his brother and serving girl. There are several translations available, and some are available rights free.

◆ *The Importance of Being Earnest* (5 M, 4 F, 3 sets): Oscar Wilde's definitive comedy depicts Victorian manners at their best and worst. With strong acting and good costuming, this explosion of period style can work, even with minimized sets. Rights free.

◆ *Life with Father* (8 M, 8 F, 1 set): All age groups fit into this delightful family comedy, which is rarely done today but still great fun. DPS

◆ A *Midsummer Night's Dream* (11 M, 9 F, flexible ensemble, 2 sets): If your actors can handle Shakespearean dialogue, this romantic comedy is a perennial favorite. Creative visual design is a must. Rights free.

◆ *Much Ado About Nothing* (variable): Another Shakespeare comedy that can work in amateur stagings, with a central story involving reluctant lovers surrounded by the foibles of others. Rights free.

◆ *The Odd Couple* (6 M, 2 F, 1 set): Neil Simon's much-loved tale presents two divorced men sharing an apartment in the 1960s. This guaranteed audience pleaser is also available in a female version and another (*Oscar and Felix*) updated to the present. SF

◆ *Orson's Shadow* (5 M, 2 F, unit set): Orson Welles directs Sir Laurence Olivier in the London production of *Rhinoceros*, and Vivien Leigh, Joan Plowright, and Kenneth Tynan are all on hand for the fireworks. A fascinating backstage comedy, with adult themes. DPS

◆ *Steel Magnolias* (6 F, 1 set): Lots of laughs prevail in this all-female look at Southern living. DPS

◆ *The Sunshine Boys* (5 M, 2 F, 1 set): Two feuding vaudevillians reunite for a TV appearance in this hilarious Neil Simon classic. SF

◆ *The Taming of the Shrew* (variable): Shakespeare's classic tale of violent romance between the shrewish Kate and the headstrong Petruchio is actually a play within a play. Many groups dispose of the external story and stick to the core play, which has lots of slapstick physical comedy. This can be successfully re-set in various times and locations and performed in a wide variety of styles. Rights free.

Musicals

Musicals require more extensive resources, but without question, they sell more tickets than any other form of theatre. Amateur groups often worry about the cost of performance rights, but did you know that a block of the most popular musicals ever written is currently available rights free?

Gilbert and Sullivan

Although written more than a century ago, the best works of librettist William S. Gilbert and composer Arthur Sullivan are still entertaining—and all are available rights free. The vocal demands are substantial, but any school with a solid music program should have little trouble with these scores. The following G&S works are quite accessible to contemporary audiences:

◆ *H.M.S. Pinafore* (6 M, 3 F, plus ensemble, 1 set): A naval captain wants his daughter to marry a member of the British cabinet, but she loves a lowly sailor.

◆ *The Mikado* (5 M, 4 F, plus ensemble, 1 set): The ruler of Japan declares flirting illegal, causing a crisis for his eldest son and the worried residents of a fictional town called Titpu. (An updated jazz version titled *Hot Mikado* is available through R&H but involves a rights fee.)

◆ *The Gondoliers* (9 M, 8 F, plus ensemble, 2 sets): One of two anti-monarchist Venetian brothers is really a king; until they figure out which is which, both men must rule an island kingdom together.

◆ *The Pirates of Penzance* (5 M, 5 W, plus ensemble, 2 sets): A former pirate is torn between his sense of duty and his love for a major general's lovely ward.

The G&S shows have been performed by all-male and all-female casts and all have been re-set in modern times. Although the rights are free, it is necessary to either rent, borrow, or purchase the scripts as well as vocal and orchestral scores, so be prepared for that expense.

Book Musicals

Many musicals can shine in amateur hands. This brief list of *book musicals* is limited to shows that give inexperienced directors and casts a distinct advantage.

- *The 1940s Radio Hour* (10 M, 5 F, 1 set): A live radio broadcast is the excuse for fun plot twists and a cavalcade of period hits. This is easy to stage and a real audience pleaser. SF

def•i•ni•tion

A **book musical** is any musical show with a plot.

- *Aladdin* (6 M, 4 F, plus ensemble, unit set): Written for the now-legendary Prince Street Players, this is a tuneful and witty take on the classic fairy tale, especially for younger audiences. (The same licensing company offers a junior version of the Disney animated film.) MTI

- *Annie* (4 M, 10 F, plus ensemble, 8 sets): The adventures of America's favorite comic strip orphan, with Daddy Warbucks, a dog named Sandy, and the evil Miss Hannigan thrown in for good measure, this perennial charmer is still hard to resist. A version for all-juvenile casts is available. MTI

- *Annie Get Your Gun* (9 M, 6 F, plus ensemble, 8 sets): Stick to the original, not the clumsy revival version. R&H

- *Anything Goes* (6 M, 7 F, plus ensemble, 4 sets): There are two versions available, both excellent and brimming with great Cole Porter songs. See which best fits your needs. TAMS

- *Babes in Arms* (12 M, 5 F, plus ensemble 7 sets): This is the original "hey kids, let's put on a show" musical, with a hit-filled Rodgers and Hart score. A great showcase for a young, talented cast, check out both available versions to see which will work best for your group. R&H

- *Big River* (14 M, 8 W, unit set): Huckleberry Finn's story, retold with great songs by Roger Miller, calls for some strong singers and a talented, multi-racial cast, but dance requirements are minimal. R&H

- *Bye, Bye Birdie* (7 M, 6 F, plus ensemble, 8 sets): This rock 'n' roll spoof of an Elvis-like star mingling with fans before being drafted into the Army has long been a staple for school and community theatre groups. TAMS

- *The Emperor's New Clothes* (7 M, 3 W, additional ensemble optional, unit set): A brilliant take on the classic fairy tale, the story is told with real wit and a catchy score. It's great for young audiences but fun for adults, too. MTI

- *The Fantasticks* (7 M, 1 F, unit set): The longest-running musical of all time, this endearing boy-meets-girl fable is an intimate charmer—great for smaller theatres. No set is needed and the costumes are a breeze, but the demanding score requires solid singer-actors. MTI

◆ *Godspell* (5 M, 5 F, unit set): The story of Christ and his disciples is set to an early Stephen Schwartz score. Tuneful and charming, this is very easy to produce and a big favorite with church groups and is also available in a junior version. MTI

◆ *Grease* (9 M, 8 F, unit set): This long-running hit about 1950s high schoolers is a real ticket seller, but the foul language and adult themes can pose a problem. A cleaned-up "school version" is available but could still offend some. SF

◆ *I Do! I Do!* (1 M, 1 F, 1 set): If you have two sensational performers, this intimate look at love and marriage (by the creators of *The Fantasticks*) is guaranteed to charm the heck out of audiences. MTI

◆ *Is There Life After High School?* (5 M, 3 F, unit set): This delightful revue looks at the way memories of high school follow us through life. Although this show failed on Broadway, it has been a winner for many amateur groups. SF

◆ *Jack and the Beanstalk* (4 M, 3 F, unit set): Another of the Prince Street Players musicals, this is a wonderful show for younger audiences, with great tunes and lots of laughter. MTI

◆ *Joseph and the Amazing Technicolor Dreamcoat* (12 M, 1 F, plus ensemble, unit set): Webber and Rice's first hit is great for young performers and family audiences. Casting note: it only adds to the fun if some or all of Joseph's brothers are depicted by girls. R&H

◆ *Lucky Stiff* (6 M, 4 F, minimal sets): To collect a massive inheritance, a young man must take his late uncle's corpse on a dream vacation. Quirky but very entertaining, with hilarious characters and a solid Ahrens and Flaherty score, this would be a great choice for college groups. MTI

◆ *Musical of Musicals, The Musical* (2 M, 2 F, unit set): A hilarious spoof of Rodgers and Hammerstein, Jerry Herman, Stephen Sondheim, Kander and Ebb, and Andrew Lloyd Webber. All you need is four great performers, a pianist, and an audience that has some familiarity with musical theatre. SF

◆ *Nunsense* (5 F, 1 set): A group of nuns put on a show to raise emergency funds. Great, inoffensive fun—even real nuns enjoy this show. Available in an all-male version (*Nunsense A-Men*). Tams-Witmark offers two sequels, but the original is the best of the convent crop. SF

◆ *Oliver* (9 M, 6 F, plus ensemble, 8 sets): Dickens's classic tale of an orphaned boy caught in the criminal underworld of nineteenth-century London inspired one of the world's most beloved family musicals. Some double casting is possible. Heavy on sets and costumes, this show can incorporate performers of all ages and has tremendous audience appeal. TAMS

- *Once Upon a Mattress* (6 M, 4 F, plus ensemble, 10 sets): This send-up of "The Princess and the Pea" is a big audience favorite. It can be heavy on sets and costumes, and you must have a comically (and vocally) gifted leading lady.

- *Radio Gals* (3 M, 4 F, 1 set): A 1927 radio show is broadcast from an Arkansas front parlor. This has lots of down-home country flavor and good-natured humor. SF

- *The Rocky Horror Picture Show* (7 M, 3 F, 1 set): The cult classic film began onstage, with all the irreverent wackiness that later graced the film version. With a hard rock score and some decidedly adult content, this has potential for college groups. Be ready to deal with *Rocky*'s oh-so demonstrative cult of fans! SF

- *Snoopy* (3 M, 4 F, unit set): This endearing sequel to *You're a Good Man, Charlie Brown* has the *Peanuts* gang in more of their comic-strip adventures, offering a fine score and at least as much fun as the original. TAMS

- *The Sound of Music* (6 M, 12 F, plus ensemble, sets): Despite the major set and costume requirements, this show is such a solid audience favorite that it is almost foolproof—even for beginners. Concert stagings (minus all those sets) go over very well. R&H

- *Stop the World, I Want to Get Off* (2M, 3 F, plus ensemble, unit set): An ordinary man takes on life and love in this allegorical musical. It's odd but easy to stage. You might prefer the semi-sequel, *The Roar of the Greasepaint, the Smell of the Crowd.* TAMS

- *They're Playing Our Song* (4 M, 4 F, multiple sets): A composer and lyricist collaborate and fall in love. Tuneful, it is a laugh-filled book by Neil Simon. SF

- *The Wizard of Oz* (variable): There are two stage adaptations of the beloved MGM film available. The less-demanding MUNY version fits most amateur groups best. And yes, this show can be done with minimal sets. TAMS

- *You're a Good Man, Charlie Brown* (4 M, 2 F, unit set): Charles Schultz's beloved comic-strip characters come to winning life in this easy-to-stage, longtime audience favorite. Available in two versions—the original and revival are both delightful, so take time to consider each. TAMS

Professional Revues

If you want the fluidity of a revue without the challenge of creating your own, some fine professional revues are available. All those listed here require simple unit sets and are proven audience pleasers.

◆ *A … My Name Is Alice* (5 F, unit set): This Off-Broadway hit offers a kaleidoscopic look at the lives of contemporary women. Two sequels are also available through the same licensing firm. SF

◆ *Ain't Misbehavin'* (2 M, 3 F, unit set): An all-black cast pays tribute to the songs of Fats Waller. Filled with laughter and pathos, this is one of the greatest intimate revues ever to play Broadway. Solid cast and musicians are essential! MTI

◆ *Cowardy Custard* (6 M, 6 F, ensemble optional, unit set): This two-act mélange of songs and scenes by Noel Coward is witty and fun, and a flexible cast size makes this a worthwhile option. SF

◆ *Free to Be … You and Me* (2 M, 2 F, plus ensemble, unit set): Based on the popular book by Marlo Thomas, this is a life-affirming show that encourages youngsters to reach beyond their boundaries. Fun and fast-paced, it has a contemporary score that can be performed by adults or kids. R&H

◆ *A Grand Night for Singing* (2 M, 3 F, unit set): This is a fast-moving, compact parade of Rodgers and Hammerstein songs with brief but witty dialogue throughout. It is sophisticated but accessible, mixing well-known hits with interesting rarities. R&H

◆ *I Love You, You're Perfect, Now Change* (2 M, 2 F, unit set): Here is a fresh, funny contemporary take on finding and keeping love. The cast can be expanded. R&H

◆ *Jerry's Girls* (3 F, plus ensemble, unit set): This delightful all-girl revue pays tribute to the composer of *Hello Dolly*, *Mame*, and *La Cage aux Folles*. SF

◆ *Putting It Together* (3 M, 2 F, unit set): Sondheim conceived this socko revue featuring some of his best songs. R&H

◆ *Red, Hot and Cole* (7 M, 6 F, unit set): The wonderful words and music of Cole Porter are packaged with style. MTI

◆ *Showtune* (4 M, 3 F, unit set): Another enjoyable tribute to Jerry Herman, this time with room for both sexes. MTI

◆ *Side by Side by Sondheim* (2 M, 2 F, unit set): This cavalcade of great songs by the dean of Broadway songwriters requires a talented, sophisticated cast. MTI

◆ *Smokey Joe's Café* (5 M, 4 F, unit set): The pop hits of Lieber and Stoller inspired this surprise, long-running Broadway hit. R&H

◆ *Stardust* (3 M, 3 F, unit set): This show presents the lyrics of Mitchell Parrish, including "Moonlight Serenade," "Ruby," and the haunting title tune. SF

- *Starting Here, Starting Now* (1 M, 2 F, unit set): A brilliant cabaret-style revue uses the early songs of Richard Maltby and David Shire. The cast can be expanded. MTI

- *Taking My Turn* (4 M, 4 F, unit set): Songs and stories about growing old make this a delightful vehicle for older performers. SF

- *Tintypes* (2M, 3 F, unit set): The early twentieth century is viewed through a wide-ranging selection of the era's popular songs. This requires some dancing but is an easy audience pleaser. MTI

- *The World Goes Round* (2 M, 3 F, unit set): This rich, entertaining revue presents songs by Broadway legends John Kander and Fred Ebb. MTI

Children's Theatre

Several smaller licensing firms specialize in children's works that never played Broadway—which is not always a bad thing! These works have been designed for juvenile audiences and/or performers.

- **Frumi Cohen Musicals** (www.frumicohen.com)—This composer specializes in family-friendly musicals based on classic stories, as well as several originals. A full production package (rights, scripts, scores, and rehearsal tapes) is just $300—worth looking into.

- **Bruce Goodman's Musicals** (plays.freeservers.com/children/childmus.htm)—Offers 35–40-minute musicals designed for elementary school performers. Very affordable—you can purchase performance rights, script, and accompaniment tapes online for less than $40.

- **Hope Publishing** (www.hopepublishing.com)—This well-known company carries more than 30 religious and general interest musicals for children, most with prerecorded accompaniment. In particular, *PT* (about Barnum) is a winner. Type "musicals" into the website search feature for a full list.

Ask for perusal copies and scrutinize them before committing to a production. Because local standards and tastes are so variable, you will have to consider which of these fits your cast—and your potential audiences.

Accompaniment: Live or Prerecorded?

Which sort of accompaniment should you go with? Whenever possible, live theatre deserves live accompaniment—even if that means nothing more than one person on a keyboard. At the very least, live musicians provide true accompaniment, working with and accommodating the singers. However, much as I hate to say it, if good musicians are unavailable or unaffordable, you may have to consider prerecorded music as a workable option. For information on using playback equipment, see Chapter 20.

Keeping It Legal: The Only Option

Anyone who performs material without paying for the rights is a thief, pure and simple! However, many talk themselves into believing that there is nothing wrong with stealing someone else's property.

I've heard all the arguments time and again. *We should not have to pay for performance rights because …*

♦ *It's for a good cause.* "Good causes" pay for things like rent, electricity, and staff salaries. Why shouldn't they pay for performance rights, too?

♦ *We're not charging admission.* So that gives you the right to steal? Raise the money for performance rights by other means (see Chapter 6), or just go ahead and charge admission.

♦ *We have no money for rights.* Yes, you do! (See the next section.)

♦ *Obtaining the rights is too complicated.* Huh? All it takes is a phone call.

♦ *The authors won't miss the money.* What a crock! Everyone has the right to be compensated for the materials he or she creates.

What's that? You say there's no way the rights holders of a Broadway show will hear about your production? That may have been true at one time, but not in an age when anybody with a grudge can play tattletale via an e-mail or a quick phone call. Every year amateur groups get burned for unauthorized productions. If caught in advance, you will have to choose between paying up or canceling all performances. If caught after the final curtain, the sponsoring organization and producer can face expensive litigation and criminal charges. Don't laugh; it happens.

Yes, You Can Afford It!

Most first-timers who complain about the cost of performance rights have not bothered to find out what that cost really is. For plays and individual songs, performance rights tend to be quite affordable. The price tag for established musicals is heftier, but often less than first-timers expect—and as I noted elsewhere in this chapter, some shows (like the Gilbert and Sullivan operettas) are now available rights free.

Plays tend to charge a flat fee, but most licensing companies base their charges for musicals on a sliding scale that includes such factors as ticket price, the number of performances, and the number of seats. If the musical you're interested in is not listed in this chapter, my website has a page listing all the titles currently available for amateurs (www.musicals101.com/alphinde.htm). When you identify the licensing company for a show that you are interested in, give them a call. They will calculate a custom-tailored price quote at no charge and with no obligation.

Budget Saver: Fewer Seats

Let me pass on an honest budget-saving technique. A friend of mine produces high school musicals in an oversized auditorium. Instead of paying top price for rights, he closes off the back sections of the space, limiting ticket sales to the best seats. This reduces the rights scale he is charged. If a production becomes a hit and starts selling seats in those blocked-off areas, he reports it to the licensing company and pays an additional fee. When ticket sales go that well, no one minds paying a bit more.

Change Is Not Always a Good Thing

Some amateur producers and directors think it's okay to alter copyrighted plays or musicals by adding or deleting material, changing dialogue, revising lyrics, and so on. For works still under copyright, don't change anything! Unauthorized changes can lead to major legal headaches, and it is foolish to think no one will catch you.

Rights for Individual Songs

Most show tunes—and pop songs, too—are handled by two organizations: ASCAP and BMI (contact information in Appendix B). If you're looking to put together a revue using a wide range of songs, both organizations offer reasonably priced blanket licensing agreements. There are some limits as to the number of songs you can do from any one musical, but these agreements make it easy to put together a wide range of songs with no legal hassles.

When Rights Are Not Available

On occasion, an amateur producer or director will develop a passion for a show that either flopped on Broadway or happened so long ago that no one has staged it in decades. When titles fall out of favor and no licensing company carries the rights, you have the dual challenge of finding the rights owners and of obtaining things like scripts, vocal scores, and orchestrations.

If you want to track down rights holders, the following organizations can help you:

- The Authors League of America for deceased playwrights

- The Dramatists Guild for current writers

- ASCAP or BMI for songwriters

Contact information for all three is listed in Appendix B.

The Least You Need to Know

- Amateur groups look their best in material that fits their resources and abilities.

- A sizeable list of plays, book musicals, and revues are well written and relatively easy for amateur groups to stage.

- Live accompaniment is best, but if prerecorded is your only practical option, go for it.

- Always pay performance rights! If material is good enough for your group to present, then it is good enough for your group to pay for the privilege.

5

Writing Original Shows: "It's Our Time"

In This Chapter

- ◆ Reasons for writing your own show
- ◆ The elements of dramatic entertainment
- ◆ Steps for constructing an original revue
- ◆ Writing original plays and musicals
- ◆ Creating original children's theatre
- ◆ The importance of copyright protection

As if it wasn't enough to put on a show, you want to write it, too? Well, you aren't alone. Many amateur groups now stage original works. The challenge is to create well-written material that fits your group's needs. Reading this chapter will not turn you into the next Arthur Miller, but it will introduce you to a few basic storytelling tools that can help you create coherent, enjoyable children's plays, revues, holiday pageants, and other stage works. Even if you don't plan to write your own show, this chapter will help you understand the basic mechanics of drama, making it easier to understand any play you choose to produce or direct.

Why Write Your Own?

In the early twentieth century, most schools and community theaters staged their own original plays and *revues*. Not until the late 1940s did most of these groups shift their energies to re-staging former Broadway hits. In recent years, an increasing number of amateur companies have gone back to creating new shows of their own.

With thousands of existing plays and musicals out there, why would you want to write a new one for your group? There are plenty of reasons:

def·i·ni·tion

Revues use skits and songs to tell a variety of stories, usually held together by common thematic content or authorship.

◆ To custom fit material to your group's talents and facilities

◆ To serve a special educational purpose

◆ To tell stories of special significance to your local audience

◆ To poke fun at local issues and celebrities

◆ To avoid the cost of royalties

◆ To prove that theatrical creativity is not limited to Broadway and its environs

Feel free to add your own reasons to this list. If you feel compelled to write a show, then that is reason enough. The challenge will be to create material that delights and perhaps even enlightens.

All forms of theatre involve acting out a story. Dramas do it with power, comedies do it with humor, and musicals add song and dance. But it all comes down to storytelling. What sort of story do you want to tell, and how? Perhaps you want to dramatize a classic fairy tale for grade-school performers or write a Christmas play for a church youth group. You might be planning a collegiate musical comedy revue or a political fund-raiser that will spoof local events. Whatever theatrical form you choose to work in, remember that your primary task is to tell a story in clear, dramatic terms. That will be easier to do if you follow the basic rules of good playwriting.

The New Basic Rules of Playwriting

Many books and teachers have laid out rules for writing plays. Some of these precepts have been around since ancient times. This fresh collection of rules, both old and new, is custom designed for the fledgling playwright.

Show, Don't Tell

This is the first rule of all writing and is particularly true of dramatic works. Heck, we call them "shows," don't we? Instead of telling what a character or event is like, show it! Actions can express a character's qualities far more effectively than words. For example, in *The Sound of Music*, no one has to state that Maria loves the Von Trapp children; from the moment she meets them, her actions make those feelings obvious.

Gremlins

Telling instead of showing is the most common hallmark of bad writing, and every playwright has been guilty of it at some point. If a play or scene you are working on seems flat or dull, odds are that you've been telling instead of showing.

Write About What You Believe

The old rule was to "write about what you know," but that doesn't wash. Start by writing about what you believe. Have something to say, a premise or core idea that makes your story worth telling. J.R.R. Tolkein did not "know" Middle Earth. He had certain beliefs, and he imagined a cast of hobbits, elves, wizards, and orks that could interact in ways that illustrated those beliefs, expressing them in dramatic terms. Tolkein's *The Hobbit* and *Lord of the Rings* trilogy gave birth to the adult fantasy genre, and it all came from the depths of his imagination. "What you know" is going to inform your writing, but don't let it limit your choice of subject matter.

Save Preaching for the Pulpit

Effective theatre may have a theme or moral, but it must express its points in dramatic terms. Instead of letting a character or narrator tell the audience what to think, let the actions of your characters do the talking. The musical *Ragtime* wisely avoided preaching about the need for ethnic equality, and instead conjured an unforgettable final image of happy children walking hand in hand—white and black, Jewish and Christian. This moment invariably leaves audiences applauding as they blink back tears. So keep your message subtle, letting actions rather than words convey it to your audiences.

Maintain Tight Focus

New writers have a nagging habit of writing plays with small armies of characters (*please* tell me you haven't fallen into the age-old beginners trap of setting your play in a bar!) or myriad settings. Experienced writers can handle such a broad focus, but do your audiences a favor and learn to walk before you try running. Keep your plays focused on a few central characters, using as few settings as possible. Simplicity and a tight focus make it easier for a production team to bring your show to life and easier for audiences to encounter your story.

Build to a Climax

Every stage show must offer a progression of ideas and events, building up to an emotional climax. When you get to that climax, bring things to a swift conclusion. Most successful dramatizations end within five minutes of reaching the climax. Once *Kiss Me Kate* resolves its plot by reuniting the contentious leads, the finale is sung, curtain calls are taken, and the audience is sent on its happy way. Follow that example, and your plays will be the better for it.

Keep Everything Clear and Logical

Theatre is live, "of the moment." It does not come with a rewind button, so playwrights are obliged to keep the flow of events clear at all times. The audience must always understand who is speaking, what is happening, and where the action is taking place. Whenever there is a scene change, the new location must be instantly identifiable, as must any new characters. Even a brief spell of unintentional confusion can cost you the audience's attention for the rest of the show, so be sure every moment clearly follows what came before and leads into whatever follows it.

Use the Mechanics of the Stage

When writing a play for amateur production, keep the mechanics of the stage in mind. Keep the number of your scenes to a minimum, and avoid having too many jumps in time and space. On the big screen, an editorial cut can take the action from a sunlit forest to a candlelit ballroom in a snap. That same transition could be a time-consuming logistical nightmare on an amateur stage.

Beyond these initial rules, you should also be familiar with the basic elements of playwriting: premise, character, conflict, plot, and dialogue. Let's look at each in brief detail.

Premise

How often have you walked out of a play or movie wondering, *What was the point?* There may have been characters and some kind of story, but none of it mattered very much. At such times, you have been the victim of storytelling without a premise, a clear central idea or belief that makes a story relevant to audiences. Plot tells you the "who, what, where, when, and how" of a story, but premise tells you the "why."

Premise goes by many alternate names—thesis, theme, main question, etc. Call it whatever you like, as long as your show has one. Every successful novel, short story, stage show, dramatic film, or TV sitcom has a premise that can be stated in one clear sentence. Some examples:

♦ *Gone with the Wind* (novel, film): with determination, you can survive any crisis and begin again.

♦ *Oklahoma* (musical): Knowing what you really want is the key to personal happiness.

♦ *A Streetcar Named Desire* (drama): Denial leads to self-destruction.

♦ *Ain't Misbehavin'* (revue): The songs of Fats Waller offer myriad lasting pleasures.

♦ *Friends* (sitcom): Friendship is a sustaining force in contemporary urban life.

♦ *Will and Grace* (sitcom): Same as *Friends;* just add gay men.

A premise makes faraway people and distant eras matter, giving audiences a reason to care. L. Frank Baum's classic children's book *The Wizard of Oz* is about a little girl carried by a cyclone to a magical land where she must deal with witches and enchanted creatures to find her way home. The premise that a brave child can triumph over adversity is admirable, but only relevant to a juvenile audience. MGM made the girl a teenager and turned her trip into an allegorical dream, during which she learns that nothing matches the importance of home and family. This new premise has relevance to people of all ages, and it helped *The Wizard of Oz* (1939) become one of the most popular films of all time.

Your premise may not become clear until partway through the writing process. That's okay! You can begin writing with little more than a situation or a few characters in mind. Go with whatever works for you. When a clear premise is in place, you will be able to trim away any extraneous ideas and shape a more effective story. You don't have to state your premise anywhere in your show. In most cases, doing so would only seem clumsy and obvious, but see what serves your material best. It's hard to imagine a better ending for *The Wizard of Oz* than Dorothy's statement that, "There's no place like home."

Characters

Next to a lack of premise, the most common flaw in storytelling is the presence of dull characters. An effective story is built around memorable personalities (real or fictional) whose experiences and actions prove the story's premise.

Memorable characters have three dimensions:

◆ Body: age, height, weight, etc.

◆ Mind-set: personality, attitude

◆ Environment: personal history, home, class, family

Sketch out this information for each of your characters. Like actors, writers use these sorts of details to understand what motivates a character's words and actions. You don't need to mention all these details in your story. The point is to know your characters, and thereby make them more believable.

Now here's the kicker. When you really know a character's three dimensions, you will never wonder what her reaction to a particular situation will be. Your protagonist may have doubts, but knowing her background and mind-set will make her actions seem inevitable to you. All your characters can only make choices that help prove your premise. In fact, your characters must be so conceived that premise-based choices come naturally to them. Their refusal to compromise makes a conflict compelling.

Conflict

In a story, the central character or *protagonist* has a specific need or desire that is opposed by another character or force known as the *antagonist*. This opposition creates *conflict*, the heart of all drama. The antagonist must be strong enough to pose a daunting obstacle to the protagonist. You must make it hard as heck for your hero or heroine to succeed! From Scarlett O'Hara to Lucy Ricardo, the size of the challenge makes the protagonist's struggle (and ultimate result) worth watching. Ideally, conflict grows from the meeting of determined, formidable opposites, like an irresistible force meeting an immoveable object. Think of Oscar (slob) and Felix (neat freak) in *The Odd Couple*, Stanley (reality) and Blanche (deception) in *A Streetcar Named Desire*, or Anna (modern West) and the King (ancient East) in *The King and I*.

The best conflicts are those a protagonist is forced to contend with. Few empathize when someone goes looking for trouble, but we all root for people when trouble comes looking for them. A heroic figure like Batman or Indiana Jones can pursue conflict, but it only becomes interesting when that trouble turns out to be far more than the character bargained for. Let's say your play is about Joey, a boy who wants to spend a hot summer day playing outdoors with his pet dog. The antagonist could be Joey's mother, who wants him to finish some chores and practice the piano. It could also be the weather, with threatening thunderclouds rolling in. It could even be the dog, who would rather relax in the air-conditioned house. Better yet, it could be a combination of all three! Joey doesn't go looking for these obstacles. The harder it is for him to get what he wants, the more audiences will enjoy watching his struggle to get it.

Plot

Plot is the line of events in a story, the things that characters say and do. Please note that good plays do not begin at the beginning of a story, but in the midst of one. Before the curtain rises, forces in the story have long been in motion, the characters developing, and the elements of conflict brewing. In fact, the central conflict must come to a head in the first few scenes. From the moment the curtain rises, use *exposition* to introduce audiences to your play's world. The *central struggle* begins at the point of attack, the event that forces the protagonist to either change that world or save it from some threat. That point of attack should come early, setting events into motion toward the *climax*, a moment that resolves the main action of the plot. The climax should come as close to the final curtain as possible, giving the audience a sense of emotional satisfaction, sometimes called a *catharsis*.

The protagonist must do more than win; he has to be better or wiser than he was before the play began. Audiences expect to see characters change and learn as they face a conflict, and the character's actions must demonstrate that change. In *A Christmas Carol*, Scrooge doesn't just proclaim that he is a new man; he joins his nephew for Christmas dinner, sends a prize turkey to the Cratchits, raises their father's salary, and changes their lives forever. Scrooge's final actions alter his world, giving audiences a fulfilling catharsis.

Dialogue

Dialogue is more than just words. It is verbal action, expressing the conflicts and forces at work in the play. Dialogue is a playwright's primary means of communicating information to the audience. It sets the play's tone and thrusts the action forward, letting us into characters' minds, conveying emotion, and stimulating audiences to think and feel. Instead of offering an exact replica of real-life conversation, dialogue is an artistic revision designed for actors to speak and audiences to hear. Clear, simple sentences are easier for actors to deliver and easier for audiences to understand.

Each of your characters must speak with a distinct personality, a unique voice. If I gave you a page of dialogue from *The Odd Couple* with the character names blacked out, you could easily tell which lines belong to Oscar and which to Felix. Strive to give your characters such singularity.

Amateur groups can create many forms of theatre, all of which involve the elements of storytelling discussed earlier in this chapter. Let's consider some of the most popular formats.

Revues and Concerts

Every song, skit, and dance routine in a revue has a tale to tell or some special light to shed on human experience. Revues first appeared during the late 1800s in Paris, at places like the Moulin Rouge and the Follies Bergere. The format did not catch on in America until Florenz Ziegfeld initiated his *Follies* in 1910, mixing political and social satire with lavish production numbers. Big-scale revues flourished on Broadway through the 1940s, when radio and television variety shows turned large-stage revues into things of the past. In recent years, intimate revues have reigned on and off Broadway, usually focusing on composers' careers or spoofing contemporary issues. Because this is a fluid format, revues can be all music, a blend of songs and scenes, or limited to skits and solo comedy routines. Three variations of the revue format are currently popular with amateur groups: musical revues, concerts, and comedy revues.

Musical Revues

Many ready-made Broadway revues centering on the work of specific songwriters are available, and these professionally designed shows can save your team a lot of effort. However, as long as you arrange with ASCAP or BMI for song royalties (discussed in Chapter 4), you can put together a tribute to most any composer, lyricist, or songwriting team yourself. You may also choose to build a musical revue around a particular decade or year, specific performer, or musical genre. If your revue focuses on living local songwriters, you will want a letter of agreement spelling out a compensation agreement for the use of their songs. Confer with an attorney for specifics.

Begin by researching your subject. Learn everything you can, trivia included. This will help you create an interesting context for specific songs. Your revue must have an overall point or story, such as the career of a songwriter or the musical profile of an era. Use songs to tell that story, with just enough connecting material (dialogue, solo narration, etc.) to pave the way.

In a musical revue, connective material should take up less than 10 percent of your total running time. The Tony-winning *Ain't Misbehavin'* keeps dialogue to the barest minimum, using a few lines here and there to create scenarios for a succession of wonderful songs.

Plan the order of songs with some sense of variety, altering between up numbers and ballads. Having several torch songs in a row can become tedious unless they are edited down into a concise medley. Likewise, placing one comedy song after another can kill the laughs. Vary the audience's musical diet! Swift pacing is also essential. Plan a smooth flow from number to number, with no prolonged pauses.

Concerts

For a scholastic music program, a concert can be an audience-pleasing, relatively low-cost option. The staging is minimal, with performers rarely doing more than standing and singing. Most concerts require no sets, and singers provide their own formal attire. Concert programming is very much like planning a musical revue. Know your subject or theme well, vary the song styles, and keep the pacing crisp.

Select the physical setup that best fits your needs. The traditional concert arrangement has musicians surrounding a conductor, with soloists beside the conductor and a vocal ensemble (if any) seated upstage. This straightforward approach works well, but don't feel bound by it. You can experiment with fresh physical arrangements, depending on acoustics and other features of your performance venue. For example, using a more Broadway-style arrangement with musicians in a pit would clear the stage for possible dance numbers.

Concert performances of Broadway musicals are becoming increasingly popular. On the downside, this format is less eye filling than a fully staged show, and you pay just as much for royalties. However, these concerts can be performed with scripts in hand, limited choreography, and no more than a few essential costumes and props. As a result, concert stagings cost less to present and require far less rehearsal time.

Comedy Revues

If you have one or more promising comedy writers in your talent pool, you might want to create a full-length comic revue with or without musical numbers. Or you might have some budding comedians who can put together a full evening of stand-up material.

To make such an evening more than just a parade of solo acts, see if you can get your comics together for group skits or improvisational bits.

You have to be careful with original comedy material. What may seem perfectly acceptable to inventive comic minds may set more tender sensibilities roaring with outrage. Righteous protest is now almost as likely on college campuses as it is in church halls. Political humor, a mainstay in most comedy revues, can inspire as much howling as sexual content. You may find it advisable to lay down guidelines to keep your comics on the reasonable side of caution, but be aware that caution can kill comedy.

Original Plays

Schools and universities with theatre departments often showcase the work of student writers. Such productions give young actors the opportunity to work on original material and allow fledgling writers to see their efforts onstage. While few of these works become commercial successes, those who write and perform in them often go on to careers in theatre, film, and television. Whatever their artistic merits, these showcases cradle the future of mainstream American entertainment.

Many community theatres present original works on at least an occasional basis, either as fully staged productions or simple readings. If you want to find new, unproduced plays, you have several paths open to you:

- Contact local universities with theatre departments

- Contact the New Dramatist's Guild (see Appendix B)

- Post a notice on theatre-related Internet chat rooms and newsgroups

> **Backstage Whispers**
>
> A number of foundations and other funding sources make special grants to support productions of new plays. If your group stages such works, be sure to research your options. The best place to start is The Foundation Center (contact info in Appendix B).

Once you get the word out, don't be surprised if you wind up inundated with submissions. You may need a committee of volunteers to sift through them all. Some playwrights may not want their works showcased by amateur performers, but others will leap at the chance. Choose as carefully as you would from established hits. And no matter how small your budget, make a point of offering new playwrights reasonable compensation for the right to stage their work. Showcasing new works does not justify cheating writers out of fair payment for their work.

Book Musicals

Any musical that tells a story is considered a book musical. Developing new book musicals is such a complicated process that that even the most seasoned amateur producers shy away from the challenge. Few amateur groups have the resources to develop these works. An experienced production team is a must. Scores have to be written, vocal and orchestral arrangements prepared, and scripts reproduced.

Even if all the special talents required volunteer their services, this process can be costly. Daunting as all this can be, a few high schools and community theatres have presented new book musicals successfully. While none of these productions has ever led a show to Broadway, they are remembered for years, becoming community legends.

Children's Theatre

I believe that anyone who has a reasonable way with words and the desire to write can learn to create workable plays for children. When writing for young audiences, try to see and hear your story through a child's eyes and ears. Because children expect stories to have a point, a clear premise is essential (does this sound familiar yet?), as are vivid multi-dimensional characters and a compelling conflict—in short, the same elements needed for adult plays. Use clear language at all times, and keep the vocabulary accessible to your target age group. Physical comedy is preferable to verbal humor, which can be difficult for smaller children to grasp.

Adaptations

If you are adapting a published story, you must determine if that story is in the public domain or still protected by copyright. Copyright laws can be rather complex, but odds are that anything published within the last 75 years or so is still protected. To dramatize such material, you must obtain permission from the author or (if deceased) the author's estate. The process of tracking down rights holders is so complex that attorneys specialize in it. The U.S. Copyright Office can help you identify who holds most copyrights. Their website (www.uscopyright.gov) even includes a search option for recent works. See the next section on "Copyright Protection" for complete contact information.

Copyright Protection

From the moment you write down or record an original song or dramatic work (including any script, melody, lyric, choreography, or pantomime), you own the copyright to that material. No one may perform, publish, or otherwise reproduce that work in any form without your consent. While formal copyright registration is not legally required, it is a great way to prevent misunderstandings.

Don't worry about a big publisher or established author stealing your work. Most copyright abuse comes from less-imposing sources. I once discovered that a songwriting partner was submitting our work to producers and claiming to be the sole author. When confronted, he said there was nothing I could do about it—until I reminded him that all my lyric copyrights were registered. I sent polite notes to the producers in question, one of whom soon invited me to work on a project. I have also found the occasional singer performing my lyrics without permission. At such times, copyright certificates make performers (and their attorneys) extremely cooperative.

In the United States, the registration process is inexpensive and simple:

1. Go to the U.S. Copyright Office website (www.copyright.gov/register/literary.html).

2. Download Form TX.

3. Send the completed form, your manuscript, and a check for $30 (payable to "Register of Copyrights") to:

> Library of Congress
> Copyright Office
> 101 Independence Avenue, S.E.
> Washington, DC 20559-6000

Copyright registration becomes effective when a manuscript arrives at the Copyright Office, but it takes up to five months to generate a formal certificate of registration.

The Least You Need to Know

- ◆ All forms of stage entertainment require a premise and one or more characters.

- ◆ All storytelling forms also require a plot that places characters in conflict.

- ◆ Children's plays use all the same storytelling elements, while keeping a child's perspective in mind.

- ◆ Always protect your original stage works by registering the copyright.

Chapter 6

Financial Realities: "A Mark, a Yen, a Buck, or a Pound"

In This Chapter

◆ Finding funding for your show

◆ Creating a responsible budget

◆ Producing within your means

◆ Avoiding budget busters

Financial concerns intimidate many creative people. If that includes you, relax. There is nothing in these next few pages that you can't handle. I will walk you though the process of building a budget step by step. Amateur productions have to pay their bills just like everybody else. That means you have to set priorities (easy enough), create a workable budget (a bit of work, but still easy), and then stick to it (ah, that's the kicker!).

Where's the Money Coming From?

It's a long way from the decision to put on a show to the glory of opening night, and along that way a lot of preliminary expenses await you. If a sponsoring organization is covering all production costs, be incredibly thankful—somebody up there likes you. The rest of us back here on Earth have to figure out where our production money is coming from.

You can't put off things like rights payments, staff fees, space rental, supplies, or publicity costs until money starts coming in at the box office. Your budget will have to indicate where the bucks for these necessities are coming from. The last thing you want is your business manager telling you there's no money to pay the bills a month before opening night.

There are several options for paying production expenses:

Backstage Whispers

Tony-winning producer John Glines once told me, "The first step in any production is to sit down and work out a sane budget. No one can be creative if bill collectors are banging on the rehearsal hall doors."

- Early ticket sales
- Organizational sponsorship
- Your pocket
- Patrons
- Corporate sponsorship
- Traditional fund-raising
- Miscellaneous sources

I have known amateur productions that used each of these options, either alone or in combination. Let's consider each in detail.

Early Ticket Sales

Most amateur productions rely on ticket sales to cover the majority of their expenses. But it is hard to generate substantial sales far in advance, and many items will have to be paid for before opening night. Once your group has a reputation, advance sales may improve, but only to a degree. You may want to consider one or more of the alternate sources listed throughout this chapter.

Organizational Sponsorship

Sponsoring organizations (schools, churches, companies, etc.) may cover all preliminary expenses on the understanding that they receive all proceeds. Such an arrangement simplifies a producer's life, but you must never take such a relationship for granted. In some cases, sponsoring groups may only cover part of your costs or will hold reimbursement until after the production is over. In an era of lean-and-mean budgeting, there may be little or no money available to support your project. If this happens, no need to give up. You just have to locate other funding. Your first option is to cover expenses yourself.

Your Pocket

If you have millions to spare and can pour unlimited finds into a production, by all means do so. You may never see a monetary return on your investment, but the psychological rewards will more than make up for it. And if you're going to be in New York City anytime soon, drop me a line. We can do coffee and talk over this great idea I have for a musical …

Okay, back to reality. Even if you're just a working stiff, when preliminary production expenses are small—say, a few hundred dollars—you may be tempted to cover them yourself. This sort of arrangement can work, but you must handle it with care. Draw up a specific, written agreement with any sponsoring organization guaranteeing that box office income will compensate you before going to any other use. Be sure such an arrangement is reflected in your budget. If you're planning to make a gift of some or all of the funds, be sure to cover that in writing so your generosity can be turned into a legal tax deduction.

> ### On Stage
>
> When I was an elementary school teacher, budget cuts left no money for the annual musical. I volunteered to cover preliminary expenses, with the written understanding that I would be compensated out of the ticket sales. The day after our final performance, my savings were restored, and the school still received a handsome amount.

Before paying for production expenses, have a clear, written agreement defining what you will spend and how you will be compensated. Even then, be sure your every expenditure is properly documented. No matter how honest or innocent you are, sloppy bookkeeping can make it look as if you're picking the production's pocket, and the appearance of impropriety can prove disastrous. Worse yet, there is always the chance that ticket sales may not be enough to cover what you lay out. Just as you would set a limit before entering a casino, be sure to limit the total amount you're willing to cover—and pick a figure that you can comfortably afford to lose.

In the heat of rehearsals, you and other members of the production team may be tempted to shell out additional bucks for unexpected expenses. Such generosity could do wonders for the production but leave personal finances in tatters. However good your cause, keep hold of your everyday cash.

Patrons

When preliminary expenses are far more than you can cover personally, it's time to consider private sponsorship. There are times when a generous individual may be willing to donate production expenses. Accept an outright gift with every possible expression of gratitude, but beware of those who give money to gain some creative control over your project. ("My granddaughter would be perfect for the lead.") Such relationships are tricky at best and can have unpleasant ramifications.

Most sponsors expect some public mention of their generosity, while others prefer anonymity. Adhere strictly to whatever terms you and a sponsor agree to. You should neither embarrass the meek with a curtain call nor deny the proud a well-earned ovation. However, all patrons should receive a heartfelt letter of thanks from the producer and/or director.

Having individuals (other than the producer or director) put up money with an expectation of reimbursement is always a bad idea. In commercial theatre, investors understand the risks, but such arrangements can wreak havoc at the amateur level. It is impossible for any amateur effort to guarantee that ticket sales will cover costs. Individual investors can say they understand this and then sing a very different tune if they wind up losing even a small part of their money.

Corporate Sponsorship

Shows affiliated with a 501(c)(3) nonprofit organization may be able to attract corporate sponsorship. Your best bets are local businesses looking for a way to give something back to the community. One of the best things about corporate sponsorship is that it comes in the form of an outright gift.

To pursue corporate sponsorship, start with companies that you or your production team members have connections to. Relatives, friends, students, golfing buddies, and old schoolmates—consider everyone you know and then find out who *they* know. A personal link can get more immediate attention for your proposal.

Businesspeople appreciate an organized, businesslike approach. You cannot expect to get funding for a vague, half-baked project. Offer sponsors a formal written proposal, with a cover letter describing your production plans, a complete and detailed budget (as discussed later in this chapter), and samples of design sketches and publicity materials. You may even want to include materials from previous group productions (if any).

Be clear as to what sort of recognition businesses can expect for their generosity. Program credit and a few warm words of thanks during a curtain speech are always appropriate, but there are limits. In this day of aggressive product placement, be sure sponsor expectations don't clash with your best interests. I once saw a production of *Bells Are Ringing* where a corporate sponsor's banner was draped over the proscenium, hanging so low that the audience could not see part of the set. A potentially effective marketing tool became a much-resented annoyance. The following year, the same company placed its banner in the lobby, and everyone was much happier.

Another option is sponsorships by individuals, particularly if your cause lacks formal nonprofit status. Be sure such support is an outright gift, and that clear written agreements spell out whatever terms are expected on both sides.

Traditional Fund-Raising

Many amateur theatre groups cover their initial production expenses by organizing traditional fund-raising events: bake sales, car washes, and so on. The simpler and less expensive the event is, the better. In some cases, auxiliary groups or PTAs put these fund-raisers together.

Many books on traditional fund-raising exist, so I will limit my advice on this subject to one overriding suggestion. Don't just do what every other group in your area is doing. Blend your fund-raising efforts into the existing culture of your community, and come up with something distinctive. Be sure your efforts don't conflict with other local events, either in scheduling or in format. Your annual preproduction fund-raiser can become as much of a community tradition as the show it helps pay for.

Miscellaneous Sources

Program advertising is discussed in Chapter 23. As you will learn, while advertising can add a helpful amount to your bottom line, it requires a serious time and talent commitment on the part of volunteers.

Creating a Budget

You must set down a budget in black and white—no red! If you have ever had to create or live by a budget (and yes, a home budget counts), you know how important this process is. Even if you don't have sponsors to impress, a detailed production budget organizes your expenditures, clarifies your thinking, and helps your group make the most of whatever money is available.

In your production budget, spell out every expenditure and anticipated source of income. Have solid numbers for each item! Get your designers and administrative team involved. Those who help build or at least review a budget are less likely to overrun it. In the early stages, this process involves some guesswork. The sooner guesses can be converted to hard figures, the sooner you will have a meaningful, workable budget.

A Model Production Budget

This budget format is designed to be flexible. Remove any items that don't apply to your production. While I have tried to include every likely line item, be sure to include any additional income source or expense your project may have.

Projected Income

Ticket sales	$_____
Sponsorships	$_____
Patrons	$_____
Program ads	$_____
Concessions	$_____
Other (specify): _____	$_____
Total projected income	$_____

Projected Expenses

Royalties and administrative costs:

Rights	$_____
Scripts/scores:	
Purchase/rent	$_____
Shipping	$_____
Administrative costs	$_____
Total royalties	$_____

Production staff:

Director	$_____

Music director $_____

Choreographer $_____

Stage manager $_____

Other (specify): _____ $_____

Total staff $_____

Costumes and Accessories:

Designer $_____

Purchases $_____

Rentals $_____

Shipping $_____

Cleaning $_____

Total costumes $_____

Makeup and hairpieces:

Purchases $_____

Fees $_____

Total makeup $_____

Props:

Manager $_____

Purchases $_____

Rentals $_____

Shipping $_____

Repairs $_____

Total props $_____

Sets:

Designer $_____

Materials $_____

continues

continued

Space rental $_____

Equipment rental $_____

Transportation $_____

Total sets $_____

Lights:

Designer $_____

Purchase items $_____

Rental items $_____

Equipment rental $_____

Transportation $_____

Total lights $_____

Sound:

Designer $_____

Operator $_____

Equipment rental $_____

Purchases $_____

Related expenses $_____

Total sound $_____

Space:

Rehearsal rental $_____

Performance rental $_____

Maintenance fees $_____

Security fees $_____

Total space $_____

Programs:

Layout costs $_____

Printing costs $_____

Shipping $_____

Total programs $_____

Tickets and public relations materials:

Layout costs $_____

Printing costs $_____

Shipping $_____

Total tickets and PR $_____

Emergency fund $_____

Total Projected Expenditures $_____

Total Projected Income $_____

Projected Gain/Loss $_____

Some clarification:

Income:

- ◆ Ticket sales: Take the number of seats you hope to sell, and multiply it by the ticket price. (See Chapter 22 for help with this step.) Then multiply the result by the number of paid performances.

- ◆ Sponsorships/patrons: When submitting a budget to potential sponsors, include the amount you are requesting from them in your calculations.

Expenses:

- ◆ General rule: For expenses that you're unsure about, set your estimate slightly higher than your best guess. Err on the side of caution.

- ◆ Administrative costs: This covers everything from phone calls to office supplies. If you have a sponsoring organization, odds are they will cover these items for you.

♦ Emergency fund: You must have a contingency fund on hand for the inevitable unexpected expense. For first-time producers, this amount should equal 10 percent of your total production budget. With experience, you may find that less will do.

Budget Busters

The numbers in your production budget are serious commitments. Our nation's leaders may get away with deficit spending, but you can't. Anything you spend beyond your budgetary limits has to be deducted from the bottom line. You'll be fine if ticket sales bring in more than expected, but you can't count on such a windfall. Once your production budget is set, you must make every effort to stick to it.

Of course, sticking to any budget is easier said than done. In the course of rehearsals and performances, all sorts of little budget busters can come along. Several of the most common are:

♦ Overestimated ticket and ad sales

♦ Unexpected expenses

♦ Undocumented expenses

♦ Forgetting to say "no"

♦ Big spenders

♦ Greed

Each of these deserves some detailed consideration.

Overestimated Ticket and Ad Sales

You know those figures you came up with for ticket and program ad sales? Well, take another look at them. Everyone I know in amateur theater has overestimated these numbers, and some never quite get over the habit. Don't do it! My advice to first-timers is to take your current estimates and cut them by one-third. Before you start screaming, I have news—this figure is still probably too high! But odds are that at least it is closer to the truth.

While downsizing income estimates can feel like a downer, it helps you plan tighter, more realistic production finances. And at least when aiming for smaller ticket sales, you may be able to reduce your royalty payments. See the discussion of rights payments in Chapter 4.

A number of amateur companies require all cast and crew to sell a minimum number of tickets and/or program ads. While I consider this practice unattractive, it is neither illegal nor immoral.

> **Gremlins**
>
> Odds are that your production will not sell every ticket. Most Broadway shows aim for operational budgets that can be covered if just 50 percent of the house is sold (gulp!). You don't have to be that careful, but keep your sales estimates on the conservative side.

Unexpected Expenses

No matter how well you plan, there is no way to foresee every contingency. "Little surprises" are bound to crop up: a few replacement bulbs here, an overnight shipping charge there. There are also things like facility maintenance fees no one told you about in advance.

Then there are some far costlier surprises: the set that has to be rebuilt or the crucial piece of equipment that shorts out and must be replaced. And yes, little things like fires, leaky roofs, or burst pipes can occur at the darndest times. You may need to hire an electrician for emergency repairs or pay for new materials. Such expenses can be steep, and you have no time for additional fund-raising when you're in the heat of production.

In theatre, as in life, it is best to expect the unexpected and accept from the start that you and others on your team are going to make a few mistakes. This is why I advise having an emergency fund equal to 10 percent of your total budget. That will cover most surprise expenses, and odds are you will not need all of it. Any unused sum automatically becomes a positive addition to your bottom line, so think of it as a no-cost form of insurance.

Undocumented Expenses

There are times when production staff will make small purchases on behalf of the production and expect compensation. This is a reasonable way to handle minor transactions, but people have been known to take advantage of such an arrangement. Make it clear from day one that all production-related expenditures must be documented by receipts (for merchandise) or invoices (for services). No compensation without documentation! Under no circumstances should a business manager accept anyone's word regarding expenses—not even your own.

Forgetting to Say "No"

Saying "no" is one of the most powerful tools any producer or director has. Designers and publicity directors can get sudden inspirations and come at you with dazzling proposals. All sorts of fascinating things might be accomplished by spending a few hundred dollars more here and a thousand or so there. However good these ideas sound, never let them endanger the budget. If the money is simply not on hand, respond with a polite but firm "no."

When production staff refuse to take no for a financial answer, I find one argument often proves effective. Tell them they can make the desired expenditure if they raise the money for it themselves. After all, the producer's job is to fund the budget. If anyone wants to add a major expense, make it that person's job to fund it. I have seen this approach turn many a "must have" into an "oh, we can get by without it."

Big Spenders

The business manager has to keep a close eye on all expenditures and alert the producer whenever there are signs of unusual or unexplained spending. Producers must be firm about budgets, keeping after each department to be sure every dollar is spent for sensible reasons. Being a financial disciplinarian can be a bummer, but it is a key part of the producer's job description.

When it comes to spending questions, producers should initially give designers and other staffers the benefit of any doubt. Keep the tone of all budget-based conversations positive and cordial. First of all, there may be nothing more at stake than an innocent misunderstanding—in which case, anger will seem silly and cause unnecessary bad feelings. Even intentional overspending is almost always done with the good of the show in mind. So there is no need to act as if someone has betrayed the team by making a questionable purchase.

It is best to correct and forget minor, unintentional errors. For more serious spending mistakes, a few words of gentle warning are usually all that is required. Your goal is to correct, never to humiliate. If advisable, have your business manager offer transgressors additional hands-on guidance with spending.

Every now and then, you'll come up against someone who refuses to listen to reason. Some have issues with authority, and some are just irresponsible with money. They will "yes" you to death, assure you they won't mess up again, and then go right ahead and keep on spending. You cannot afford to let such a person have access to the till. One loose spender can turn a successful amateur show into a money loser.

That is why I hold to a strict "three financial strikes and you're out" policy:

- One serious spending mistake is automatically forgiven as human error.

- A second mistake means a stern warning to tow the line, or else.

- A third mistake means the permanent withdrawal of authority to spend another dime.

> **Backstage Whispers**
>
> Advice from an experienced amateur producer: "When it comes to money mess-ups, three times is the end of the discussion. Honest or not, that's someone we cannot allow near the till."

Invoke this policy only when absolutely necessary. You run the risk of the offender quitting, but that beats having all your efforts endangered by one irresponsible person. Some organizations have found it helpful to reduce this to a two-strike policy; go with whatever works best for your group.

Greed

In some cases, one strike is more than enough. Anyone who is caught stealing supplies or funds must be dismissed immediately. Such incidents are rare, but not nearly as rare as they used to be. Thievery can devastate your production budget and demoralize the entire company. Accusations must never be made lightly, but once you are certain something inappropriate is going on, take decisive action. If major theft or damage occurs, notify the police and take whatever legal steps are necessary.

The Least You Need to Know

- There are many sources for early production funding, ranging from sponsors and patrons, to general fund-raising, to your own pocket.

- You must create a detailed, realistic production budget covering every expected source of income and all foreseeable expenditures.

◆ When preparing your budget, beware of overestimating income and underestimating expenses—almost everyone does it, especially first-timers.

◆ The producer and director must know how to say no to unnecessary expenses and rein in anyone whose spending endangers the budget.

◆ There is no room in amateur theatre for financial dishonesty. Anyone caught stealing supplies or funds must be dismissed immediately.

Part 3

Building Your Team— "Side by Side by Side"

Don't you hate those endless acceptance speeches on awards shows where actors thank a dozen or more people you've never heard of for "making it all possible"? Well, theatre is a team effort, and the many members in such a team must work together. So building your production team is more than a question of finding enough people; you must find people with the ability and cooperative spirit required to make your show a winner. The next few chapters discuss how to organize and select the best people for your project, bringing together a small army of volunteers and paid staff. What? You didn't know anyone in amateur theatre gets paid? More surprises (mostly pleasant ones) lie ahead.

Chapter 7

Selecting Production Staff: "You for Me and Me for You"

In This Chapter

- ◆ Finding volunteers and hiring professionals
- ◆ Using a production organizational chart
- ◆ Deciding how many people you need on your team
- ◆ Considering personality as well as ability
- ◆ Providing contracts for paid staff
- ◆ Considering background checks for certain positions

Like most sports, theatre is very much a team effort, and the members of a team must work together. One of the keys to keeping a team effort harmonious is having a well-defined organization where everyone understands the placement of responsibility. This chapter teaches you how to organize the best team for your project. This is more than a question of finding enough people; you must find people with the ability and cooperative spirit required to get the job done well.

Building a Strong Team

You've probably seen those classic advertisements featuring a team of massive horses pulling a wagon loaded with barrels of beer. Each of these powerful animals is capable of pulling a full share of the load, making a massive chore no real strain on any one of them. Before diesel-powered trucks roamed the planet, wagon drivers had to master the art of matching heavy loads to the number of horses on their team. Taking on a load with two horses too few would risk exhausting all of them.

Gremlins

You know the old saying that "a chain is only as strong as its weakest link"? Well, you will never learn the truth of this faster than in the theatre! In most team sports, you can keep weak players on the bench, but when it comes to putting on a show, everyone has to be "on the ball."

Now I'm not suggesting that you should think of your production staff as a team of horses—although I have heard them referred to as far worse. My point is that when planning your team, keep in mind that every position requires a tremendous investment of time, effort, and ability. Having too few team members risks overtaxing the whole bunch.

It is common for amateur stage productions to have volunteers combine jobs. Taking on any two of the major production jobs discussed in Chapters 8, 9, and 10 can work out well enough, but anything more than that is crossing the fine line between martyrdom and recklessness. Sure, having fewer team members can streamline things, but it can also send the production (and the martyrs in question) flying down a fast track to collapse.

Is it possible to pretty much run a show single-handed? Sure, as long as you keep the production compact, have a downright obedient cast and crew, and resign yourself to having no free hours or personal life until the production closes. Your call.

Backstage Whispers

"You have no idea what a poor opinion I have of myself—and how little I deserve it."
—William S. Gilbert

In the late 1800s, William S. Gilbert was the driving force behind a series of acclaimed comic operas that he wrote with composer Arthur Sullivan. Gilbert served as librettist, lyricist, director, and co-producer for *H.M.S. Pinafore*, *The Pirates of Penzance*, *The Mikado*, and 10 more shows. He had to fill these jobs because no one else at the time understood the new levels of professionalism Gilbert was aiming for.

The good news is that it is no longer impossible to find people who can share in and support your creative vision! So why do so many first-time producers and directors make the mistake of taking on too many production jobs at one time? Some are convinced that no one else will get those jobs done capably. Well, however gifted and energetic you may be, your time and talents can only stretch so far. The more tasks you take on, the less you will be able to invest in each of them—and the weaker your overall results will be. Accept the fact that you're going to need help. You (and yes, I mean *you*, kiddo) cannot do it all.

Other first-timers assume it will be impossible to find willing volunteers. Nonsense! People in every organization and community will be happy to help put on a show. But it is up to you to reach out and find them. Teachers, truck drivers, secretaries, retirees, real estate brokers, school kids, ministers, office executives, doctors, store clerks— I have seen all these and more volunteer to handle offstage chores with the same enthusiasm you would expect from stars in the spotlight. All someone had to do was ask.

Finding People

Putting together a production team comes down to hiring the right person for each job, whether he is paid staff or a volunteer. The idea of "hiring" people can sound intimidating, but don't worry! This process requires good judgment, determination, and a sense of organization—the same basic qualities it takes to handle most aspects of producing amateur theatre.

In House

You start by reaching out to those in the school or organization presenting your show. Go with whatever method best fits your group culture—post a sign-up list or offer an e-mail address or phone number where people can ask for more information. Be as specific as you want about the kind of help you're looking for, right down to listing open job titles. Even if you don't get a full slate of people right off the bat, you may be surprised by the number of people who express interest.

Networking

Networking is another source of production talent. The hit play *Six Degrees of Separation* took its title from the theory that no more than six acquaintances stand between any two people on the planet. While that may not be a mathematical certainty, I've seen it confirmed by my experience in amateur theatre. A few contacts making phone calls can lead to valuable, talented people.

Encourage early joiners to assist in the recruiting effort. Every person already on your team has a personal network of family, friends, and neighbors he can reach out to. Stage crew can be your best source for finding more crew volunteers, and your publicity director or lighting designer may be able to link you up with a promising stage manager or costume seamstress. Be sure to encourage your own friends, relatives, and neighbors to get into the talent search.

Public Notices

If your production reaches out to the general community for its cast and audiences, it makes sense to do the same when putting together your production team. Try a free notice in the local paper or flyers posted on bulletin boards ("Putting On a Show: Help Wanted"). There may be some people you would rather *not* work with, but you can usually find jobs for everyone who wants to take part.

Checking References

When someone unknown to you offers his services, avoid making any automatic commitments. If anyone claims important experience, verify those claims. With professionals or volunteers, ask for references and then call them. If one of your designers is not all he claims to be or your electrician wouldn't know a license from a short circuit, the time to find out is now, not on opening night.

Your Organizational Chart

Many people automatically ignore organizational charts, but I urge you to pay serious attention to the one shown here. Like everything else in this book, it is designed to simplify your life. Most amateur production staffs are a blend of paid professionals and volunteers, so egos can be fragile. While you can't prevent all personality clashes, having a clear production hierarchy can minimize friction.

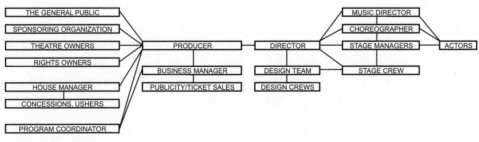

Model organizational chart.

This chart defines the chain of responsibility linking everyone in your amateur company. Everyone should know to whom to bring questions or concerns. I have maximized it to give every person required for a large-scale musical production.

Because this chart is designed to empower, not to tie your hands, let's make a few clarifications:

- ◆ The producer may deal directly with any company member at any time. However, once a show goes into production, the producer should always respect the intermediate people in the chain of command (particularly the director), including them in important decisions.

- ◆ I have included all members of the design team in one box because they must all serve as absolute equals, with the director settling any creative disputes.

- ◆ All members of the company can communicate with each other at any appropriate time. However, production concerns should be passed through proper channels.

- ◆ If someone perceives a genuine emergency at any time, the organizational chart becomes irrelevant. Speak up!

On Stage

During a community theatre dress rehearsal I took part in some years ago, the cast began noticing signs of smoke. It turned out that a light just above the stage had shorted out. A stagehand said that she had noticed the problem earlier but did not say anything because she had no way to contact the lighting designer mid-rehearsal. The director held an immediate full-company discussion of basic emergency procedure—when you see physical danger, instantly get the word to the stage manager or another person in authority.

Team Planning: Do You Really Need *All* These People?

While shopping in a large home improvement store, I could not help overhearing as a man wearing tattered overalls and a slightly panicked expression spoke to a clerk:

Customer: "Can you tell me everything that I need?"

Clerk: "Sure, if you can tell me what it is you want to do."

Customer: "How the heck am I supposed to know that?"

Do you really need all the people included in the model organizational chart shown earlier? The simple answer is, it depends. If your show has no sets, there would be no point in having a set designer. And if your event is for a guaranteed audience (students in a school, company employees, etc.), then publicity and ticket sales may be nonissues.

Trim the chart to custom fit your needs. Read through the job descriptions in the chapters that follow. If it is clear that a particular position would be a waste of your people power, leave it out. When you are not sure, fill as many of the chart positions as you can. You can always reassign someone to an understaffed department mid-production.

Ability and Personality Both Count

Professional qualifications are just one factor in selecting your production team. It is equally important for you to consider a prospect's personality. You work with a person, not his job record. The last thing you want to do is make the mistake of "hiring a resumé."

In *Sunday in the Park with George*, Stephen Sondheim observes that "Art isn't easy." Well, that goes triple for a collaborative art form like theatre. Every one of the people involved in a production brings special talents to the mix, and ego is the handmaiden of talent. That is why the theatre is a parade ground for creative egos, and wherever a number of them parade about at the same time, scrapes and bruises become inevitable. While you cannot hope to prevent such clashes altogether, you can minimize them by judiciously choosing who works on your production.

I know one professional actress who is considered a Broadway star. Fans follow her every move, and her name on a marquee sells tickets. Onstage, this vocal powerhouse delivers with a vengeance, winning unfailing cheers and rave reviews. But she takes increasing liberties with her performance over the course of a run, and her backstage behavior is infantile. Fans wonder why she only works on Broadway once every decade or so. The reason is that it takes 10 years for memories of her behavior to fade. Eventually, someone breaks down and hires her again, only to find her as impossible as ever.

> **Backstage Whispers**
>
> "Bad manners, Mr. Bornay. The infallible sign of talent."
>
> —Socialite Joan Crawford responding to rude violinist John Garfield in the 1946 film *Humoresque*

The era of the "irreplaceable talent" has passed. Artistic temperament may have been tolerated and even expected at one time, but no one needs to put up with it today. There are many people who could step in and get most jobs done without causing angst. If you find yourself considering a qualified talent attached to an obnoxious ego, ask yourself some frank questions:

- Is there no one else in a 50-mile radius who can handle this person's job?

- Will replacing this person jeopardize the production?

- Is this person really irreplaceable, or am I just talking myself into believing that?

If your answer to any of these points is a firm, honest "yes," start practicing meditation techniques and fasten your seatbelt—it is going to be a bumpy run. I discuss the very real challenge of working with difficult people in Chapter 14 (in the section "Prima Donnas and Tantrums"). Some of those suggestions may prove helpful, but when it comes to difficult production staff, the best cure is early prevention. Whenever possible, don't hire a headache.

Of course, there are times when a potential source of trouble winds up working on a production whether you like it or not. When your boss's wife or kid is in the cast or one of the local nabobs takes a production job so he can second-guess your every move, you have to decide whether it's worth it for you to take on such *tsurris*.

def•i•ni•tion

Tsurris (pronounced *tsoo-riss*) is a Yiddish word meaning "troubles" or "aggravation." It is frequently heard in theatrical circles, as in, "Oh he's got talent, but with his attitude he's guaranteed tsurris."

There is little point to investing your time and effort in amateur theatre if you aren't enjoying it. So think long and hard before forcing yourself to work with aggravating people. Life is too short! I have talked myself into such scenarios over the years and always lived to regret it. Mind you, a successful opening night makes a wonderful tonic for all kinds of ailments, including the regret one suffers from working with toxic colleagues, but at least be honest with yourself about what you're getting into.

Contracts for Paid Staff

I suggest having a written agreement with every person involved in your production. But with paid members of your production staff, a written contract is essential. For some reason, the idea of contracts freaks out some people. If you are one of them, relax—I promise this will be easy.

You hire paid members of your production staff as consultants, not as full-time employees. As such, there is no need for any complicated paperwork. If your school or sponsoring organization has an existing system regarding contracts and compensation for paid consultants, just go along with whatever the established system requires. If no such system exists, you will want to create a basic *letter of agreement* for each paid staff member. These letters are binding legal agreements, but no legal mumbo-jumbo is required—just straightforward English. As a first-timer, you may want a friendly attorney to double-check such agreements before signing, but if the terms are basic and clear, that won't be necessary.

def•i•ni•tion

A **letter of agreement** is just that—a letter defining the basic terms of a legal agreement.

Letters of agreement allow two parties to define the terms of a simple business relationship. You say you're uncomfortable making such written commitments? Well, if you want people to make commitments to you, you have to be ready to make some in return. In this case, you, as a producer, want to know that someone will deliver particular services in a timely, professional manner, and your staff members will want to be paid in the same way.

A letter of agreement for a paid staff member should include the following:

Backstage Whispers

"God is love, but get it in writing."
—Gypsy Rose Lee

- ◆ Clear descriptions of all the staff member's responsibilities

- ◆ All required deadlines or due dates connected with this person's duties

- ◆ The amount and terms of payment

- ◆ Signatures of the staff member and producer

A typical letter of agreement could be worded as follows:

Letter of Agreement

Between Henry Ford High School and Emma Goldman

Date: _____

Emma Goldman agrees to serve as choreographer for Henry Ford High School's production of the musical *Ragtime*. Ms. Goldman will:

- Attend all preproduction planning sessions and auditions.

- Create choreography for all musical numbers.

- Submit plans for all dance numbers by March 15.

- Train the students at 12 dance rehearsals in April and May.

- Be available for up to six additional dance rehearsals if needed.

- Assist at all technical and dress rehearsals in the first week of May.

In exchange for Ms. Goldman's services, Henry Ford High School will pay her a flat rate of $_____, payable within 30 days of the final performance.

Signed and agreed,

_____   _____

Jay P. Morgan, Producer   Emma Goldman

Background Checks

You must consider running background checks on anyone in your group who will be working with money or children. Both are irresistible lures to the unscrupulous and the unhinged. You may have lived next door to someone for five years, but that does not mean you know about his past. Recent headlines make it clear that "harmless" people in every community have criminal records.

This can be a sensitive and upsetting issue, but you cannot afford to overlook it. Various websites make it easy and affordable to research criminal records. Have volunteers sign a waiver granting permission for a background check. While such permission may not be legally required, it is best to be upfront about such a procedure. If someone objects to having his background checked, you are probably better off without him on your team.

There are situations where running a background check could be inappropriate. You are not looking to insult anyone—only to avoid harm. For example, there is little point in investigating your business manager if she is an established figure in the community or an employee of your sponsoring organization. Likewise, teachers and administrators taking part in a school production have (one hopes) been hired based on their records.

One additional suggestion—make it a policy to have more than one responsible adult present when anyone is working with children. This simple procedure can prevent all sorts of misunderstandings.

The Least You Need to Know

♦ Taking on too many jobs leads to burnout. Be easy on yourself and share the workload.

♦ You won't know how many people are interested in working on your production until you ask around.

♦ Having a clear production hierarchy clarifies lines of responsibility, prevents misunderstandings, and simplifies the production process.

♦ Select production staff based on personality as well as ability.

♦ Every staff member should have a formal letter of agreement spelling out their duties and any compensation they are to receive.

♦ It is a good idea to run background checks on any staff members who will be working with children or production funds.

Chapter 8

The Executive Team: "You Gotta Have Heart"

In This Chapter

◆ The responsibilities and relationship of the producer and director

◆ The choreographer's special role

◆ The special challenges faced by the musical director

◆ The stage manager and stage crew's demanding jobs

◆ The need for a business manager

The executive team for any amateur production has to be the crème de la (available) crème. Select these people as carefully as you choose leading performers, because they, too, can make or break a show. The difference is that because the producer, director, music director, stage manager, and business manager get little if any glory and applause, good production leaders are often in shorter supply than eager performers.

The Producer

Standing at the head of any production's organizational chart, the producer has the final say on all major business decisions. Old movies have spawned lots of popular misconceptions about what a producer does. If you have visions of glamour and power, this is not the job for you. Oh sure, on opening night you will be applauded and congratulated, but in the months leading up to those few glittering hours, the amateur producer faces enormous responsibility.

> **Backstage Whispers** _____
>
> A Tony-nominated producer was cleaning out a Manhattan loft he had used as an experimental performance space. Several volunteers helped with grungy, backbreaking work, but no one put in more effort than the producer. After hours of hauling, sweeping, and scrubbing, he paused, wiped perspiration from his forehead, and announced, "This is what I really love about the theatre—the #!&%ing glamour."

The producer is the one person in any theatrical enterprise who can never say, "That's not my department." Producers are responsible for—and therefore concerned with—every aspect of a production. If a hallway is dirty and there is no one else on hand, the producer picks up a broom and starts sweeping. (You should only hope that a dusty floor is your biggest problem!)

The amateur theatre producer is responsible for …

- ◆ Overseeing the cast and crew. This includes having final say when hiring or letting go of paid staff and volunteers.

- ◆ Creating and using a clear production hierarchy so every question can be referred to the right person for resolution.

- ◆ Keeping the production team coordinated and on track.

- ◆ Setting and sticking to a production budget, reining in anything (or anyone) that endangers the bottom line.

- ◆ Securing funds for the production and finalizing all business decisions.

- ◆ Scheduling the overall production.

- ◆ Setting and enforcing deadlines for creative and technical staff.

- ◆ Scheduling use of rehearsal and performance space.

- ◆ Settling serious disputes between cast and crew members.

- ◆ Serving as the production's official spokesperson to vendors, authorities, and the community at large.

- ◆ Providing a safe and secure environment for cast, crew, and audience.

The producer and director must have a basically harmonious relationship and maintain a common front. It helps if both can maintain a clear division of responsibilities. But there are times when the lines of demarcation blur, especially when dealing with expenses or the possible replacement of company members. While a producer can overrule a director, the inelegant use of that authority is a sign of poor leadership and will lead to bad feeling on both sides. The producer and director must settle any disagreements in private. Dissension or even subtle tension between these two people soon becomes evident to everyone else involved in a production, and this can have a disastrous effect on morale.

On Stage

Curt Ebersole has served as producer and musical director at Northern Valley Old Tappan High School for more than 20 years. Has he ever considered directing as well as producing? "Are you kidding? If I didn't have another faculty member on hand to direct, I wouldn't stand a chance. As it is, I always spend the week before opening night wondering if I am going to find time to eat dinner or get the laundry done. Trying to produce, conduct, and direct at the same time would be impossible."

At times, keeping a show on budget means a producer has to confront various members of the production team about expenditures. This should always be done in private, with the director present to offer the producer complete support. If you are a first-time amateur producer, there is no need to feel uneasy about such discussions. Overspending is almost always done with the best of intentions—those little things that pave the road to you-know-where. Keeping everyone on the financial straight and narrow gives a production a far greater chance of financial success.

The Director

Teacher, guru, traffic cop, and cheerleader, the director is the creative commander of any theatrical production. A director is a problem-solver who is on hand to instruct, inspire, enlighten, coordinate, and see to it that audiences get the best show a cast and crew can offer. A director's duties include ...

- Coming up with an overall production concept (discussed in Chapter 13) and communicating it to all members of the production team.

- Scheduling and running fair auditions designed to encourage unknown talent to reveal itself.

- ◆ Finalizing all casting decisions.

- ◆ Scheduling and running effective cast rehearsals.

- ◆ Staging all dialogue scenes and those musical numbers that involve no dance movement.

- ◆ Helping performers develop their characterizations.

- ◆ *Integrating* all creative departments, making sure the various elements fit together.

- ◆ Creating a well-ordered, nurturing production environment.

- ◆ Setting and upholding standards and deadlines for cast and crew.

- ◆ Teaching by example.

- ◆ Balancing the needs of the production with the needs of individuals.

- ◆ Encouraging the artistic growth of staff, cast, and crew by creating opportunities for them to learn new skills and expand their personal horizons.

def•i•ni•tion

Integration means getting all the elements in a production to harmonize. When asked what made *Oklahoma* into a groundbreaking integrated musical, Richard Rodgers replied, "The orchestrations sounded the way the costumes looked."

This is one job where personality and imagination count as much as (if not more than) professional credentials. I have seen directors with all-amateur credits helm many first-rate stage productions.

A good director understands that no one can automatically command authority and respect. These are things one earns by a consistent display of competency, fairness, and intelligence. Hollering sessions have the opposite effect. Amateurs of all ages quickly lose respect for directors who make the fatal mistake of displaying bad temper or arrogance. Think back on the times when people in authority have been angry with you. Who impressed you more, the ones who screamed or the ones who kept their cool?

When Directors Produce—or Producers Direct

Jazz legend Louis Armstrong once said, "When some people don't wanna know, you can't tell 'em." That certainly applies to first-timers who think they can simultaneously produce and direct an amateur show. A recent e-mail from just such a person asked, "Why do I need someone else to produce? This is a neighborhood show with only a few dozen people. From what I see, producing is a few little side jobs I can handle in my spare time." Despite my detailed pleas to the contrary, that director served as her own producer. When her production neared its opening, she dropped me another e-mail stating, "Why didn't you warn me this was going to be so hard? I have no idea how I am going to get through half of the things I need to do."

It is feasible to serve as producer-director for a small production with simple requirements. However, any show with more than one set and a handful of actors is another matter. You may see yourself as a small-town Hal Prince, but you'll be setting yourself up for a series of royal headaches. Months from now you will be drowning in responsibilities and wondering what you've gotten yourself into—and will have no one to blame but yourself. No awards are given for "Burnout of the Year," and it is far nicer to share the glory of a success than to tell to your cast or audiences that "there wasn't enough time to do it all."

If you are determined to do this double duty, nothing I say is likely to stop you. But before taking on such a load, do yourself a favor and take the time to ask around. I have never had great difficulty locating someone willing to lend a hand. Somewhere nearby, there is someone with either the organizational flair required to produce or the creative instinct one needs to direct. Develop a working partnership, and you just might spare yourself a working ulcer.

> **Gremlins**
>
> Each job on the executive team is multifunctional. Assume that more than one of these titles is the equivalent of working on more than one production at once. As someone who has tried this in the past, I speak from experience—don't do it! Share the burden.

Assistant Director: Do You Need One?

The overwhelming majority of amateur productions get by without having an assistant director on staff. However, for elaborate productions or in situations where a director has other concerns (work, family, or health issues) that may interfere with his commitment to a production, an assistant director can be a valuable asset.

This is the perfect position for someone who wants to gain directorial experience. An amateur theatre company that wants to survive over time will want to nurture and develop new production talent. You can tailor this job to meet your production's special needs—running rehearsals the director cannot be on hand for, supervising specific aspects of production, prompting lines and cues, or taking care of whatever other tasks need doing. When in charge, an assistant director speaks with all the authority of the director. Therefore, it is essential that a director and her assistant work together like two hands on the same body.

There have been cases where a producer-director dumped so many duties on an assistant director that the designation became something of a joke. If someone handles most of the major items on the director's list of responsibilities, it is ridiculous to say he is "assisting." In such cases, "associate" makes more sense. Giving directorial credit where it is due will earn the increased respect of everyone connected with a production.

The Music Director

In musical theatre, the music director (MD) is in charge of all the musical elements and materials. During actual performances, while the director, choreographer, and designers become little more than spectators, the MD is still hard at work, leading the cast through every musical turn.

The music director's responsibilities include …

- Taking part in the audition and casting process, helping assess the musical ability and potential of each performer.

- Recruiting and supervising all musicians, both professional and volunteer. Finding the right people can be a challenge on a tight budget, and pit musicians (whether paid or volunteer) can have egos that more than match the ones onstage.

- Recruiting and supervising any other musical staff. When a rehearsal pianist and/or vocal coach is required, they should report to the MD.

- Scheduling and running effective orchestra rehearsals. The trick is determining the number of these rehearsals based on the budget and the musicians' level of talent.

- Coordinating the rental, purchase, and distribution of all sheet music, including orchestral and vocal scores. In most organizations, this is handled in partnership with the producer and director.

- Running effective vocal rehearsals for the leads and chorus. It is up to the MD to be sure every song in a show meets its musical and dramatic potential.

- Creating recordings of dance music to be used in dance rehearsals. This can free up the MD or rehearsal pianist for vocal rehearsals.

- Obeying all relevant copyright laws. Rehearsal recordings, photocopying of music, and any changes to the score must be handled within legal guidelines. When in doubt, consult the rights holders.

- Making sure the piano is tuned and well cared for.

- Conducting all major rehearsals and performances. When the curtain goes up, the performers must rely on the MD to set the pace and sidestep potential disasters.

- Maintaining any space reserved for musicians, including the pit and backstage. Cleanliness and safety mean as much here as anywhere, especially with the ever-increasing presence of electronic equipment. It is also the MD's responsibility to be sure these areas are cleared and cleaned after a production ends.

- Supervising the ongoing use and final return of all rented scores, including cleanup. This tedious task can best be handled by inviting the musicians to a "cleanup" party, handing out erasers and having them clean up their scores before food and drinks are served.

As with the stage director and choreographer, the MD must have extraordinary patience and persistence to work with people at varying levels of musical talent and experience. The MD's tasks can be divided among several people, including a rehearsal pianist and vocal coach, but one person should have a clear position of musical authority.

With the increasing use of prerecorded accompaniment, some might be tempted to think there is no need for a music director. Wrong! During rehearsals, the music director can make the score more accessible to cast members with little or no musical experience. In performance, even the most experienced performers need a conductor to cue songs and keep them on beat. It is madness to leave the control of a prerecorded score in the hands of overworked *techies* who have little knowledge of music and might not have full visual contact with the people onstage.

def•i•ni•tion

Techies is affectionate theatre slang for members of the stage and technical crews.

The Choreographer

In a musical production, the choreographer is in charge of staging all dance sequences and intricate group movement. Amateur musical productions are now expected to present dance with all the care lavished on other elements of the production. If you decide to do a show where dance is a major element, you have to have someone who will do it well, planning dances that are entertaining to watch and safe to perform. That is why your choreography ought to be handled by someone with professional dance and a solid understanding of musical theatre staging.

The choreographer's duties include …

♦ Taking part in the audition and casting process.

♦ Working closely with the director and music director to plan all dance sequences.

♦ Attending all creative staff meetings.

♦ Working with the designers to be sure all sets and costumes will allow for proper dance movement.

♦ Designing varied dance sequences that can be performed safely. The goal is to provide stylistic variety while causing no injuries.

♦ Running safe, affirmative dance rehearsals. Realistic goals and an upbeat attitude are far more inspiring than exhausting sessions and dictatorial methods.

♦ Attending all tech and dress rehearsals where last-minute tweaking can make all the difference.

In both professional and amateur theater, it is not unusual for one person to serve as both choreographer and director—but only if the person in question has experience in both domains. When the jobs are not combined, it is vital that the director and choreographer work together. The separation between dialogue scenes, songs, and dance sequences must appear to be as seamless as possible.

Choreographers must try to build confidence while teaching the basics of stage movement. Amateurs of all ages are afraid to "look silly," but this can be a particular challenge with self-conscious teenagers. Even so, with the right blend of patience and persistence, a choreographer can turn inexperienced high school kids into show-stopping tap dancers in a matter of weeks.

The Production Stage Manager

The production stage manager (PSM) handles two very different jobs. During auditions and standard rehearsals, the PSM is the director's ever-ready assistant. Once the production reaches tech rehearsals, the PSM must become a commander, supervising final rehearsals as well as all performances. Remember the TV series *M*A*S*H*? Well, the ideal PSM has to be a Corporal Radar who can morph into Colonel Potter.

This position requires an exceptionally organized and responsible person the director can trust. In most school productions, this is the highest production position entrusted to a student. In other amateur companies, the PSM can be any age, as long as he or she is reliable, has a positive attitude, and (when possible) possesses a degree of backstage experience.

A production stage manager's responsibilities include …

- Assisting the director in every aspect of the production process, from auditions to *strike set*, so it is vital that these two people work well together.

- Attending and assisting at all meetings, auditions, and rehearsals.

- Processing and posting audition and rehearsal schedules (some knowledge of basic computer programs is a plus).

- Collecting and collating information from performers, including maintaining a production contact sheet and an emergency contact book.

- Maintaining lines of communication between the director and all cast and crews.

- Creating and maintaining a *prompt book*.

- *Prompting* dialogue at all rehearsals and performances.

- Recruiting and co-supervising the stage crew.

- Maintaining rehearsal attendance records, keeping the director informed of absences and poor attendance patterns.

def•i•ni•tion

Strike set occurs after the final performance, when all sets, props, and other production materials are cleared out of the performance space.

To **prompt** is to assist actors by calling out forgotten dialogue or lyrics. Also sometimes known as "cueing."

The **prompt book** is a photocopy of the script annotated with all the stage directions and cues used in a particular production. The stage manager compiles this book during the rehearsal process and uses it as a guide to running tech rehearsals and performances.

Cues are signals to actors or crewmembers.

- Coordinating different rehearsals.
- Maintaining all rehearsal areas at the start and end of every session.
- Handling chaos with calm.
- Calling the *cues* for final rehearsals and performances.
- Supervising strike set.

There is no way to overestimate the PSM's importance. Good stage managers are the unsung heroes and heroines of every successful amateur production. When you find one, thank the higher powers for your good fortune, and treat this living treasure accordingly.

> **Backstage Whispers**
>
> Stage managers must be prepared for all sorts of challenges. During a national tour in the 1930s, actors Ethel Barrymore and Louis Calhern both had a few drinks too many before curtain time and wound up forgetting their lines in the middle of a shared scene. The stage manager stood in the wings whispering and then shouting the next line, until the great Barrymore proclaimed, "We know the line, young man. We want to know who says it!"

The Assistant Stage Manager

Because the PSM is responsible for such a dizzying array of tasks, it is not unusual for professional productions to use several assistant stage managers (ASMs). As amateur productions become more complicated, this job is becoming a regular part of the team.

The PSM must work closely with any ASMs. You can assign an ASM any variety of tasks that would otherwise fall to the PSM, such as maintaining the prompt book, cuing at rehearsals, or coordinating the stage crew. All ASMs should answer to the director, with the PSM as more of a team captain than a boss.

The Stage Crew

While computerized hydraulics control most Broadway set changes today, amateur productions still rely on human power to get things on- and offstage. Train the stage crew to handle …

- The construction, load-in, and maintenance of all set elements.
- The troubleshooting of common backstage problems.

- The operation of any special equipment (smoke machines, etc.).

- All staging cues required by the production.

- The striking and storing of all sets and related equipment.

By working on set construction, amateur stage crews gain a hands-on knowledge of the set pieces they will have to work with in performance. In close consultation with the director and designers, the PSM creates schedules for the stage crew that fit around the times the performance space is needed for cast rehearsals. It is not unusual for members of the cast to lend a hand in set construction and decoration, and some actors may even double as stagehands during performances, but the director and PSM must plan such double-duty assignments with care. Most actors have enough to worry about in the midst of a performance without having to move major set elements around.

I am always amazed at how many talented, energetic people volunteer to join stage crews. Most audiences never notice the crew unless something goes wrong, but such gaffes are usually the fault of the creative team. If sets are not completed until the final dress rehearsal, the stage crew is bound to have trouble maneuvering in the dark on opening night. Be sure your stage crew is given ample rehearsal time with all sets and the full cast on hand. Properly trained and equipped, a stage crew will do its job with the same devotion one expects from the performers in the spotlight.

The Business Manager

Even the most capable amateur producer can have trouble with the fine points of bookkeeping. If your production is affiliated with a school or sponsoring organization, odds are procedures exist for handling bills and staff expenses. As a courtesy, you may want to confer with the "powers that be" on how they wish to handle the following items. However, if you are not blessed with preexisting institutional support, you will need a dedicated, detail-oriented person with the accounting know-how required to serve as business manager.

A business manager's responsibilities include …

- Assisting in the development and review of the production budget.

- Paying all bills and salaries in a timely, professional manner, keeping production staff, licensing companies, vendors, and the community at large happy and on your side.

- If appropriate, setting up a separate business checking account for production expense. Depending upon an organization's way of doing business, this is either a necessity or a nonissue.

- Alerting the producer to any unexpected expenses or questionable expenditures.

- Reviewing all income, including ad, concession, and ticket sales. The most honest volunteers can make mistakes, and a business manager can resolve these before they become problems.

- Preparing a final financial report. If your business manager is not a professional bookkeeper or accountant, have a pro assist in preparing this document.

The business manager is part bookkeeper, part financial whistle blower—but getting other team members to mend their budget-busting ways is the producer's job. Any business manager who finds the producer refusing to stick to the budget should think about locating the nearest exit.

The Least You Need to Know

- Members of the executive team must work together to coordinate crucial aspects of the production.

- The producer secures the funds, sets the budget, has the final say on all business issues, and serves as official spokesperson for a production.

- The director works directly with the designers, performers, and crews, overseeing all creative aspects of a production.

- The choreographer stages all dance sequences.

- The production stage manager acts as the director's main assistant during rehearsals and then runs all final rehearsals and performances.

- The stage crew builds, maintains, and maneuvers all set elements.

- The business manager oversees expenditures and assists the producer in keeping the production on budget.

The Design Team: "The Colors of My Life"

In This Chapter

- ◆ Getting the right designers for your show
- ◆ Defining key creative production positions
- ◆ Selecting creative support teams
- ◆ Meeting audience expectations

Ah, theatrical design! The glamour, the magic ... the mountainous effort! In a large-scale stage production, for every hour that goes into rehearsing performances, at least five hours of labor go into the creation of sets, costumes, lighting, and sound. And each of these elements requires a talented, knowledgeable designer. Having the right designers on hand will literally put your performers in the best possible light.

The Right Designers for Your Project

A paying audience expects that the design and technical elements of any live event will be handled effectively, making the performance attractive, easy to see, and clearly audible. Amateur productions are not excused from this standard. You may charge a fraction of Broadway's price, but that doesn't mean audiences will accept a poorly presented product. And why should they? Sloppy design and technical elements are the surest signs of an "amateurish" production. Chintzy sets or shabby costumes distract from even the best performance, and your cast's efforts will be wasted if the audience cannot clearly see and hear what is going on.

So if you are going to have sets, costumes, lighting, or sound, you must have people on hand with the creativity and technical know-how required to make each of these features a strong point rather than a distraction. This does not mean that your designers must be professionals in these areas, but they should have solid experience. As a fledgling producer or director, the last thing you need is a lighting designer who doesn't know a "fresnel" from a "gobo." (More on those when I discuss lighting in Chapter 19.)

Productions have very specific needs. I recently took part in a benefit concert that involved four professional singers, a pianist, and yours truly serving as narrator. The performers provided their own formal attire (no costume designer) and used a simple platform stage decorated with floral sprays (no set designer either). A physical production could not be much simpler. But the 300-seat performance hall had a high vaulted ceiling, with no stage lighting or sound system. So the producer arranged for a professional to install and operate portable lighting and sound equipment. With one basic light plan, five microphones, and two quality loudspeakers, our presentation looked and sounded great.

It is important—and at times quite difficult—for creative people to keep their roles in perspective. When a designer acts as if his or her contribution (sets, costumes, etc.) is the most important factor in a show, it can lead to unreasonable creative and financial demands that throw the entire project off balance. I cannot tell you how many times I have seen a good performance *hijacked* by design elements that got out of control. The simple, foolproof remedy for this is having a producer or director who is willing to keep all the production teams in synch with the overall creative concept. Holding the line is not always easy in the face of touchy artistic egos—but letting those egos run unchecked risks wasting your entire team's effort for the sake of indulging one or two people. By making sure that all your designers stay on the same track, you can avoid major misunderstandings and reap handsome creative dividends.

def•i•ni•tion

Hijacking is when a production is overwhelmed by one element that is either mishandled or allowed to get out of hand. A great performer can steal a show—sets that fall apart, ill-fitting costumes, bad lighting, or a howling sound system can hijack it, making it impossible for audiences to appreciate the performance.

The Set Designer

The set designer (also referred to as the scenic designer) creates the physical playing environment for a production. This can range from providing drapes and floral displays to using flats, drops, and three-dimensional elements to create a series of semi-realistic settings. This job should go to someone with at least some practical experience in creating stage settings.

The scenic designer's responsibilities include …

- Working closely with the director and other production team members to plan all scenic elements. The design team must coordinate the use of color and space, keeping every production element in line with the director's overall vision. The production elements must all fit into the space available, while leaving adequate space for the actors to move in comfort and safety.

- Helping create and stick to the set budget. It is vital for the director, producer, and scenic designer to come up with a workable figure. A gorgeous setting that sinks a production's finances is not successful.

- Creating blueprints, sketches, and/or set models for complex set designs—all crucial for multi-set productions.

- Obtaining all supplies required for set construction and decoration. If a designer plans on using it, he or she is responsible for finding, buying, or begging it.

- Creating a work schedule for the set construction team. This must be a practical, workable plan that coordinates with other planned uses of the performance and backstage spaces—and the availability of your team members.

- Supervising the construction and timely completion of all scenic elements. Although a separate job in professional theatre, amateur production designers oversee the building of sets in accordance with the overall production schedule.

- Consulting with whatever experts are needed to create safe, stable, effective settings. As in other design departments, this job requires someone who is not afraid to ask for advice or assistance from more experienced hands (shop teachers, carpenters, etc.).

- Completing the set in time for final rehearsals. The technical and dress rehearsals will be useless if the cast and crews do not have finished sets to work with.

- Supervising the installation of set elements. The designer must be on hand to assist in the assembly, hanging, and storage of all scenery.

- Assisting in the installation of lighting. Set elements may have to be moved or altered to allow safe and effective lighting.

- Assisting in the training and supervision of the stage crew. Working closely with the PSM, the set designer shares responsibility for making the designs actually work onstage.

- Being present for all rehearsals involving set elements. This includes all technical and dress rehearsals where the set designer may be called on to make repairs or adjustments.

- Maintaining clean and safe conditions in all performance and set storage areas. I think it's fair to say that most amateur theatre injuries occur in connection with the building or use of sets. The designer must take every reasonable precaution during construction, especially in regards to the use of power tools or other heavy equipment. That done, the designer must also work with the director and PSM to be sure set elements, ropes, and so forth create no hazards backstage.

- Supervising the placement of set elements at the end of every performance. The designer must be sure the sets and the performance area are always left in good order, creating no hazards of any kind.

- Supervising set strike and final cleanup. The stage and backstage areas must be left looking as good if not better than they did before the production. This includes the proper disposal or storage of any leftover set elements, supplies, and equipment, including any hazardous materials.

The most underrated challenge for set designers is to build and install set elements without disturbing the rehearsal schedule. As a production nears opening night, everyone will want dibs on the performance space. While it is vital that the stage crew have time to install and practice working with all set elements, other aspects of the production must be given their share of time and attention. The set designer has to know which set issues should be given priority and when it is advisable to defer to other departments. The best sets won't look like much if they are not properly lit or if they clash with the costumes.

The Costume Designer/Coordinator

Depending on the nature of your production, this will either be one of the easiest or most demanding positions on your production staff. A play or musical set in contemporary times will need nothing more than a coordinator who makes sure that every cast member has lined up the right clothes for their characters. Costumes for a basic elementary school production (such as a holiday pageant) can be handled by sending home simple guidelines and letting parents dress up the little settlers, angels, and shepherds. But a large play or musical, particularly one with a period or fantasy setting, will require a designer/coordinator whose talent as a seamster matches his or her organizational flair.

There was a time when it seemed like every housewife in America could master a sewing machine and a dress pattern. In our consumer-driven age, such people have not disappeared, but they are getting harder to find. While creating your own costumes is usually the most economical option, you may find rental necessary for some if not all of your costume needs. In that case, the designer/coordinator will have to oversee the selection, use, washing, and eventual return of these rental items.

The costume designer's duties include …

- Working closely with the director and other production team members to plan all costumes. The design team must coordinate the use of color and space, keeping every production element in line with the director's overall vision.

- Helping to create and stick to the costume budget. Costumes that sink a production's finances are not successful.

- Creating the design and safe construction of original costumes. This requires some practical experience. It is also important to be sure sewing machines and other equipment are only handled by capable, well-supervised volunteers.

- Supervising all costume crew. In large productions, the designer will need assistance to acquire, care for, and store costumes and accessories.

- Coordinating the selection, alteration, storage, cleaning, and eventual return of all rented costume elements. This is a potential headache if mishandled.

- Planning and coordinating homemade costumes by giving performers or parents easy-to-follow instructions for creating appropriate costumes.

- Making sure all costume elements allow for easy movement. Performers have to be able to dance, fight, and just plain move comfortably at all times.

- Taking measurements of all cast members. This process should be handled early on in the rehearsal process.

- Purchasing all fabrics, thread, and other costume materials.

- Purchasing or renting all costume accessories, including gloves, hats, umbrellas, neckties, boots, period shoes, etc.

◆ Providing performers with lists of all required costume items. Even when the production provides costumes, actors must come up with appropriate undergarments, contemporary footwear, and other personal items.

◆ Delivering all costume elements on time. Every costume and accessory must be clean, fitted, and ready for use before the first dress rehearsal.

◆ Attending all costume rehearsals and performances. The costume designer is needed at these times for fine-tuning, repairs, and troubleshooting.

◆ Providing emergency repair supplies for all costume rehearsals and performances. A well-prepared costume designer should have an ample stockpile of sewing needles, thread, fabric tape, pins and safety pins, irons, and ironing boards on hand.

◆ Handling or supervising all last-minute alterations. Even the most accurate measurements can't keep performers from gaining or losing a few pounds.

◆ Keeping food and costumes as far apart as possible. The consumption of anything other than water by anyone working in or near costumes must be forbidden. That includes crew as well as performers. A last-minute splash of cola can ruin months of preparation.

◆ Maintaining a checklist of all costumes and accessories. This will facilitate a quick daily inventory.

◆ Supervising an inventory after every rehearsal and performance. Every costume and accessory should be checked and stored before calling it a night.

◆ Supervising the ongoing cleaning, alteration, and repair of all costume items. The closing performance should look as fresh as the first dress rehearsal.

◆ Assisting in strike set. When the production ends, those costumes won't disappear by themselves. The costume designer/coordinator is responsible for the return, storage, or disposal of all costumes and accessories.

Designers have to appreciate how much effective costumes can add to a performance. As an amateur actor, I have found that the right outfit added immeasurably to my sense of characterization. So I am never surprised when I see how costumes can boost the overall level of performance, regardless of a cast's age or degree of experience. It is one thing to think you are a character—looking the part is often the crucial step in making a role come to life. This is why every costume element must be comfortable. Clothing that is too tight makes it impossible for actors to concentrate on their performances, and loose or ill-tailored clothes look so ridiculous that they distract audiences.

Period costumes can be a particular challenge. Actors will need ample time to accustom themselves to any items that are not found in contemporary fashion. Designers must be sure capes, hoop skirts, and other capacious costume elements can co-exist with the sets and fit in with the director's and choreographer's plans for stage movement.

On Stage

In a college production, I wore a series of glitzy costume pieces, including a heavy sequined cape. The cape was not ready until dress rehearsal, and it quickly became apparent that several bits of business the director and I had been planning would not work—the cape was far larger than we had expected. Unwilling to admit defeat, the director insisted that I stick to the planned business. Opening night went well until the final scene, where I spoke my last line, turned with a flourish—and made my exit cape-less. The sparkling material had caught on the set, where it hung like a dead drag queen. The director agreed to some changes, and at all remaining performances, I made my final exit intact.

The biggest mistake most first-time designers make is trying to handle all aspects of costume care single-handedly. If a production requires any more than a dozen costumes, recruit one or more volunteers to lend support. Seams and hems come undone, and zippers and buttons can give way during the heat of rehearsals or performances. There are often far too many urgent repairs for one or two pairs of hands to handle. Even if every stitch holds (and trust me, they won't), costumes can land all over the place after rehearsals or performances. With proper organization and a few extra pairs of capable hands, postperformance inventory can be handled in a matter of minutes.

The Lighting Designer

There are three indispensable elements in any kind of performance—the performer, the space, and the light. The latter is the responsibility of the lighting designer, who must create a lighting plan and oversee the crew that installs and operates the lights. Because this involves heavy equipment, ladders, and high-voltage wiring, someone with extensive experience must handle this job. A lighting designer's responsibilities include …

- Designing lighting that will illuminate the playing space effectively, suggesting the mood or time of day required in each scene.

◆ Working closely with the director and other production team members to plan all lighting elements. The design team must carefully coordinate the use of color and space, keeping every production element in line with the director's overall vision. The sets and lighting equipment must fit in the limited space available.

Backstage Whispers

When Cecil Beaton selected some exquisite pastel fabrics for costumes in *My Fair Lady*, lighting designer Abe Feder reacted by saying, "Very pretty, but would you mind bringing them over to my studio?" He then showed the production team how those subtle colors disappeared under stage lights. Instead of being annoyed, Beaton was delighted to discover the problem before thousands of dollars were wasted.

◆ Helping create and stick to the lighting budget. No production was ever turned into a hit by a costly lighting effect, but many have been marred by insufficient lighting.

◆ Creating blueprints for complex light plans. This is particularly helpful for large, multi-set productions.

◆ Purchasing all lighting supplies; spare bulbs and gels are a must.

◆ Creating a work schedule for the light team. This must be a practical, workable plan that coordinates with other planned uses of the performance and backstage spaces.

◆ Supervising the timely installation of all lighting equipment. This has to be done in accordance with the overall production schedule, with everything in place before the start of technical rehearsals.

◆ Assisting in the training and supervision of the light crew. The lighting designer is part teacher, part team manager.

◆ Being present for all technical and dress rehearsals. Last-minute adjustments are an unavoidable part of this job.

◆ Maintaining clean and safe conditions. Every bulb, wire, connection, outlet, and control board must be placed and used safely.

◆ Having a licensed electrician inspect and verify the safety of all electronic wiring and equipment. If your lighting designer is not a licensed electrician, bring one in to inspect all lights and wiring. There has not been an amateur theatre fire fatality in many years—keep it that way.

◆ Assisting with strike set and final cleanup. All lighting elements, supplies, and equipment must be properly stored, returned to their owners, or disposed of.

First-time lighting designers can succumb to one of two extremes—underkill (too little lighting) or overkill (too much). You can avoid this in several ways. One is to schedule one tech rehearsal devoted primarily to lighting issues. This will give you a chance to see what works and what doesn't, as well as ample time to make adjustments before the first performance. It is also a good idea to contact lighting designers working with other amateur groups in your area. Aside from creative advice, these colleagues can point you toward reliable suppliers—and can come through in a crisis with advice and loans of valuable equipment. Keep in mind that whenever a gracious favor is given, you must be ready to return the favor in kind.

The Lighting Crew

Intimate productions may be able to get by with little more than a lighting designer, but most productions will need several people to hang and operate the lights. Some amateur groups treat the lighting crew as part of the stage crew, but I think they deserve to be a distinct component in your team.

Gremlins

Give potential "weak links" an assistant. I worked on a community theatre production where the longtime lighting board operator started missing meetings and rehearsals. At my suggestion, the producer assigned a light board assistant, with the official excuse that it was always wise to train new team members. When the main operator dropped out of the show one week before opening night, her assistant handled the final rehearsals and performances with calm efficiency.

The lighting crew should meet early on in the rehearsal process, but their actual work does not begin until three or four weeks before opening night. The designer should make an effort to pass on to all crewmembers the skills needed to light your production effectively.

Lighting crew members should be trained to handle such tasks as ...

- Identifying, loading in, focusing, and maintaining all lights and related equipment.
- Reading and following a *lighting plot*.
- Troubleshooting common lighting problems.
- Operating any special equipment, such as the *light board*, spotlights, etc.

◆ Recording and running light cues.

◆ Striking and storing lighting equipment.

def•i•ni•tion

The **light board** controls all stage and house lights. Manual light boards include a series of switches and dimmers, while newer boards are programmed and operated by computer.

The **light plot** is a written plan listing all elements of a production's lighting system and all lighting cues.

Everyone in the lighting crew needs a clear sense of commitment to handling the almost invisible job of lighting a performance. I say "almost" invisible because a few crewmembers may work in full view of the audience, including the spotlight and lighting board operators. It should not be hard to find volunteers who are happy to handle these demanding tasks. As is the case with most technical staff, treat them as a crucial part of the team, and they will deliver.

If your lighting crew has more than three or four members, appoint a crew chief. In school and youth productions, it is customary for this position to go to a student. The lighting crew chief assists the lighting designer and supervises crew projects in the designer's absence. However, this is a position of responsibility, not one of authority. Any problems or disputes that arise in the light crew are best handled jointly by the director and lighting designer.

The board operator handles the lighting board for all rehearsals and performances. For most manual light boards, two operators are advisable, but for newer computerized boards, one operator is all you need. During tech rehearsals and performances, the operator takes all cues from the PSM.

The Prop Manager

Any handheld item that is not a costume element is a stage property or prop. The prop manager is in charge of the design, creation, and care of all props, including any edibles or drinkables required onstage. This job calls for a strong sense of organization, as well as a genuine streak of ingenuity.

A prop manager's duties include …

◆ Conferring with the director and all designers. Every prop will have to fit in with the production's overall look, so the director and designers will have to indicate the size, style, and color of important props.

- Helping create and stick to a prop budget. Once a budget is set, the prop manager cannot spend a penny more—unless it comes out of pocket.

- Creating a prop list. This scene-by-scene list of all required props becomes the prop manager's bible.

- Designing and constructing all original props. From period telephones to flaming torches, props do a lot to complete an effective stage picture. Some helpful books are listed in Appendix B.

- Obtaining items to be used as props. If a scene requires common objects that can be purchased or borrowed, there's no need to reinvent the wheel.

- Balancing realism with safety concerns. Weapons and other potentially harmful objects must be built or altered so they can pose no threat to performers, crews, or audiences.

- Recruiting and supervising prop crew. If it is clear that additional hands are needed, the prop manager must find and train assistants.

- Running prop inventory before and after all dress rehearsals and performances. Proper preparation prevents embarrassed improvisation.

- Maintaining the prop table(s) during all major rehearsals and performances. Performers making hurried entrances and exits can misplace props. The prop manager makes sure each prop winds up in its rightful place.

- Storage, return, and disposal of all props during strike set. The prop manager gathereth, and the prop manager giveth away.

Inexperienced producers and directors sometimes make the mistake of not having a prop manager, leaving it up to the actors to create and keep track of the props. It always seems like a nice idea—until somewhere in the midst of tech rehearsals when essential props begin to disappear. If your production involves more than a dozen props, a prop manager is a must-have. For complex productions, it is a good idea to have a full prop crew that can maintain prop stations on both sides of the performing area.

The Sound Designer

The sound designer is responsible for all the sound effects and electronic amplification for a production. This position requires a solid knowledge of sound equipment, as well as practical experience providing sound for public performances. This is no small matter. Anyone who has ever heard a sound system howl thanks to a misplaced microphone can understand how tricky it is to create effective amplification for live performances.

The sound designer's responsibilities include …

◆ Working closely with the director to understand the production concept and assess all sound needs. The number and type of microphones, speakers, sound effects, and required crew varies from show to show.

◆ Conferring with the costume designer on the use of any body mikes. The designer needs to know well in advance if microphones and power packs will have to hide in costumes or wigs.

◆ Helping create and stick to a sound budget. You must do what you can to give the producer and director a realistic idea of what good sound equipment will cost, and then do your best with whatever they feel the production can afford.

◆ Maintaining inventory of all existing sound equipment. You must know what you have in hand to calculate your needs before a new production. This also means keeping an ample supply of replacement batteries and other essentials on hand throughout the production process.

◆ Purchasing, renting, or borrowing all required equipment. From speakers to body mikes to wiring, the sound designer must find it all.

◆ Maintaining all sound equipment. All microphones, wiring, speakers, etc. must be kept in good working order.

◆ Scheduling timely load in and testing of all sound equipment. Install and test all equipment well before the first tech rehearsal.

◆ Training and supervising any sound crew. Any assistants should be fully trained to use all required equipment and handle basic troubleshooting. If the stage crew hangs the sound equipment, the sound designer should closely supervise this process.

◆ Attending all technical rehearsals and performances. These are the times that try sound designers' souls, when there is almost always trouble in need of shooting.

◆ Supervising sound strike and final inventory. All sound equipment must be returned, properly stored, or (if beyond repair) replaced.

In amateur productions, it is customary for the sound designer to run the sound system at all rehearsals and performances. Some school and youth productions hand this job over to a student, but the sound designer should be on hand to assist and troubleshoot.

For large productions with complicated sound requirements, a sound crew may prove useful, but in most cases, one or two capable individuals can handle all sound system issues.

The Least You Need to Know

- ◆ All production designers have to coordinate their efforts to meet audience expectations for quality design and technical elements.

- ◆ The set designer designs and builds all set elements and helps train the stage crew in how to handle them.

- ◆ The costume designer designs, constructs, purchases, rents, or borrows all required costume elements, including accessories.

- ◆ The lighting designer plans, installs, and oversees the use of all lighting.

- ◆ The prop manager must provide and oversee the use of all handheld stage properties.

- ◆ The sound manager plans, installs, and oversees the use of all sound effects and equipment.

Chapter 10

The Support Team and Volunteers: "All You Need Is a Hand"

In This Chapter

◆ Job descriptions for key production team positions often filled by volunteers

◆ The house manager, ushers, and concession staff

◆ Times to use volunteers, and times *not* to

◆ Managing your volunteer help

Volunteers are the backbone of amateur theatre. Even when professionals are on hand to provide guidance, volunteers get most of the physical work done both on- and offstage. Their enthusiasm makes up for any lack of experience, giving amateur productions an irresistible aura of energy and fun. In this chapter, I discuss several positions that usually go to volunteers and consider attitudes and policies that will make your production a happy, welcoming place for volunteers to be.

The Role of Volunteers in Amateur Theatre

Without a doubt, volunteers are the heart and soul of amateur theatre. They can fill any of the roles I have discussed in previous chapters and handle myriad smaller tasks: set construction and decoration, costume construction, hair and makeup, playing in the band, backstage help, crew (particularly assistants), lobby décor and cleanup, late-night drivers—and positions specifically relevant to kids' theatre, such as drivers for car pools, cast party coordinator, child wranglers for very young casts, and backstage chaperones for all ages through high school. (Just typing out the possibilities leaves my head spinning!)

There may also be quite a few "almost volunteers" who receive something nominal for their efforts. An experienced person may offer to set your lights for $100. Some high school and college students will work as stage crew for restaurant gift certificates or to earn community service points, either to complete their resumés or to meet scholastic requirements.

So the positions I discuss in this chapter are the tip of the iceberg, the most prominent jobs handled by volunteer hands. They constitute only the beginning, rather than the end, of volunteer staff possibilities.

The Publicity Coordinator

The publicity coordinator puts together and executes a publicity plan that will get the public's attention and fill your seats. This job calls for someone who is organized and energetic, who either has a knack for writing and graphic design, or who can build a team to get the work done.

The publicity coordinator is in charge of …

- ◆ Planning a comprehensive publicity campaign.
- ◆ Creating a logo.
- ◆ Generating posters, flyers, and all other publicity materials.
- ◆ Writing and circulating press releases to all local media.
- ◆ Supervising publicity photos of rehearsals and the final production.
- ◆ Inviting local press and community leaders to attend performances for free.
- ◆ Creating lobby displays.

Odds are that plenty of people are interested in seeing your production, but other things are clamoring for their attention. It takes a sustained and focused effort to reach as many potential ticket buyers as possible. The place to begin is with a detailed plan. Based on the general production schedule (discussed in Chapter 11), the publicity coordinator must schedule dates for all design submissions, identify promising excuses for press releases (auditions, first rehearsal, etc.), and decide which events to invite the local press to. The coordinator must run all publicity materials by the producer for final approval and then get those materials posted or distributed to all the right places in a timely manner. For a detailed discussion of publicity, see Chapter 21.

In professional theatre, advertising firms and press agents who specialize in theatrical projects handle publicity. But dedicated volunteers can excel in this position. If your publicity coordinator is under the age of 18, it might be wise to provide additional adult guidance, just to avoid missteps that could be caused by inexperience or ill-aimed high spirits.

Gremlins

Why is adult guidance necessary? Consider this: the student publicity coordinator for a high school production of *Stalag 13* was looking for a way to boost ticket sales and decided to have several cast members in Nazi uniforms stage a mock raid at a local shopping center—not realizing the date in question was a Jewish holy day. A faculty adviser got wind of this idea the day before it was set to happen and was able to avoid what might have been a very embarrassing incident.

The Program Coordinator

Amateur theater programs were once nothing more than a simple sheet of paper naming the cast and production staff. Now, most amateur groups turn out handsome, professional-quality booklets that add a touch of glamour while at the same time providing some much-needed advertising income. As a result, putting the program together has become a full-time job calling for someone with strong sales skills, a great sense of organization, and (if possible) some previous experience in program planning. Because computer skills are required and young people can excel at sales, this job is not limited to adults.

The program coordinator has to ...

- ◆ Plan layouts for every page in the program, using a computer program your printer can handle.

◆ Estimate the number of programs needed.

◆ Gather and organize program information for everyone involved in the production, including cast bios (if you are including them) and any sponsors or patrons.

◆ Work closely with the printer on design options, scheduling a definite materials submission deadline, time for proofreading the final draft, and a safe delivery date for the completed programs.

◆ Sell advertisement space to local businesses, community leaders, and organizations, as well as friends and family of the company.

◆ Assist in designing ads when necessary.

◆ Have all program contents collated, proofread by at least two reliable people, and then sent to the printer ahead of deadline.

◆ Be sure the programs are in hand on time.

◆ Create any program inserts, such as fund-raising flyers or lists of late additions to the cast and crews.

Even if you opt for a simple, ad-free program, it will be necessary for someone to organize the production credits and then create and run off the results. This is not something the producer or director can throw together the night before opening.

Fair warning: many producers have unrealistic hopes for program ad income. Printing costs can be high, and first-time groups can have a hard time making the program do much more than pay for itself. Having a good salesperson as your program coordinator makes a major difference. Some groups make ad sales a separate job. You must find someone willing to get out and pound the pavement, seeking businesses and local organizations that will be willing to buy space—along with the friends and family members who will be happy to add a page congratulating their loved ones in the company. I discuss the fine points of creating programs and selling ads in Chapter 23.

The Box Office Manager

The box office manager handles ticket sales and seating, bringing the art and commerce of theatre together. That is why the box office manager must be an organizer, banker, and diplomat all at the same time. This position requires someone of impeccable character, extraordinary organization, good mathematical ability, common sense, and a people-friendly attitude.

The box office manager is expected to …

- ◆ Work closely with the business manager.

- ◆ Create ticket sale spreadsheets.

- ◆ Set up advance ticket sale procedures via phone, mail, and/or Internet.

- ◆ Process all advance ticket orders.

- ◆ Manage the box office for all performances.

- ◆ Create seating charts for performances (if you are using assigned seating).

- ◆ Prepare ticket sales reports for each performance and a final report for the entire run.

As with any position where cash is handled, select the box office manager with care and give him detailed, ongoing guidance and supervision. In school productions, it is not unusual to have an adult volunteer serve in this position with a small team of responsible student assistants. At the very least, an adult should double-check all box office figures on a daily basis from the time ticket sales begin. With a daily check, you can catch innocent errors and thwart unscrupulous efforts.

On Stage

A longtime high school director who wishes to remain anonymous recalls one student box office manager who excelled at every facet of the job except the math. There were always a few dollars too many or too few in the till. Instead of assuming dishonesty and replacing anyone, the director arranged for an adult with bookkeeping experience to go over the sales figures with the student every day for a week. The discrepancies evaporated, and an enthusiastic kid got well-earned praise for a job well done.

The House Manager and Staff

Too many amateur productions treat house staff as an afterthought. However, these people are the first members of your team that audiences see, so they set the tone for all that follows as they greet and guide members of the audience to their seats. Have you ever had an evening at the theatre marred by an usher who placed people in the wrong seats? Then you know why everyone on the house staff should be trained to handle their responsibilities in an efficient and pleasant manner.

Of course, it helps if the house manager sets the right tone for the rest of the team. A house manager is expected to …

- Recruit and train concession workers and ushers.

- Organize all sales tables.

- Create and post any directional signs.

- Supervise the seating of audiences.

- Close the auditorium doors and cue the stage manager that the audience is seated and ready at the start of each act.

- Handle any audience problems (illness, disputes) during a performance.

- Open doors and assist audiences after each act.

- Be sure the house is clean and all audience members have left at the end of every performance.

- Maintain a "lost and found" collection as needed.

The house manager must be an organizer, motivator, and problem solver, setting an upbeat tone for the entire house staff. Beyond that lies the challenge of dealing with the general public. Audience members can get into bizarre arguments ("How am I supposed to see around that hair, dude?"), behave disruptively ("These are important phone calls!"), or suffer unexpected health problems. The house manager must be ready to referee disagreements, stop or expel troublemakers, and call for an ambulance or other emergency assistance.

On Stage

From an e-mail: "As house manager for our community theatre for fourteen years, I have had to deal with everything from serial talkers to geniuses chomping on carrots during a performance. I had to hold a performance once. A woman collapsed in the aisle and had to be taken away in an ambulance. But in truth, the most I usually had to worry about was an inexperienced usher sticking people in the wrong seats."

In extreme situations, the house manager may have to disrupt a performance. So this job calls for someone with solid judgment. While a responsible student can usually serve as house manager, it is a good idea to have an adult with some degree of authority on hand to provide backup.

Ushers

Determine the number of ushers you will need based on the size of your audience, with at least one for each aisle. They must be trained in using the seat numbering system (if any) and in guiding audience members to their seats in a swift and courteous manner. If you have open seating, you will still need several ushers to handle audience questions and (when possible) disarm potential disputes. Encourage ushers to pass on any serious problems to the house manager. All ushers must know the way to rest rooms, water fountains, public phones, and emergency exits.

Concessions

Entrust soda, snack, and souvenir sales to people who can handle money and merchandise responsibly. These volunteers will be expected to set up concession tables, haul supplies, make change, clean up after themselves, and account for all sales (and all unsold merchandise) at the end of every performance. The concession staff gets little thanks, yet their efforts add a great deal to an audience's comfort and enjoyment. Pick people who will help make your audiences feel welcome.

Security

In the past, security was not a concern for amateur theatre groups, but as Cole Porter observed, "times have changed." Unreasonable people can ruin the theatrical experience for everyone on- and offstage. Audience and company members must feel they are in a safe environment. Some facilities may have professional security staff, but you may have to arrange for such a presence. Be sure to clarify this issue when booking rehearsal and performance facilities.

Anyone who refuses to cooperate with house staff may need to be escorted from the premises. The house manager should have adult security staff available to assist in such situations. In some cases, local law enforcement officials are willing to be on hand—either as volunteers or for a reasonable fee. This is one area where you do not want to stint.

Volunteers and Friends

As the months of production pass by, you will be amazed at how much volunteers are willing to do to make your show a success. They will pour countless hours into every aspect of the production, and although their efforts may lack polish, few in the professional world could hope to match their dedication. The last thing any producer, director, or house manager wants to do is to take volunteers for granted. Even the most enthusiastic helpers have to feel that their efforts are appreciated. The ill-treated employee may stick around for a paycheck; volunteers stick around because what they do matters and is recognized.

The best "pay" for any volunteer is an ongoing diet of good old-fashioned praise. Many amateur producers and directors can fall into the habit of taking good efforts for granted. Make a point of remarking on every job well done, and do so publicly whenever possible. Did the stage crew work overtime getting part of the set painted? Let the whole company give them a cheer! When a performer makes real progress, let him know you've noticed. It will only take a few seconds, but such praise can make any volunteer feel like a million bucks.

Even the most encouraging leader can unintentionally overlook someone's contribution. There may be someone whose name is absent from the program or who does not get mentioned during a "thank you" speech. When such things happen (and they will), go out of your way to apologize and do whatever you can to make up for it. Never let any volunteer feel that his efforts have been overlooked. The smallest cog on the tiniest wheel in your production team plays a valuable role.

> ### On Stage
>
> I once volunteered to serve as stage manager for a cabaret revue showcasing the work of several friends. It was demanding work, with never so much as a word of thanks or encouragement from anyone. Naturally, I wound up feeling used. When the same group asked me for a repeat unpaid effort a year later, they were surprised to learn that I was "too busy with other projects"—another way of saying, "I'm *not* out of my mind."

One of the best by-products of appreciative leadership is that the entire company can develop a healthy habit of mutual encouragement. Instead of actors and tech crews operating as separate cliques, they become one cooperative group, genuinely pleased with each other's work and enjoying a common sense of accomplishment. If you see your company behaving this way, you will have succeeded in building a team. In my opinion, that is at least as important as putting on a good performance.

When *Not* to Pinch Pennies

So if volunteers are such a wonderful resource, why not use them to fill every production job? In simple terms, some jobs require a paid professional. If you're building your own home, family and friends can handle plenty of chores. But certain elements of design and construction require professional hands. It's the same way in amateur theatre. In certain key positions, the guidance of a pro is the only option.

Think you can't afford to have any paid staff? Sure you can. It may require rethinking your budget and doing some extra fund-raising, but that beats having your show ruined by inexperienced hands. Your entire company and the people who will be in your audience deserve the best you can offer them. This is particularly true when it comes to directors, choreographers, and designers. For the sake of safety and technical proficiency, get the best people you can afford. If you are unwilling to pay for a few key team members, you may as well consider dropping the idea of doing a show altogether.

Finding (and Keeping!) Great Volunteers

When you announce your plans to put on a show, volunteers will either inundate you or not show up at all—it tends to be either feast or famine. A great way to drum up additional helpers is to have your cast and crewmembers speak to any family, friends, and neighbors who might be interested.

People volunteer their time and talent for various reasons. But even the most dedicated volunteers have busy lives. Regardless of their age, it is a safe bet that everyone involved in your production has other things they could be doing, other commitments they set aside so they could be part of this show. Keeping them focused and motivated during the long process of putting on a show may sound difficult, but the challenges built into the process usually keep everyone fascinated. The one proviso is that the folks in charge must avoid letting the rank and file feel as if their time is being wasted. If you call volunteers in for a day or evening of work, be sure they have something constructive to do. A sense of accomplishment will keep them coming back to do more. Keeping rehearsals well organized and giving people a day or evening off whenever they are not needed will do a lot to keep your campers happy.

Treating all volunteers with respect helps, too. I have seen directors and designers rage at crewmembers and then react in shock when the victims of such verbal attacks walk out and leave a production shorthanded. Hello! Did these big shots think they were yelling at blocks of wood? Volunteers are people, and nothing obliges them to put up with rude or inconsiderate behavior. Human beings are going to make their share of unintentional mistakes. Gentle correction and encouragement accomplishes far more than bluster and spleen. Volunteers invest the living gold of their time and energy in your show—if you're wise, you'll treat them well.

As Strong as Your Weakest Link

As I've noted earlier, in any group effort, the team is only as strong as its weakest link. Volunteers become weak links when they are forced into jobs they are either unwilling or unqualified to fill. When you ask someone with no math skills to run your ticket sales or fail to provide young children with adult supervision, there are bound to be problems. It's great to show your confidence in individuals by giving them responsibility, but be realistic. Let people earn your confidence with their deeds.

By the same token, let deeds tell you when someone is in the wrong job. If it ever becomes obvious that a volunteer is not up to a particular job, step in tactfully. In a private chat, ask if he's enjoying his duties—if the answer is no, moving him to another production job may be the answer to his prayers. If the answer is yes, ease his workload by giving him an assistant or perhaps additional supervision—whatever it takes to keep this volunteer and your show both humming merrily along.

"Contracts" for Volunteers

Just as your paid staff should have written contracts, so, too, should all your production volunteers. I don't mean contracts in the technical sense, but a written commitment statement. Although these documents carry no legal weight, they do have a very real psychological value. This is particularly true with young children and teenagers, but commitment statements can have an impact with volunteers of all ages.

I find it useful to have all cast and crew sign such a statement at the first rehearsal. It helps people understand from the very beginning just how serious a commitment they are making to your show. I've seen slackers renew their efforts because they signed a letter promising to give their all. You will find a model version in Chapter 15.

Friends and Allies: Keeping in Touch

In the course of putting your production together, you will meet a wide variety of people in your community who express interest in, and perhaps outright enthusiasm for, your project. Exchange business cards with such people, or at the very least ask for an e-mail or snail-mail address. Take the time to save this information in a "friends file," a list of businesses and individuals who are rooting for you. Be sure they receive any publicity mailings, as well as invitations to fund-raisers and other events related to your show. Whenever you bump into these supportive people, take a moment to find out how they are doing—and let them hear how the show is going, too.

These friends and allies will provide you with the kind of word-of-mouth publicity no amount of money can buy. People do a lot of talking at the coffee shop, the firehouse, other local theatre groups, the senior center, church events … the very places your target audience hangs out. Surveys tell us that word of mouth is the most effective sales tool today, so do what you can to cultivate it.

And you never know who your community allies might link you with. They all have relatives, friends, and neighbors—and some of them are bound to be people you want to know. You may have a hard time arranging a meeting with a local big shot or potential corporate sponsor, but walls come down when a cousin or close friend provides a personal introduction. Professionals call it "networking"—old-timers call it "common courtesy" or "being a good neighbor." Whatever you call it, do it.

Parties

Many first-time directors and producers ask about holding special events for their volunteers—barbecues, pizza parties, or the like. This is a laudable idea, in moderation. A well-run production should give those involved enough satisfaction to keep them happy. A "thank you" event can be an effective morale booster or a great way to make up for any bumps or mismanaged steps. Pick a day when it will be convenient for all company volunteers to be on hand, and hit them with something simple and satisfying. If your company includes anyone under drinking age, opt for an alcohol-free event such as pizza and sodas or an afternoon cookout. All-adult groups can add beer or have a wine and cheese party—just be sure no one is "overserved."

You may find your cast and crew spontaneously scheduling their own get-togethers. As long as everyone is happy and well behaved, there is no reason to discourage such socializing. During the college productions I took part in, most of the cast and crew made a point of heading out for a postrehearsal bite every Friday night. Rehearsals ended at 11 P.M., and by 11:30, we would descend on a local diner for burgers. This reinforced company spirit, and some of the friendships formed over heaps of steaming french fries survive to this day.

The Least You Need to Know

◆ Volunteers usually handle several key production positions.

◆ Be sure all volunteers on your production team have ample supervision.

◆ The box office and house managers may need special backup, especially if they are school age.

◆ While volunteers are invaluable, use professionals in positions requiring special expertise.

◆ All volunteers deserve to be treated with respect and appreciate well-earned praise. Verbal abuse is never an option.

◆ Do your best to match each volunteer with the right position. Your team is only as strong as its weakest link.

Part 4

Going into Production—
"Putting It Together"

After months of planning and dreaming, it's time to begin the nuts-and-bolts work of putting on your show. In Part 4, we create a detailed production schedule and then quickly move from planning to auditions to rehearsals. As set and costume construction get underway, the technical elements start percolating, and in a matter of weeks, your team will have a show on its hands. There will be ups and downs, but with a little guidance, you'll find ways to survive and thrive. So roll up your sleeves and get ready for some of the most exhausting—and satisfying—work you've ever done.

Production Calendar: "One Brick at a Time"

In This Chapter

- ◆ Giving your production enough time to happen
- ◆ The art of scheduling rehearsals
- ◆ A detailed model production outline
- ◆ Tailoring the timeline to your team's needs

While preparing this book, I canvassed dozens of friends and acquaintances with extensive experience producing and directing amateur theatre. When I asked them what would have helped them most when preparing for their first-ever production, they all responded that a timetable or model production calendar would have made a real difference. So this chapter offers exactly that: a detailed production timeline that outlines when you should take key steps.

Giving Yourself Time

Every amateur show needs a well-planned production schedule, just as surely as it needs a well-planned budget. For some reason, this idea seems to shock a number of otherwise sensible people. My website's subsection on producing amateur musical theatre attracts hundreds of e-mail queries every year, and I am always a bit terrified when I get messages that go something like this: "We're set to open our show in four weeks. When should we start rehearsals, and how many should we plan on?"

Ye gods! I know Cole Porter's *Kiss Me Kate* says it takes four weeks to "rehearse and rehearse," but that figure is for seasoned professionals. Amateur troupes, whatever their level of experience, need several times that period to do a full production. Every amateur production has its share of first-timers who are learning by doing, and even those with battle scars must balance their involvement in a production with the demands of a busy life.

> **On Stage**
>
> Musical Theatreworks in San Francisco gives its young casts a whopping five months of rehearsals, working three to four days a week. As an independent youth theatre company, they can set their own timeframe. As company founder Carolyn Miller explains it, "This company is about learning, not just about the production. We work on every element, bringing it to a high level."

For a fully staged play, book musical, or revue, I advise you to use a 13-week production period, with preparatory meetings occurring months in advance (readings and concert stagings you can prepare in perhaps half that time). This may sound like a lot of time, and it is, but it will all seem like the blink of an eye as you near opening night. If you have the luxury of planning well in advance, relish it, and give your team as generous a period for rehearsals as your budget and facilities will allow. Remember the old adage about the "five P's of success: *proper preparation prevents poor performance!*"

"Just No Time at All?"

Sometimes, circumstances leave you with less than an optimal time frame to work with. Other events may get in the way, leaving you with only a handful of weeks to put a production together. If this happens to you, go with the common wisdom of every great spiritual master the world has ever known, and simplify. No time to build sets or construct costumes? Minimize or do without. Numerous professional and amateur groups now offer partially staged concerts and readings. A simple and effective presentation beats the heck out of a full-scale but half-baked effort. If the material is too ambitious to handle in the time at your disposal, switch to something your team is more likely to handle well.

Scheduling Rehearsals: When and Who?

Scheduling rehearsals is an art, but one that you can learn with relative ease. Confer with the members of your executive team, as well as people who are likely to be in your cast. What are the most convenient evenings or weekend afternoons? Leave in time for participants to eat lunch and/or dinner, and expect to have regular breaks so people can check their cell phones or answer the call of nature.

Work with a calendar in front of you, figuring in all major holidays and religious feasts. It is also unrealistic to compete with special local events like the "big game," or to expect folks to show up on Academy Awards night. Identify and work around these dates as best you can. If you find such an event pops up along the way, canceling a rehearsal makes more sense than demoralizing or even losing valuable people.

Budget your time, and plan what basic material you will cover at each session. This will enable you to stagger the list of company members needed at rehearsals, especially in the early weeks. Try to give people days off whenever possible. These free nights are much appreciated and make more sense than having the entire company sit about, doing nothing for hours at a time.

All rehearsals should have a set routine:

- Have everyone sign in on arriving. Make it clear that no one is allowed to sign in for others.

- Begin on time with physical and/or vocal warm-up exercises.

- If separate rehearsal sessions take place at the same time, be sure no one is expected in two or more places at once.

- End all sessions on time. People tend to respect your time if you respect theirs.

Avoid delaying the start of any rehearsal for more than 5 or 10 minutes, even in bad weather. In Chapter 15, I discuss the importance of making it clear from day one that latecomers will be locked out. Stick to this policy throughout the rehearsal process, and you will save every member of your company untold amounts of wasted time.

A Model Calendar

Following is a model amateur production timeline that covers all the aspects of a full-scale musical production.

Beginning Six Months Before Opening

- ◆ Assess your people power and facilities.

- ◆ Select your show.

- ◆ Set the date for all performances.

- ◆ Lay out a full production and rehearsal schedule.

- ◆ Check with other local theatre organizations to avoid scheduling conflicts.

- ◆ Reserve performance rights, along with renting or purchasing all scripts and scores.

- ◆ Line up all executive, creative, and support staff.

- ◆ Hold production team meetings as needed.

- ◆ Finalize budget in consultation with production team.

- ◆ Order required supplies.

- ◆ Reserve the facilities for auditions, rehearsals, and performances.

- ◆ Plan and hold fund-raising events as needed.

Three Months to Opening

- ◆ Confirm reservations for all rehearsal and performance spaces.

- ◆ Design initial publicity mailer (postcard or brochure) and send it to the printer.

- ◆ Have full set of tickets printed and ready.

Thirteen Weeks to Opening

- ◆ Hold a full preaudition production staff meeting.

- ◆ Arrange for director to confer with choreographer, musical director, designers, and publicity coordinator to review creative concept and production plans.

- ◆ Select audition materials.

- ◆ Prepare all scripts and other rehearsal materials.

- ◆ Have the PSM begin constructing the prompt book.

- Announce auditions.
- Have sign-ups for auditions and all production crews.

Twelve Weeks to Opening

- Promote auditions and recruit crew.
- Instruct the PSM to prepare production information packets for all cast and crew.

Eleven Weeks to Opening

- Hold cast auditions and callbacks.
- Finalize and announce cast.
- Finalize poster and flyer design; have these items printed.
- Hold first full company meeting, attendance mandatory for all; distribute production packets.
- Collect contact, emergency information, and any other required forms for all company members.
- Distribute scripts.
- Suggest children's theatre groups hold a preproduction meeting for parents and other adult volunteers.
- Have the PSM post a full rehearsal schedule that includes date, time, location, and required personnel for each session the following week.
- Have every crew post work schedules that include date, time, location, and required personnel for each session the following week.

Ten Weeks to Opening

- Begin rehearsals for Act I.
- Have rehearsal props ready as needed.
- Begin music rehearsals.
- Take costume measurements.

◆ Begin set and costume construction.

◆ Begin distributing posters and flyers.

◆ Begin ticket and program ad sales.

◆ Send out publicity mailing to potential ticket buyers.

◆ Begin program planning.

◆ Create rehearsal accompaniment tapes (if any).

◆ Have the PSM post a full rehearsal schedule that includes date, time, location, and required personnel for each session the following week.

◆ Have every crew post work schedules that include date, time, location, and required personnel for each session the following week.

◆ Require box office staff to make weekly ticket sale report to the business manager and producer.

Nine Weeks to Opening

◆ Continue blocking and refining Act I.

◆ Stress basic blocking, character development, and memorization during rehearsals.

◆ Have the music director continue music rehearsals and recruit/hire orchestra.

◆ Finalize the logo design.

◆ Finalize the master list of required costumes and props.

◆ Instruct the prop crew to start borrowing or shopping for props, furnishings, etc.

◆ Inform the costume crew to shop for accessories.

◆ Remind the costume designer to prepare a list of any personal costume items that cast members must provide for themselves (tights, undergarments, shoes, etc.).

◆ Instruct the makeup crew to shop for wigs and makeup.

◆ In consultation with the costume designer, have the makeup crew research appropriate styles of hair and makeup.

◆ As construction continues, remind the set and costume designers to coordinate use of color.

◆ Begin ticket sales and keep a weekly account of all ticket orders.

◆ Have the PSM post a full rehearsal schedule that includes date, time, location, and required personnel for each session the following week.

◆ Have every crew post work schedules that include date, time, location, and required personnel for each session the following week.

◆ Remind the box office staff to make weekly ticket sale report to the business manager and producer.

Eight Weeks to Opening

◆ Director continues blocking and refining Act I.

◆ Cast has memorized all musical numbers for Act I.

◆ Choreographer begins rehearsing major numbers with the cast.

◆ Cast members receive list of personal costume items.

◆ Executive and design team schedules a meeting for sometime next week.

◆ The producer and business manager meet to review ticket and ad sales and to compare budget to actual expenditures.

◆ The producer and director inspect ongoing set and costume construction.

◆ The cast and crew are encouraged to push ticket sales.

◆ The sound crew creates a master sound cue list and researches all necessary sound effects and music.

◆ PR finalizes the program cover design.

◆ The group keeps encouraging ticket and program ad sales.

◆ A photographer takes publicity photos (for use in press releases, posters, etc.).

◆ PR finalizes major press release and sends it to all local media.

◆ If a production T-shirt is planned, PR finalizes the design and places the order.

◆ Crews create full checklists of costumes, accessories, and props.

◆ Have the PSM post a full rehearsal schedule that includes date, time, location, and required personnel for each session the following week.

- Every crew posts work schedules that include date, time, location, and required personnel for each session the following week.

- The box office staff makes a weekly ticket sale report to the business manager and producer.

Seven Weeks to Opening

- Cast is off-book for all of Act I.

- Choreographer completes all dances for Act I.

- Cast does first full run-through of Act I this week, using any completed props and set elements. All designers and crews are in attendance.

- Full executive and design teams meet to review progress in all departments.

- The musical director distributes orchestral scores to musicians.

- The lighting and sound designers create technical plots.

- PR finishes program ad sales and prepares the final program layout.

- PR makes follow-up calls to the media to verify materials were received.

- The sound crew makes full inventory of existing sound equipment (if any).

- The director keeps encouraging ticket sales.

- The PSM posts a full rehearsal schedule that includes date, time, location, and required personnel for each session the following week.

- Every crew posts work schedules that include date, time, location, and required personnel for each session the following week.

- The box office staff makes a weekly ticket sale report to the business manager and producer. The budget is adjusted as needed.

Six Weeks to Opening

- The cast begins rehearsing blocking and choreography for Act II, reviewing Act I as needed.

- The musical director finishes teaching score.

- By week's end, the cast is entirely off-book.

◆ The musical director rehearses the orchestra.

◆ The costume designer begins fittings for any completed costumes.

◆ The lighting and sound designers complete *lighting and sound plots*.

◆ The PR team completes the program design and gets producer's approval.

◆ The house manager begins recruiting ushers and concession staff.

◆ The master costume and prop lists are rechecked and updated.

◆ The producer and business manager follow up on any questions from the previous week's staff meeting.

◆ The producer keeps encouraging ticket sales.

◆ The PSM posts a full rehearsal schedule that includes date, time, location, and required personnel for each session the following week.

◆ Every crew posts work schedules that include date, time, location, and required personnel for each session the following week.

◆ The box office staff makes a weekly ticket sale report to the business manager and producer. The budget is adjusted as needed.

Five Weeks to Opening

◆ The cast continues rehearsing blocking and choreography for Act II, reviewing Act I as needed.

◆ Anyone still on-book faces a firing squad!

◆ The full program is finalized and sent to the printer.

◆ The PSM makes sure the prompt book is updated and complete.

◆ The producer and director inspect progress on the sets, props, and costumes.

◆ The house manager finishes recruiting ushers and concession staff.

◆ The cast keeps encouraging ticket sales.

◆ The PSM posts a full rehearsal schedule that includes date, time, location, and required personnel for each session the following week.

- Every crew posts work schedules that include date, time, location, and required personnel for each session the following week.

- The box office staff makes a weekly ticket sale report to the business manager and producer. The budget is adjusted as needed.

Four Weeks to Opening

- The cast rehearses staging, music, and choreography for Act II.

- A complete run-through of Act II is done by week's end, using any completed props and set elements. All designers and crews are in attendance.

- The cast rehearses material from both acts, as needed.

- The PSM posts a full rehearsal schedule that includes date, time, location, and required personnel for each session the following week.

- Every crew posts work schedules that include date, time, location, and required personnel for each session the following week.

- The box office staff makes a weekly ticket sale report to the business manager and producer. The budget is adjusted as needed.

Three Weeks to Opening

- The cast begins complete run-throughs of both acts at alternating sessions, focusing on any scenes or numbers that require special attention.

- The completed set elements are introduced whenever possible.

- The producer extends invitations to groups that will attend the dress rehearsal.

- The director and design crew meet to be sure all design elements are coordinated.

- The lighting crew begins gathering any borrowed or leased equipment; secure storage is provided.

- The lighting and sound designers place orders for any rentals.

- The final publicity buildup to opening night begins.

- The props crew organizes prop storage and placement (stage right versus stage left).

- Hair and makeup designs are finalized.

◆ Mail-ordered tickets should be mailed out no later than this week; from here on, new orders must be picked up at the box office.

◆ The costume designer assigns dressers for leads, if needed.

◆ T-shirts should be ready and in hand; store or distribute, as preferred.

◆ Programs should be delivered, proofread, and then stored until opening night.

◆ Everyone keeps encouraging ticket sales!

◆ The PSM posts a full rehearsal schedule that includes date, time, location, and required personnel for each session the following week.

◆ Every crew posts work schedules that include date, time, location, and required personnel for each session the following week.

◆ The box office staff makes a weekly ticket sale report to the business manager and producer. The budget is adjusted as needed.

Two Weeks to Opening

◆ All rehearsals become full-cast run-throughs of an entire act, with at least one complete run-through of the entire show, using set elements, props, and costumes.

◆ First orchestra rehearsal with full company occurs.

◆ When crews require stage area for tech work, hold rehearsals in alternate space.

◆ If the facility is available, the lighting crew begins hanging lights.

◆ All sets and costumes should be completed.

◆ Now is a great time for last-minute publicity events, press coverage, interviews, etc.

◆ Delivery of all rented costumes and equipment should be verified; each department must follow up as needed.

◆ Everyone keeps encouraging ticket sales!

◆ The PSM posts a full rehearsal schedule that includes date, time, location, and required personnel for each session the following week.

◆ Every crew posts work schedules that include date, time, location, and required personnel for each session the following week.

◆ The box office staff makes a weekly ticket sale report to the business manager and producer. The budget is adjusted as needed.

One Week to Opening

- When necessary, hold a complete load in of all lighting and sound equipment.

- The director and PSM assign dressing rooms.

- All backstage areas are set up; the PSM inspects for any obvious hazards.

- All rented or borrowed equipment should be in hand by this week.

- All costumes, props, and sets are completed.

- The costume parade takes place. Alterations are to follow, as needed.

- First tech rehearsal for tech teams in the performance space occurs; the PSM calls the cues; all tech and design staff must be in attendance—performers do a full run-through in an alternate location under the ASM and musical director.

- The full production team meets after first tech to hammer out any obvious problems.

- The second tech rehearsal involves the full company; the PSM calls the cues; the full production team is in attendance. (Note: with complex productions, you may opt to have a separate second tech session for each act.)

- Special rehearsal to clean up problems identified during the techs is held.

- The house manager meets with the ushers and all house staff to go over seating plans, the art of giving directions, and pointers on handling common audience problems (illness, ticket disputes, etc.).

- All staff keeps encouraging ticket sales!

- The PSM posts a full rehearsal and performance schedule that includes cast and crew sign-in times for the following week.

- The box office staff makes a weekly ticket sale report to the business manager and producer. The budget is adjusted as needed.

Opening Week

- Preliminary dress rehearsals (optional) are held to familiarize cast with sets, costumes, and props.

- Final dress rehearsal is held; full company must be in attendance, invited audience is optional.

◆ The director, producer, choreographer, and designers give final notes.

◆ The day before opening, the cast takes a break; the crews make last-minute adjustments.

◆ Opening night: the house opens to cast and crew two hours before curtain time.

◆ Cast and crews are to be on hand one hour to curtain time.

◆ The PSM calls "half-hour" and "15 minutes" warnings; calls "places" just before the performance begins.

◆ The audience enters the auditorium a half-hour to official curtain time.

◆ The curtain is held five minutes as a courtesy to late arrivals.

◆ After the performance, the lock-up team makes sure the entire facility is cleared.

◆ Any additional performances repeat the pattern set on opening night.

◆ Always encourage ticket sales!

◆ The PSM posts a full schedule for any remaining performances, including cast and crew sign-in times for the following week.

◆ The box office staff makes a weekly ticket sale report to the business manager and producer. The budget is adjusted as needed.

Any Additional Weeks

◆ All performances repeat the pattern set on opening night.

◆ Cast and crews are to be on hand one hour to curtain time.

◆ Everyone pays special attention to all safety and security procedures.

◆ The director and/or musical director schedule "brush-up" rehearsals, as needed.

◆ The PSM posts a full schedule for any remaining performances, including cast and crew sign-in times.

◆ Keep encouraging ticket sales!

◆ During the final week, the PSM posts a schedule and list of required personnel for strike set.

◆ The box office staff makes a weekly ticket sale report to the business manager and producer. The budget is adjusted as needed.

After the Final Performance

- The producer oversees the striking of the set ASAP, clearing all production materials from the performance space. The PSM assists in coordinating all efforts.

- All rented or borrowed materials are cleaned and returned to the owners immediately.

- A cast party (if any) is held.

- The box office staff makes the final ticket sale report to the business manager and producer.

- The business manager pays all outstanding expenses and stipends and completes and submits the final production financial report to the producer.

- The entire executive and design staff holds a postmortem to assess production and discuss preliminary plans for a next show.

- The producer and/or director send thank you notes to all the company members.

Tailoring Your Calendar

This calendar is only a model, an ideal production schedule for a large-scale musical. Do not feel bound by it! Tailor it to your production's specific needs. If you are doing a concert or a drama, deduct those elements that do not relate to your show.

The Least You Need to Know

- Every amateur production must have a carefully planned production calendar, outlining each week of activity.

- Planning can begin months in advance, but the ideal production period for large-scale amateur musicals is 13 weeks.

- Schedule rehearsals with an eye on the calendar, recognizing holidays and special events.

Chapter 12

Auditions and Casting: "I Hope I Get It!"

In This Chapter

- ◆ The way to schedule, publicize, and run humane auditions
- ◆ The dangers of precasting
- ◆ The value of callbacks
- ◆ Making difficult casting choices
- ◆ The best way to announce final casting
- ◆ Alternative actions when auditions draw too few people

Performers love to share audition "war stories." Hours of tense waiting, auditors who refuse to pay attention, construction going on next door while a volleyball team practices overhead, accompanists who seem to play with hooves rather than hands … and then someone else gets the coveted part! No wonder so many performers approach auditions with the same enthusiasm they otherwise reserve for root canal work.

The good news is that you can minimize audition angst. Can you make it pain free? Not quite, but a combination of organization and sensitivity will take much of the terror out of this process for performers and auditors alike.

Scheduling and Staffing Auditions

Have auditions on more than one day and time to make it easier for interested people to show up. For example, schedule one weekday evening session and another on a weekend afternoon. Two to four audition dates are usually sufficient for even the largest amateur productions.

When scheduling auditions, be aware of what else is happening in your community. Try to pick days and times that are not dominated by other popular activities. If a major event moves into conflict with you, consider rescheduling. You don't want other groups to view your show as competition, and there is no point in having auditions that a large part of your talent pool is likely to miss.

Reserve your audition space before making any announcements. Choose a quiet, relatively private location that is properly equipped (piano, adequate lighting and ventilation, etc.). You will need several rooms: one for the actual auditions and at least one separate waiting area. Schedule ample time, have backup dates in case of callbacks, and be sure to get the piano tuned for any musical auditions.

I see no good reason for exposing performers to an intimidating platoon of judges. Broadway productions keep the casting committee small, and so should you. Limit the people sitting in on auditions to those golden few who have a real say in casting decisions. In many cases, the director is the only one needed. When appropriate, the producer may have input. For musicals, add the musical director, choral director, and choreographer to the list, but you probably don't need to expand the committee further than that. The production stage manager (PSM) and one or two adult volunteers can be on hand to keep things moving. Allow no other production staff at auditions.

> **Gremlins**
>
> If you have worked with a performer time and again in a variety of roles, it might not seem necessary to have them audition again. But having everyone audition anew affirms that your group gives new talent a chance to be heard on an equal footing with veteran performers.

Performers should face the auditors in private. Have parents, friends, and other auditioning performers wait in a separate space. Never allow sponsors, donors, or casual observers to sit in. Their presence helps no one and is a potential distraction.

The Perils of Precasting and Typecasting

My advice on *precasting* is simple—don't do it. It is natural to have certain performers in mind when you decide on a particular show, but it is unwise to plan the casting for all your leads in advance. Even if performers express great interest in your show, there is no guarantee that they won't opt for other commitments. It's hard to compete with a job promotion or a spot on a school athletic team.

Typecasting rules in Hollywood, but there is no excuse for it in amateur theatre. Barriers like race and physical type have been smashed time and again, with excellent results. Audiences walk into a theatre prepared to suspend belief, so unless you're doing a play like *Othello* or *Show Boat* where race is a specific plot issue, consider casting "outside the box." Of course, there are limits. If Cinderella is two feet taller than Prince Charming, even the most understanding audience will have trouble taking their romance seriously.

def•i•ni•tion _____

Precasting is selecting actors for specific roles before auditions can begin.

Typecasting is selecting an actor based on physical type or personal reputation, rather than on ability.

When Performers Refuse a Role

Some otherwise cooperative actors may be dead set against taking a particular role. If you can accommodate a performer's preferences without harming a production, by all means do so. In my senior year of college, I told my director before auditions that I was tired of playing a series of bad guys and wanted to try something different. He was caught off guard but knew I was an enthusiastic team player. I scored a surprise success in my first comedy part while a classmate did a grand job as the bad guy.

Never promise a role to anyone before auditions are over. Telling someone on day one that they're a shoo-in leaves you in an awful bind if a newcomer wows you on day two. Everyone trying out has the right to expect a fair hearing, so keep an open mind until all interested parties have had a chance. You can't be sure what unexpected talent is out there.

Getting the Word Out

With your schedule and audition staff in place, use whatever announcement process is most likely to reach most of your target talent pool. Options include the following:

♦ In-house newsletters

♦ Church and synagogue bulletins

- Handouts at group events

- P.A. announcements

- Bulletin board postings

- Website postings

- Newspaper listings

- Press releases

If you are part of an ongoing theatre company, consider announcing future casting calls in the program of your current production. Go with whatever best fits your group or community culture. Use as many methods as you can. The larger your potential talent pool is, the stronger your final cast is apt be.

Audition announcements should include the following:

- The name of the show and some descriptive information

- Performance days and dates

- The days, dates, times, and place of auditions

- For new or lesser-known plays, a list of available roles with brief explanations ("Tom Carson: a beloved grandfather with an eye for the ladies")

- An explanation of what performers will be expected to do at the audition

- Instructions on how to sign up for an appointment

- Notice of any open audition rehearsals

- Whom to contact with questions

Include each of these points whether an announcement is in written or oral form. A written version could look something like this:

OPEN AUDITIONS FOR THE BAXTER STREET PLAYERS

For their spring production of **MY FAIR LADY,** which will be presented on the first two weekends in May. Everyone is welcome to try out!

WHERE
Anderson High School Auditorium
32 Baxter Street, 2nd Floor, Ourtown

WHEN
Saturday, February 20th from 2–6 PM
Sunday, February 21st from 2–6 PM

HOW TO SIGN UP
Make an appointment by signing up at The Magic Cut Salon, 48 Main Street, Ourtown.

Auditioners must be prepared to read any scene from the play and sing a verse from at least one of these songs: "I Could Have Danced All Night," "With a Little Bit of Luck," or "On the Street Where You Live." An accompanist will be provided.

OPEN PREAUDITION REHEARSAL
Join us to go over songs and audition scenes at the Anderson H.S. Auditorium on Thursday, February 18th from 7 to 9 PM.

QUESTIONS? Contact Bess Bennett at (222) 333-4444 or bb@baxterstreet.org.

Audition Material

Some directors prefer to let performers select their own material for preliminary auditions, but this is not always practical, especially for musical auditions. It takes a gifted pianist to sight-read dozens of songs without rehearsal. To simplify the process, my advice is to assign specific material, a limited list of monologues and songs from the play you are presenting or material in a comparable style. The PSM will have to make cuttings of scenes (approximately 2 to 3 minutes or 1 to 2 pages in length) and possibly sheet music (16 to 32 bars) available for advance review through a local library or other accessible facility.

In my view, performers should memorize all audition materials. By announcing auditions at least two weeks in advance and providing assigned materials, you give performers ample time to master a scene and/or a song. This gives you a better idea of what an individual will be capable of in performance. Assigned readings and songs help level the playing field. You can always use cold readings later on in the selection process if you want.

Getting young children to audition can be a challenge. It is reasonable to ask them to memorize brief passages of the material they will be expected to perform onstage. When it comes to songs, you may have to be flexible to accommodate the inexperienced. In a pinch, encourage children to sing whatever they know—holiday carols, TV jingles, even "The Birthday Song."

Preaudition Rehearsal

To take some of the nervous sting out of musical auditions, it's a great idea to hold at least one open preaudition song rehearsal. Participants get to communally sing through various songs several times, perhaps trying certain numbers in different keys for different vocal ranges. Such sessions give newcomers a chance to learn a little about the show and see what the group dynamic is like. The director can field individual questions at some point during this rehearsal and give performers an idea of which scenes to prepare for the formal auditions.

> ### On Stage
>
> Carolyn Miller of Musical Theatreworks takes an innovative approach to auditions: "We begin with three weeks of pre-audition music rehearsals so that the students can become well acquainted with the music. This helps the students to be better prepared for auditions and makes them much more confident. It also gives us a chance to discuss the audition process, what to expect, what we're looking for, and how to succeed."

Preaudition rehearsals first caught on in schools and youth groups, but even adult community theatre casts now find these sessions useful. Americans do much less public singing than in previous times, and even those with solid vocal talent may have few opportunities to perform. A preaudition rehearsal makes it easier to involve the uncertain souls who may prove invaluable to your production.

By Appointment or All Together?

Performers hate waiting around for hours to audition. When you announce the audition, provide a means of signing up for specific audition time slots on a bulletin board or perhaps at a local office or store. You can post a sign-up list or ask interested people to contact the PSM (via e-mail, phone, etc.) for a specific time. If this is too time-consuming for you, assign people to a specific hour on one of your audition days, and tell them to arrive a few minutes early. Your PSM can then assign specific five-minute slots in the order that performers arrive.

For musical auditions, an effective alternative approach is to run all performers through a common training session, teaching them a song and a few dance moves from the show. This provides a chance to see potential cast members in action and gives some sense of how they respond to direction.

"I've Got to Get Into This Show"

Unless you've overestimated community interest, your announcement will set off a flurry of excitement and activity. It's amazing how much passion performers of every age group bring to amateur theatre. For those who care, your show will be of tremendous importance. They will be delighted to take on any role or backstage job. Treat these people like treasures, for that is what they are.

Others audition with only one goal in mind—a leading role. A director I know was delighted when more than 20 women tried out for his church production of *Hello Dolly*. When he announced the cast, all but five of those women refused the roles offered to them. They wanted Dolly or nothing. The director eventually assembled a fine cast, but having too many people who wanted the star role proved a major time-eater.

> **Backstage Whispers**
>
> Veteran community theatre director Louise Guinther says, "I find it useful, especially with children, to make it clear from the start that no one is auditioning for a specific role when I'm directing; it's their job to show me what they've got and mine to decide what to do with it."

The only people who hate auditions more than actors are the ones who have to run the blasted things! Difficult as it is to risk disapproval, it's even harder to risk casting the wrong person in a crucial role. Throughout the audition process, make it clear that you're looking for team players, not prima donnas. If someone tells you he wants one role and no other, thank him for his honesty—and keep him off your cast list. Anyone flaunting his inflexibility this early in the process will not be an asset in the demanding weeks ahead. By the same token, it's a waste of your time to cast people who cannot be bothered with auditioning.

Performer Information Forms

When performers arrive for auditions, have them fill out a form giving the following information:

- Name and full contact information (including parents, for young actors)

- Height

- Age range (if relevant)

- Role preferred

- Special skills

- Any backstage talents (sewing, tech experience, etc.)

- An indication of whether they're willing to sing or dance (for musicals)

- Any possible conflicts

Then use these forms to keep track of individuals as they go through the audition process. An alternative is to have auditioners put this information on a large index card. Some directors find it useful to take a Polaroid or digital picture at the audition and staple it to the form. This little trick can prevent embarrassing mix-ups. To save on film or photo paper, you can take a picture of two to four auditioners at a time, then cut up the resulting photo and paste the appropriate face to each audition form.

An auditioner may want an unsuitable role. Many performers have no idea what their real strengths are, so I prefer to have open auditions without specifying the role anyone is trying out for. Disappointments are minimized, and you can give those who show promise a second chance during callbacks.

Evaluating Performers

When performers enter the audition space, take a moment to make each one feel at ease. Some will be a bundle of nerves no matter what you say or do, but a little goodwill can ease the worst of their fears. Be patient. If the audition material includes dialogue, have a member of the audition committee or an assistant stage manager (ASM) read with the performer. The musical director or rehearsal pianist can run each auditioner through a song.

An audition is like a job interview. Would you appreciate an interviewer who noshed while your future was on the line? All members of the audition committee must give every performer their undivided attention. No snacking or cell phone interruptions allowed! Some judges seem to go without food for days, building a ravenous appetite for mid-audition grazing. Sneaking a gulp of water or making a quick call home between sessions is okay, but not while people are performing.

Hollywood has immortalized those unfeeling, professional directors who cut an audition piece short with an abrupt "Thank you! Next, please!" In case you hadn't guessed, this is not an option in amateur theatre! Volunteer performers who put themselves on the line deserve a chance to be heard from start to finish with decorum. Even if their efforts make you want to cringe, don't.

Take notes on each performer, concentrating on the following criteria:

◆ Acting ability: Kate Hepburn or Paris Hilton?

◆ Voice: range, singing ability, variation of tone

◆ Appearance: general physical description, special characteristics

◆ Moves: awkward, graceful, poised?

These notes will help you keep track of the people you see, so be sure to include any standout details. Thank each performer as his audition ends, and tell him when you will announce casting decisions. Keep as close to schedule as possible. If performers show promise and you want to see or hear them do more, have a callback session.

Dance Auditions

If dance is a major factor in your show, the choreographer may want to run a separate dance audition. This can involve teaching groups of performers a basic assortment of steps, looking to evaluate flexibility, attitude, coordination, and the ability to pick up a routine. Some prefer running several sessions with small groups; others go for one large common audition. This may sound like the opening scene to *A Chorus Line*—but that's hardly a bad thing!

Callbacks

At the end of preliminary auditions, there are often some unanswered questions. You may have two or more performers who would do justice to a particular role. Callbacks allow you to take a second look. Invite these performers to return for a more detailed session. Give them selected material from the play and two to three days to prepare.

Scheduling for callbacks should allow much more time per performer. If a second look is not enough to resolve any doubts, have a third. Multiple callbacks are standard procedure. Performers who don't show up for callbacks are not committed to your production, so you can scratch them from your list with a clear conscience.

> ### On Stage
>
> Treating auditioners with respect can reap real dividends. I was one of three actors up for the role of Arthur in a college production of *Camelot*. The director had each of us prepare the same scene and song; then he worked with us in a joint callback session that lasted more than two hours. Each of us would have been a solid choice, but the final decision came down to the good of the play. By discussing the decision in a frank yet sensitive manner, the director had no trouble keeping all three of us in the cast. The actor cast as Arthur did a great job, and the two "losers" (myself included) had a blast in scene-stealing supporting roles.

Callbacks are a good time to learn how potential cast members look and sound together. Have different combinations perform joint scenes and songs. With all that auditioners have to memorize, readings with script in hand are acceptable for this part of the process.

Casting Children

The auditioning process is very much the same for children as for adults. The one major difference is parents. Under no circumstances should parents be allowed in the room during auditions, not even to serve as the child's accompanist. Trust me on this: the last thing you need is a stage-struck parent turning into Mamma Rose and cheer-leading from the sidelines. If parents are insistent, be equally firm about having them wait elsewhere. But try to respond to rudeness with courtesy. With performers under the age of 18, you will have to obtain written parental consent for their participation in your show.

Casting Critters

Shows as diverse as *Annie, You Can't Take It with You,* and *Peter Pan* require live animals in the cast. Because animals can be difficult to handle, many amateur groups cast humans in key animal roles. Don't be too hasty making this decision. Animals are such guaranteed audience pleasers that they can be worth the aggravation.

Age and size matter in animal casting. Kittens tend to be more docile than adult cats. Adult dogs tend to be calmer than puppies, and smaller breeds can pose less of a physical challenge backstage. The key factor is how an animal responds to being onstage surrounded by strangers. To find animals that are people friendly, have them brought in when a large number of cast and crew are on hand. You'll soon know if noise or a crowd rattles them. An owner must agree to be on hand to supervise his animal at all times, including all rehearsals and performances. Even a well-trained animal can prove temperamental, and few things can ruin a performance more quickly than ill-timed animal noises from offstage.

Understudies

Years ago, I attended a college production of *Fiddler on the Roof*, which went out of its way to let audiences know that its star was performing under duress. The actor playing Tevye had developed pneumonia on opening day. Rather than cancel the run, Tevye dragged himself through performances with an oxygen tank offstage and a car whisking him back to a hospital bed every night. The sympathetic applause was tremendous. The performance was terrible and did no favors for the play or the audiences.

An increasing number of amateur groups are assigning understudies for all major characters. Understudies can be actors with smaller roles or members of the ensemble. Be aware that further understudies may be needed to handle any lines or business your star understudies leave behind. For shows with small casts, it is advisable to have additional actors on standby. It can be hard to find volunteer actors willing to serve as understudies with no promise of getting a chance to go on. Some organizations remedy this by having more than one set of leads per production or double-casting. This provides an automatic backup cast and gives everyone a moment in the sun.

Double-casting also means quite a few additional rehearsals and a second set of costumes, but it keeps a show running if a major cast member can't appear.

Have understudies on hand for all lead rehearsals, and give them at least one opportunity to run through scenes and dance routines. Odds are you will not need them, but it is good to have coverage in case of emergency.

Gremlins

When double-casting, you must give each actor equal rehearsal time. There is no point in having one first-rate cast and one that is half-baked.

Making Choices: Diplomacy vs. Practicality

After auditions and callbacks are over, you have to make a decision. Aside from the criteria mentioned earlier (acting ability, voice, appearance, movement, and/or presence), your final casting involves an additional question: how will the major players look and sound together onstage? Determine if there is sufficient contrast in sound and appearance for the audience to tell one character from another, or if differences are so radical that they might distract. You must also be aware of any obvious personality clashes. Two strong actors could energize a show or cause endless headaches. A strong director may be able to keep egos in line, but choose your colleagues for this project with care.

The classic challenge for musical productions is choosing between the actor with a weak singing voice and the gifted singer with a limited acting range. No simple rule covers this scenario. Much will depend on the material itself and on the overall style of your production. Give all members of the casting committee a chance to discuss the options. Hold additional callbacks, giving the actors in question a more thorough test. Delay the first rehearsal if you have to—it's worth it when major roles are at stake. If there is still no consensus on casting a role, the final decision traditionally rests with the director.

Diplomatic issues can pose a casting challenge. It can be difficult for your friends, relatives, co-workers, or devoted company members to learn they did not get particular roles. Before announcing your cast choices, take the time to confer with anyone who auditioned for a major role, either in person or by phone. This can be done in a day at most. Explaining your decision in a private meeting can do much to soothe bruised egos and makes it clear no insult is intended. Most people will appreciate this courtesy and take the decision well.

During these discussions, some auditioners will tell you they are unable or unwilling to be part of your show. They may have a new commitment or unexpected travel plans, or perhaps they are not interested in the role you offer them. In my opinion, it is a waste of energy trying to talk these people into reconsidering. Only enthusiastic volunteers will do. If someone expresses outright anger at your casting decisions, respect his feelings without buying into them. Let him vent. A lot of emotional energy is invested in amateur auditions, so be prepared to forgive things said in the heat of this moment.

After you confirm the acceptance of key cast members, post a complete cast list on a public bulletin board or web page. Your cast announcement should include the date and time for the first rehearsal, as well as a reminder that cast and crew must bring a pen to fill out preproduction paperwork. Do not be surprised if even at this stage some people decide to withdraw. This may involve a bit more shuffling, but it cannot be helped.

When Many Are Called but Few Show Up

No matter how well you plan, you can wind up at the end of auditions with only a fraction of the people needed to put on a particular show. This does not mean you have made a fatal mistake, but it is time to reevaluate your plans.

What kind of interest did you uncover? If you are short one crucial player, think about how you might go about recruiting that individual. On the other hand, if half a dozen people auditioned for two dozen roles, see what other titles would fit your talent pool. When singers are few but actors abound, you may have to replace that musical with a comedy. You may have been aiming for *Carousel*, but that is no reason to talk yourself out of presenting a smashing *Barefoot in the Park*.

The Least You Need to Know

- Use careful scheduling and publicity to encourage a good turnout for auditions.
- Make your expectations clear, and treat all auditioners with courtesy.
- Auditions involve the performer and the audition committee—period. Allow no outsiders.
- Callbacks are a great way to compare your strongest candidates.
- Consider assigning understudies for major roles.
- Confer with cast members before announcing your final choices.

Chapter 13

Basic Stagecraft:
"We've Got Magic to Do"

In This Chapter

- ◆ Ways a director develops a production concept
- ◆ The basics of stage geography and blocking
- ◆ Creating the all-important prompt book
- ◆ An overview of choreography
- ◆ Creating simple musical staging
- ◆ Working with creative and technical crews

I've addressed the next two chapters to the director, especially the first-timer who is trying to figure out how to get cast and crew headed toward a common goal—namely, an audience-pleasing performance. Sure, it's a challenging task, but don't worry. The guidelines on the next few pages offer you a road map that you can turn to as needed in the weeks ahead.

The Production Concept

From day one, everyone involved in a production will be turning to the director for answers. That is why a director's work begins long before the first rehearsal—in fact, before the first preproduction meeting. After studying the script in detail, the director must come up with a *production concept*, an overall approach or vision that will bring every aspect of the production together to clearly express the inner meaning of the material being performed.

def•i•ni•tion

The **production concept** is the director's vision or understanding of a play. It keeps all the creative and technical aspects of a production moving in a common direction.

The production concept is where artistic theory meets physical reality. No amateur group can match the resources of a multimillion-dollar Broadway production. Instead, the director must come up with an approach that fulfills the dramatic needs of the material, accenting a theatre group's strengths while living within its financial and physical resources. The original professional staging of *Les Misérables* relied on a massive turntable and costly hydraulic sets. Many amateur groups have staged this musical without a turntable in sight, thanks to directors using imagination and theatrical know-how to concoct new, alternative approaches.

In film, the director has the final say over everything an audience sees and hears. In the theatre, that ultimate power belongs to the performers, the ones standing onstage facing the audience. A stage director is on hand to guide, inspire, and empower those performers, helping them understand the author's meaning and then communicate that meaning to an audience. The director's production concept supports the actors by giving every element of the production a common focus.

However good a concept may sound, it has to work in performance. Several key aspects help develop an effective production concept.

Knowing Your Material

Take your job title literally! The production team will look to you for a sense of direction, to serve as a tour guide. A good tour guide can make grand boulevards and little side streets equally interesting. To be that kind of guide, you must know the play better than anyone else on your team. That means reading through the material over and over again, becoming intimate with every line and developing a deep understanding of the author's creative intentions. Immerse yourself in any articles, reviews, or scholarly books you can find discussing the show and its previous incarnations. Learn everything you can about any historical period or event depicted in the show. In short, become the resident expert on the material your group is performing.

It is not necessary for a director to memorize every line, although it will blow the cast and crew's minds if you do! However, you must make an effort to understand every reference, inference, allusion, twist, and turn in the text. The company's respect for and confidence in you as a director are not accorded as an automatic right; you must earn them. When people turn to you with a question, you must be ready to provide them with answers they can use. Actors and crews want to trust your judgment. The better you know the material and its meaning, the more confidence your company will have in you.

Trust the Author

Once you understand what the playwright or songwriter is saying, your job is to get that message across to your audience. Most audience members give little thought to the author's premise. All they want to see is a believable presentation of an interesting human drama. By identifying the show's premise, your team will be in the best possible position to express it effectively. Some directors feel that they have to improve or "fix" material, reshaping it to suit their concept and taking it in directions the author never envisioned. Simply put, this is bad direction. A production concept is only valid to the extent that it gives audiences access to the author's message. Trust the author! Let the content and meaning of every line come through, and the material will work its magic.

Countless "impressive" productions have made directors look brilliant while leaving the material in the dust. For example, a number of actresses (including the legendary Sarah Bernhardt) have played the title role in *Hamlet*, winning publicity points without shedding any fresh light on Shakespeare's tragedy. An insightful feminine perspective on the Danish prince would be innovative and meaningful; without that perspective, a woman playing a man is mere transvestite stunt casting. Some contemporary directors fall in love with a particular special effect or staging gimmick ("Let's have all the actors double as the orchestra!"), which wins applause but does the material no favors. Be sure your staging serves the play.

> **Backstage Whispers**
>
> At the opening of a pretentiously staged drama, actress Tallulah Bankhead whispered to critic Alexander Woollcott, "There is *less* to this than meets the eye."

A production concept can respect the premise and still be creative. In 1980, the New York Shakespeare Festival presented a rollicking centennial revival of Gilbert and Sullivan's *The Pirates of Penzance*. The athletic choreography, synthesized orchestrations, over-the-top comedy, and sexy cast made this a serious departure from traditional G&S stagings. However, the setting was still Victorian England, and aside from one line in one song, every word was by Gilbert. The author's original spoof of social pretensions was intact, Sullivan's music was well served, and both neophytes and lifelong G&S devotees were equally delighted with the results.

On Stage

One of the best amateur stagings I have ever seen was a modern dress production of Sondheim and Lapine's *Into the Woods* at New York City's Professional Performing Arts School. Contemporary clothes (the princes dressed like modern royals; Cinderella wore glitzy dance club attire) made the relevance of these characters all the clearer. The results were fresh, exciting, and 100 percent in tune with the authors' intentions. It also saved a bundle on costuming!

Abstract production concepts are very popular in opera, but they can pose a major problem for amateur theatre groups. A university production of Rodgers and Hammerstein's *South Pacific* reset the action in a military insane asylum, with the inmates acting out the play as if it were some sort of demented fantasy. Not a word or note of music was altered, and the production earned tons of publicity, but the "fascinating" concept obscured the authors' ideas. Small wonder that the rights holders shut down the production. (Yes, it can happen!)

One Team, One Direction

Every creative and technical element in your show must be in line with the director's production concept. Nothing less than an artistic crime occurs when direction, design, or any other element distracts an audience from the play. Serve the play; never smother it.

A director must rein in anything that might interfere with the communication flow among author, actor, and audience. Be prepared to nix any set, costume, or lighting effect that threatens to get in the way. A brilliant touch may dazzle viewers to the detriment of what matters most. Egos may bridle, but the play is what matters. If the audience has to sit in darkness for several tedious minutes at a crucial moment waiting for a gorgeous set to fall into place, the set is being put ahead of the play—and the play is bound to suffer.

Gremlins

An uncontrolled actor can do tremendous harm to a show. In the 1976 revival of *Fiddler on the Roof*, Zero Mostel "accidentally" splashed his hand into a milk can during "If I Were a Rich Man." He spent a full verse shimmying and squirming as if the milk were working its way down his body, and then pulled off his boot to pour the milk out. The audience howled all the way, and a classic showtune was wasted for the sake of an actor's ego.

Likewise, the director has to keep actors in tune with the text. It is okay to experiment with different stage *business* during rehearsals, but only keep those "bits" that serve the text. By the time of your first public performance, every gesture must serve the text. Improvisations are a popular rehearsal tool, but in performance, everyone must stick to the script—unless you're presenting stand-up comedy. Whether the lines were written by Will Shakespeare, Oscar Hammerstein II, or Joe Schmo the Third, you owe it to your audiences to deliver the material as written. If your actors think they can do better than the playwright or lyricist, tell them to write shows and songs of their own.

def•i•ni•tion

Business is any nonverbal stage activity, such as pouring a drink, dialing a phone, and so on.

Beats

An audience will go along on almost any fictional journey, but you must keep that journey smooth and logical. To accomplish this, a director has to identify the dramatic *beats* in any scene or song and be sure each one is clearly expressed. Beats can be subtle or over the top, but they all contribute to the fabric of a performance. Your production concept must assist the performers in hitting their beats.

For example, let's look at an excerpt from the first scene of *Peter Pan*, set in the nursery of a townhouse in Edwardian London. Mrs. Darling has just put her three children to bed. The following happens:

def•i•ni•tion

A **beat** is a specific moment in a script or song; also a specific dramatic effect or bit of stage business.

- ◆ Mrs. Darling closes the window shutters.

- ◆ Mrs. Darling asks the nightlights to guard her sleeping children and exits.

- Tinker Bell appears at the window and flies into the nursery.

- Tinker Bell gets caught in a jug.

- The shutters fly open.

- Peter Pan flies in, and the shutters close.

- Peter finds Tinker Bell and frees her.

- Peter searches for his lost shadow and finds it.

- Wendy awakens and asks Peter who he is.

- Peter bows and introduces himself.

Each of these beats must be expressed clearly for the audience to follow the action. Skip so much as one, and the logical progression of the story is interrupted. Most of the beats in the preceding scene are subtle—the exceptions being the entrances of Tinker Bell and Peter Pan, powerful moments that must be as dramatic and thrilling as possible.

Stage Geography

To simplify the rehearsal process, all cast, crew, and designers must learn basic stage geography. Stage regions are defined from the actor's perspective; in other words, as they relate to an actor facing the audience. This map gives the full layout for a traditional proscenium stage, but you can adapt it to fit almost any performance area.

A traditional stage grid: basic vocabulary for directors, actors, designers, and stage crew.

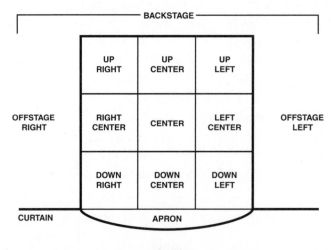

By using this system, you can direct the placement and movement of actors and set elements ("King Arthur, begin your soliloquy up right center, gradually move downstage, finishing down left center").

The sooner everyone in the company is comfortable with stage grid terminology, the better. Use these directions religiously from first rehearsal onward, and soon everyone will get the idea.

Blocking

The first job of stage direction is to give performers instructions on when to enter and where and how to move, stand, and sit onstage. This staging process is known as blocking, probably because Victorian directors used to plan out their stagings in miniature toy theatres using small wooden blocks to represent the actors. While most directors can work out basic blocking in their imagination, planning things out in advance with wood blocks or toy figurines can be helpful. Others prefer to sketch out their ideas on paper, using x's and o's to represent the actors. Experiment to find the preparation technique that works best for you.

Stage blocking is not an exact imitation of the way people behave in real life. While blocking must look naturalistic, always keep several factors in mind:

◆ Visibility: when speaking, performers' faces should be seen by the audience.

◆ Audibility: it is easier to be heard when facing the audience.

◆ Practicality: the placement of sets and costumes must be figured into the staging of any scene.

Of course, these considerations sometimes clash. It's up to the director to decide which needs take precedence at any given moment.

Several basic blocking tricks can be of particular use to first-time directors, such as *dressing the stage* and *cheating*. This may sound complicated or distracting, but it really isn't. In fact, you've been watching stage and television productions use these techniques all your life.

def•i•ni•tion

Dressing the stage means to spread the performers over as much playing area as you can while keeping the key players visible and audible.

Cheating is when actors face each other yet angle their bodies and faces ever so slightly toward the audience.

Following vs. Creating

The stage directions found in an acting edition are not eternal truths. In most cases, the playwright didn't write them. They are based on blocking used in the original professional production. It is all right to follow these directions, but you are not obliged to do so. You are free to give your audience something new by creating your own blocking, as long as your staging serves the author's intentions. When presenting *Hello Dolly*, be sure Dolly makes her iconographic descent down the stairs at the start of the title song. There are many ways to stage *Fiddler on the Roof*, but the Jewish residents of Anatevka must wear traditional orthodox clothing. Changing their attire might help you make a particular point, but it will not give your audience a real sense of the very specific time and people *Fiddler* depicts.

Simplicity

Many first-time amateur directors worry about making a good impression, putting much of their energy into superficial details. Lavish production values, ambitious special effects, complicated staging tricks—all of these can get in the way of the show. To avoid this, you must keep the production concept simple enough to fit your company's resources. Don't fear simplicity—embrace it. If all a scene needs is two people on a bench, go with it. Never be afraid to let your audience use its imagination. Theatre-goers love to take part in the creative process by filling in details with their mind's eye. If your performers are energetic and well prepared, they will be able to take audiences anywhere you want them to go. Give them a throne, and they will imagine the rest of the throne room.

The great thing about taking a simple approach is that it usually makes it easier for a production to keep its focus clear—and its finances in the black. If you concentrate on the quality of the performances, the personal and artistic growth of company members, and the clear expression of the author's ideas, all the other creative elements will work out.

Blocking a Performance

There is no great secret to creating your own blocking. The process has three basic steps:

1. *Think out a scene in advance of rehearsing it.* Set aside a few nights (or a weekend) before rehearsals begin to go over every scene and/or song in your show. There is no need to work out every move ahead of time—just find the major beats in

each scene and consider how you can place the performers to make those beats clear to the audience. Pay special attention to all entrances, major dialogue moments, and exits, keeping in mind the sets, costumes, and other production elements your cast will be working with.

2. *Have your performers work through these ideas in rehearsal.* Teach them blocking a few pages at a time, making sure the cast only marks scripts in pencil. This will make changes easier. If something you've planned does not work, toss it or adjust it. Let performers experiment with business and build on your initial plan. That is part of what rehearsals are for. The director has the final say on blocking, but some healthy give-and-take allows actors a chance to contribute. Use what works; discard the rest.

3. *Fine-tune the blocking as rehearsals progress.* If you see you can improve a particular bit of blocking, change it. A willingness to adjust blocking will reassure cast and crew that you have the best interests of the show at heart. However, it is best to freeze blocking by the time you reach first dress rehearsal, giving the cast and crew time to become accustomed to every move.

The Prompt Book: Your Production Bible

The director and the production stage manager (PSM) must work together to set up the prompt book. This will be the bible the PSM uses to assist at all rehearsals and to cue the tech and dress rehearsals as well as all performances. Using a large three-ring binder, hole puncher, and numerous tab sheets, put all the following items in one place:

- Contact sheets for cast, crew, production staff, and other volunteers
- Full production schedule
- Cast list
- Detailed rehearsal schedule
- Attendance sheets for cast and all crews
- A list of all known scheduling conflicts
- Clear photocopy of the complete script, with tabs for each scene (Yes, photo-copying of scripts is a no-no, but this is the one accepted exception.)

- Costume and prop lists (if any)
- Blank pages for additional notes (to insert as needed)

If some of these items are not ready before rehearsals start, create a binder tab for them and add the pages later.

This book must be neat and so well organized that you can find any important fact in a moment. As rehearsals progress, your PSM will turn the prompt book into the master production script, noting every bit of blocking, plus all lighting, sound, and set cues. Make all notations clearly in pencil. Some PSMs find it helpful to use colored pencils for technical cues. For particularly complex scenes, insert additional pages to allow full notation of all cues.

Staging Musical Numbers

Through the early twentieth century, most musicals used dance as an occasional diversion, stopping the story every now and then so talented hoofers could "strut their stuff." That all changed after *Oklahoma* (1943) turned dance into a basic storytelling tool. Today, most book musicals and revues require some choreography. Amateur productions of shows with formal dance requirements like *West Side Story*, *Hello Dolly*, or *Crazy for You* require the services of an experienced choreographer. However, many shows and individual numbers have simple requirements, and any director with decent stage sense can handle them.

On Stage
When the musical *Call Me Madam* was having pre-Broadway tryout performances in Boston, the book writers kept making little changes to the libretto—a cut here, an addition there. Just days before the New York opening, leading lady Ethel Merman put her foot down, saying, "Boys, as of right now I am Miss Birdseye of 1950. I am frozen. Not a comma!"

For example, *The Music Man* requires formal dance in such numbers as "Seventy-Six Trombones," "Marian the Librarian," and "Shipoopi." I could not imagine doing justice to these without the guidance of a capable choreographer. However, intimate numbers like the various quartets and love songs can be presented with little or no dance involved. Get your performers to time their movements and gestures to the music, and you will have the "look" of formal dance even though there is none. Give your performers some guidelines and invest a few rehearsals in developing their approach to such numbers. You can stage even full-ensemble pieces like "Iowa Stubborn" and "Trouble" in a straightforward manner, putting soloists downstage of the ensemble for maximum visibility and audibility.

As with the blocking of dialogue scenes, musical staging should be "frozen" during the last weeks of rehearsals to allow performers time to get accustomed to the physical requirements of each number.

Fights and Battles

From *Richard III* to *Tom Sawyer* to *Camelot*, plays and musicals have been thrilling audiences with stage fights. The more realistic the fighting, the more potent the risk to the actors onstage. Keep several guidelines in mind when staging such sequences:

- ◆ **Never use real weapons.** Safe, convincing prop knives, swords, and guns are available. No effect is worth risking the safety of your cast.

- ◆ **Keep it brief.** Make the physical struggle as quick and dramatic as possible.

- ◆ **One move at a time.** Start by going through all fight scenes move by move, and then run them in slow motion before attempting a full-speed rehearsal.

- ◆ **Keep it cool.** An overenthused co-star once plowed into me during a fight rehearsal, leaving me in pain for days. Urge performers to keep a cool head during staged fights.

- ◆ **Rehearse, rehearse, rehearse!** It is almost impossible to overprepare for fight scenes.

You might want to call in someone with gymnastic or acrobatic experience to stage complicated fight moves.

Treat Crews with Care

In the heat of rehearsals, directors can begin to take the stage and tech crews for granted. These behind-the-scenes people are every bit as important as anyone onstage and can be just as sensitive. Remember, they are either volunteers or sorely underpaid, and you need their time and talent to make your show happen. No one can stand in the spotlight unless someone else aims that spotlight.

Why bother to mention this? I have seen too many volunteer crewmembers needlessly offended by high-handed directors or designers. If stagehands are goofing around or not showing up when needed, by all means call them to task, but in private. Never reprimand crewmembers in front of their peers. As the weeks of rehearsals go by, make a point of thanking the crews every time you can. End a few rehearsals by having the cast give the crews a round of applause, and single out those who make a special effort. Such gestures go a long way toward building company spirit, helping crew and cast to become a cooperative working unit.

The Least You Need to Know

- ◆ A director's production concept must match the author's intentions with an amateur company's limited resources.

- ◆ An effective concept makes it easy for an audience to grasp all the crucial dramatic moments, or beats.

- ◆ The process of blocking scenes begins with the director's careful preplanning and then continues while interacting with performers in rehearsal.

- ◆ The PSM must maintain the prompt book as the master record of all blocking and technical cues.

- ◆ Not all musical numbers require extended formal choreography. Some can be staged very simply.

- ◆ Stage and tech crews deserve to be treated with respect and applauded for their efforts.

Chapter 14

Working with Actors: "Playing Hide and Ego Seek"

In This Chapter

◆ Treating actors with respect

◆ A director's primer on the art of acting

◆ Basic acting techniques amateurs can use

◆ Dealing with actors' egos and stage parents

First-time directors can be a little uneasy about working with actors. If you have ever acted onstage yourself, you will have a better idea of what acting is like, but former acting credits are not a requirement for this task. Some of the greatest directors have little or no acting experience. Like all arts, acting involves a combination of talent and technique. While there is no way to learn talent, amateur actors can learn basic techniques with surprising speed. By familiarizing yourself with the essential building blocks of an effective performance, you can help a cast of amateurs discover and develop their acting skills.

Handle with Care

In live performances, the director is not the primary storyteller—the performers are. They must communicate with an audience while contending with props, costumes, technical cues, audibility, and the infamous uncertainties of memorization. Your highest duty as a director is to empower your performers, reinforcing their ability to express the author's intentions.

Regardless of their age, sex, or degree of experience, performers are a vulnerable breed. They put themselves in a director's hands, seeking guidance and feedback. By breaking down their inhibitions, instilling a sense of discipline, and building their confidence, you can help them give their best. A cast that has been nurtured and encouraged will deliver far better work than people who are treated like trained dogs. Amateur actors respond to sensitive direction with amazing energy and dedication.

Let's start with a quick overview of the art of acting, followed by a discussion of some basic techniques that will help you work effectively with actors.

The Actor's Art

The art of acting has come a long way from the time Thespis (born 435 B.C.E.) stepped out of a Greek chorus to recite lines as an individual performer. The Romans copied the Greek model, staging plays in vast outdoor arenas that often held more than a thousand spectators. It's a safe bet that subtlety took a backseat to audibility.

Theatre moved indoors during the Italian Renaissance. Along with the development of stage lighting and set design, enclosed theatres forced *thespians* to redefine their art. From that time onward, the trend moved toward more naturalistic acting. Actors received no organized training. They learned by doing, using technical skills (specific conventions, movements, and gestures) to develop a character, building a performance from the outside in.

def•i•ni•tion

In tribute to Thespis, we still refer to actors as **thespians.**

Now known as technical acting, this traditional approach is still taught at such respected institutions as Britain's Royal Academy of Dramatic Arts. Many amateur actors pick up their craft in the same experience-based manner, learning by doing.

In the early twentieth century, Moscow Art Theatre director Konstantin Stanislavski developed a very different training theory. His actors learned to identify the motivation behind every word and action in a script, giving characters past histories and analyzing their unspoken thoughts and feelings—in other words, building performances from the inside out. In America, the Group Theatre and Actor's Studio refined Stanslavski's system into what is now known as the "Method." Such eminent actor-teachers as Stella Adler, Lee Strasberg, and Uta Hagen made the Method the dominant form of training for American actors.

Some of the Method's basic principles can be useful to amateur directors and actors trying to develop multi-dimensional performances in a limited period of time. You and your cast can use all or none of these ideas. It's a question of what works for each individual.

The Method

There are almost as many variations of the Method as there are acting coaches, but all share certain principles:

- Physical and mental relaxation
- Character biographies
- Text analysis

- Substitution
- Emotional and sensory recall
- Showing vs. coaching

Physical and Mental Relaxation

According to Stanislavski, mental and physical tension are "occupational diseases" that prevent actors from giving committed performances. To open the way to good acting, preface every rehearsal and performance with relaxation exercises for the entire cast. Such exercises prepare the mind and body for creative activity and help mark rehearsal time as something special and separate from the rest of the day.

You can choose from a wide variety of relaxation techniques. Quiet meditation, physical stretching, visualizing a common image … you can find dozens of more options in books on meditation. (For a few specific titles, see Appendix B.) Try one technique, or alternate among several on different days. If your cast balks at a particular technique, drop it from the list.

Character Biographies

It is now common practice for directors to ask each actor to create a detailed biography for his or her character, describing any past experiences that may contribute to that character's behavior in the play. A page or two in length, these biographies or "backstories" begin by utilizing information in the script. Actors are then free to fill in missing details. Encourage your cast members to get creative in these biographies. You can always help them revise or remove any ideas that don't jibe with the author's intentions or your production concept.

Text Analysis

When the director or an actor is uncertain about how to play a scene, take character biographies to the next level. Beginning with a careful reading of the script, analyze the emotions and objectives (both spoken and unspoken) a character has in that scene, identifying a clear *motivation* for every word and action.

def•i•ni•tion

Motivation is the conscious or unconscious cause of a character's words and actions.

To get at the truth of any character, actors and directors play the "what if" game. To illustrate, let's look at one of the characters in Shakespeare's classic tragedy *Hamlet*. Ophelia assures her father that Prince Hamlet expressed his love for her "in honorable fashion." Many scholars, actors, and theatregoers have accepted that statement at face value. But is Ophelia telling the truth? What if Ophelia and Hamlet had a sexual relationship? Isn't a girl likely to lie to her controlling father about such a thing?

What clues does the action of the play offer us? When Ophelia returns Hamlet's love tokens, he flies into a violent rage. Later, when Ophelia spurns his attempts at flirtation, Hamlet hurls sexual innuendoes at her in front of the entire royal court. After Ophelia hears rumors that Hamlet has killed her father, she is driven to madness and suicide. At her funeral, Hamlet leaps into the young woman's grave, grapples with her grieving brother, and proclaims that he loved her more than "forty thousand brothers" could. Does this sound like the behavior of people who had nothing more than an "honorable" dalliance?

Premarital sex was common in Shakespeare's time, and male royalty were infamous for taking sexual advantage of female courtiers. So the actions of the characters may suggest that Hamlet and Ophelia's relationship was far from innocent. Of course, this is one of many ways to interpret Shakespeare's words. My point is that you should dig into the text of whatever play you are doing and see what you can find. Mining for unspoken or unconscious motivation works just as well with musical comedy as with classic tragedy. Whenever your actors get stuck, a little text analysis can save the day.

Backstage Whispers

When asked if Hamlet had ever slept with Ophelia, actor John Barrymore replied, "Only in the Chicago company."

Substitution

Substitution involves an actor grasping elements in a character's life by comparing them with elements in his or her own life. This technique helps actors empathize with situations they may not have a direct experience of. For example, in *A Streetcar Named Desire*, Blanche DuBoise has dark secrets about her sexual past. Odds are most amateurs attempting this role won't have the same nightmarish experiences in their past. To empathize with the character's feelings, the actor can recall a personal secret (sexual or otherwise) she would rather the world didn't know about. The content of the secret is irrelevant and need not be revealed to anyone else—the fear of discovery is what matters. This puts an actor in contact with the feelings motivating Blanche's words and actions.

Emotional and Sensory Recall

Recall is a first cousin to substitution. Having identified a character's motivation, the next challenge is to communicate the resulting emotions to an audience. Method actors delve into their personal past to find times when they experienced similar emotions. To strengthen this recollection, the actor identifies a physical action or sensation connected with it. In other words, how was the body affected by that particular emotion? Did you stand tall and proud, hunch over in exhaustion, or collapse with grief? Perhaps a particular object comes to mind: a tie someone wore, a book that was in hand at the time, the door that slammed shut in your face. An actor invests this emotional and sensory memory into his stage performance, letting a very real memory enliven a fictional character's actions.

As an example, there is a moment in the second act of *Hello Dolly* when Horace tells Dolly that he will never marry her. Her plans thwarted, the resilient Dolly swiftly moves from disappointment to triumphant anger, bidding Horace farewell with the rollicking "So Long, Dearie." To express this tricky emotional transition, an actor looks into her personal past for a moment when she reacted to a disappointment with victorious anger. Then she identifies a physical memory connected with that moment, such as the way her body felt as she stormed off or the sound of a friend who shouted "You *go* girl!" Once she reconnects with that memory, the actor channels it into her performance, using it to help shape her vocal inflections, timing, and physical actions.

Showing vs. Coaching

Old-school directors gave actors specific instructions for every move and inflection. Some would go so far as to read dialogue aloud and then order actors to deliver exact imitations. Such line readings are the antithesis of Method acting and are almost unheard of in professional theatre today. In amateur theatre, the practice can still be appropriate, but only in select circumstances.

A director's first option is to coach, making suggestions that encourage performers to master dialogue on their own. However, line readings may be helpful when working with younger actors or with dialogue that utilizes arcane or stylized wording. This doesn't just mean the works of Shakespeare, Wilde, or Gilbert. To twenty-first-century teenagers who think of the 1960s as ancient history, even Neil Simon's dialogue can be a challenge ("What's this 'oi-vey' stuff, dude?"). If an actor makes numerous tries and cannot deliver particular lines effectively, it is acceptable for a director to sit down in private and suggest specific inflections. Make it clear that the actor has not failed or done anything wrong. A director is there to help, and this is just another form of help.

Physical Basics

In the process of imitating life, actors may have to use their body in ways that rarely occur in their everyday experience. Even common activities like using a telephone or lighting a cigarette become self-conscious challenges when performed in a spotlight. Here are some basic areas of concern.

Pacing

One of the hallmarks of an amateurish performance is slow pacing—that is, dialogue or business that stumbles along at a mind-numbing pace. This can happen when actors tire of rehearsing a scene or try to add some ill-timed "dramatic" pauses. In many cases, a simple request for the cast to kick up the energy level will set this right. If a scene seems to defy conscious adjustment, you have several time-tested options:

- Make a clear audio- or videotape of the scene and play it for the cast.

- Have the actors run the scene at top speed, jumping in on each other's last words. This forces them to pay fresh attention to the material.

- Have the actors perform the scene while jogging in place. Between the laughs and general breathlessness, this can do wonders to revitalize a tired performance.

You may have the opposite problem, with actors who speak too quickly. If so, tell 'em to slow down! Keep at them for a few rehearsals, and consider using the taping/playback technique mentioned earlier.

Gestures

Put most people onstage, and you would swear they had never used their hands before. When anyone in your cast has problems with gestures, give them a simple rule—when onstage, move a hand only when you have a deliberate reason to do so. Eliminate all other gestures, and the result will be a simpler, more focused performance.

Gestures must also fit the setting. Times and fashions change. Some of the gestures that come naturally to the hip-hop generation may be inappropriate for characters from an earlier era. So directors must be vigilant in editing gestures that seem out of context—unless you are aiming for an anachronistic effect.

Diction

A sequence in the movie *Singing in the Rain* depicts silent film actors preparing for their first sound roles. They are seen working with diction coaches, rolling their r's and polishing their vowels in a hilarious parody of classical stage speech (arrround the rrrocks …). You won't have to do anything that drastic with your actors, but proper diction is vital to good acting. All your efforts to put on a show won't mean much if your cast mumbles or muffles its lines.

You must always encourage your actors to speak and sing clearly. Ever so often during rehearsals, plant yourself in the last row of seats. If you cannot understand the actors, let them know. As a director, you don't have to be nasty about this, just persistent. Every time a line is difficult to understand during rehearsals, point out the problem and have the cast run through that particular scene or song until every word is easy to understand.

> **Backstage Whispers**
>
> Songwriter Cole Porter occasionally sat in the balcony during rehearsals with a silver whistle, which he blew whenever he had trouble hearing a lyric. He never needed that whistle for one performer whose audibility and diction were matchless. As Porter said, "I'd rather write songs for Ethel Merman than anyone else in the world. She sounds like a brass band going by."

Accents

Any American who has seen an episode of the long-running British TV series *Eastenders* knows that a real Cockney accent can make some words incomprehensible to untrained ears. That is why professional productions of *My Fair Lady* use modified accents. While it is important to depict characters realistically, accents must be tempered by the audience's need to understand what is being said. If your play calls for accents, have your actors use them with care. Even when using exaggerated accents for comic effect, every word must be understood.

Another challenge with accents is consistency. The musical *Nine* is set in Italy with mostly Italian characters. But in the 2002 Broadway revival, some cast members used Italian accents; others didn't; and several had accents that came and went from one line to the next. It would have been simpler and less jarring if the entire company had avoided synthetic accents altogether. In some cases, the use of accents is inappropriate. *The Mikado* is set in a Japanese village, and all the characters are natives of Japan. It is unnecessary and offensive to have any of these characters speak with accents.

Memorization: Get Off Book!

Unless you are doing a staged concert with scripts or scores in hand, you must encourage your cast to memorize their material as quickly as possible. True acting requires emotional and physical interaction between performers, and these things cannot take place until actors are *off book*, with lines memorized and scripts cast aside. Some actors assume they can memorize dialogue at rehearsals. Ha! Emphasize that everyone will have to memorize on their own time. Like it or not, all actors have to do their homework.

def•i•ni•tion

Off book is that golden state when actors have their lines memorized and can rehearse without referring to scripts.

Make it clear that everyone must be off book by a specific date. Give them two to three weeks at most. Openly praise anyone who is off book early, and point out in the days leading up to the deadline that it is no joke. Some will cling to their scripts until the last possible moment. After the deadline passes, it is okay for actors to study their scripts during free time, but they must keep scripts out of their hands while rehearsing. You can count on some wailing and gnashing of teeth, but stand firm. If some actors have to ask the stage manager for line after line, let them. When it is apparent that you mean business, the power of embarrassment will kick in and lines will soon be memorized.

As actors begin working off book, expect some stumbles. It's one thing to have all your lines memorized, but what about all the cues leading up to them? It may take a few rehearsals to make all the necessary connections. On top of that, blocking and establishing eye contact with other performers can be major distractions, so be patient. As actors begin to listen and react to each other, real performances can begin to take shape.

Listening and Reacting

Human interaction is the essence of drama. When memorization is secure, actors must concentrate on listening and reacting to everything their fellow actors say, sing, or do onstage. Whenever practical, staging should require actors to look at each other during conversations or shared musical numbers. This creates a more naturalistic visual sense of give and take. Aside from facing each other, they must look as if they are listening to each other. Actors "reciting lines" at each other is a sure formula for boredom. When the interaction in a scene seems weak, have actors run through the scene, replacing the dialogue with their own words. This forces them to think about what is being said, rather than just memorize and recite their lines.

The best stage actors always excel at the art of listening—or at least *looking* as if they are listening. By concentrating on what others say, they make their presence count, even if they have nothing to say themselves.

Working with Props

Even if your properties list involves nothing deadlier than a princess telephone, give your actors ample time to rehearse with props. The sooner they get comfortable with stage props, the more natural the result will be.

> **On Stage**
>
> One of the funniest moments in the musical *Carnival* comes when a philandering magician sings his mistress a love song while he simultaneously runs swords through her in a trick box. I played that magician in my college production, and to my horror, the sword box was not finished until opening night. We used real swords from our director's collection, and I was very nearsighted. If I was uneasy about this, my co-star was downright terrified. Our director told us both to get over it. In desperation, I devised a bit of business. On opening night, I pulled out a pamphlet boldly marked "Sword Box: Directions" and pantomimed being unable to read it, giving myself an excuse to slip on glasses and insert the swords accurately. Our director was annoyed, but my co-star and my conscience survived the run unscathed.

Holding Back

With the exception of tech rehearsals, a director should encourage the full company to make the most of every session. A lifeless rehearsal is a wasted rehearsal. Keep the energy level pumped! A quick jog around the block can do the trick, as can a brisk round of calisthenics. Have the stage crew join in, too, if you like. Keep it simple, fun, and quick and then get everyone right back to work.

If individual actors are ill or have strained their voices, it is okay to let them speak softly though a rehearsal or two, but don't let holding back become a habit. One of the purposes of rehearsal is to get an actor's body accustomed to the physical requirements of a performance, and that includes the process of using the voice full out. If it becomes obvious that someone is not up to the physical demands of rehearsing, you may have to replace him or her. This may seem unkind, but it is not half so cruel as wasting the efforts of everyone else connected with your production.

Prima Donnas and Tantrums

You can find many books about how to deal with difficult people, but few present ideas on handling difficult theatrical egos. Show business abounds with prima donnas, both on- and offstage. And lest anyone should feel that I am sexist, please note that in theatrical circles, the term "prima donna" is applied to men as well as women. It fits anyone who, at a given moment, feels the need to prove that they are "top of the heap." Based on a lifetime of experience, here are some specific suggestions for dealing with these demanding, maddening creatures.

Never Argue, Never Humiliate

During rehearsals, make it clear that the director's creative decisions are not open to argument. Cast members with questions can bring them up in private after that day's session. If anyone interrupts rehearsal to start an argument, don't play along. Tell them to bring it up in private after the session is over, end the discussion, and resume the rehearsal. While you can't prevent an actor from making a scene, you can refuse to co-star. If necessary, walk away and have everyone take five. Arguing is not an option.

> **Gremlins**
>
> Whenever somebody ignites your anger, talk to that person in private. A public flash of rage or caustic wit could win you a laugh, but it is not worth hurting—and perhaps losing—a crucial team member. Volunteers may not be perfect, but their hours of unpaid effort entitle them to respectful treatment. If your temper gets the better of you (and it happens to the best of us), apologize quickly, and be sure your apology is every bit as public as your outburst.

Likewise, a director must always avoid embarrassing anyone in front of the other cast and crewmembers. It is fine to tell a performer to move to a different location or adjust his volume, but serious stylistic corrections should always be made away from the ears of peers. One on one, the actor's ego is not at stake, and neither is director's.

Egos on Parade

Every actor has at least two personalities. Deep down inside, right next to the "vulnerable artist," you'll find the "show-off," ready and waiting for any opportunity to shout, "Look at me!" Directors pray for the show-off instincts to come through during performances, but rehearsals can be another matter, especially if several cast members unleash their inner show-offs at the same time.

Parading egos can be amusing now and then, but you can't let them get out of hand. A firm but gentle "That's enough!" usually does the trick, but sometimes a more creative approach is required. In a college production, I had to swing on a rope for a bit of mock swashbuckling. I had never done such a thing before, so my first attempt in rehearsal was clumsy. In seconds, other men in the cast leapt in to show me "how to do it right," with each confident entrant looking more inept than the last. Putting an end to this nonsense, our director grabbed the rope and flew across the stage with Errol Flynn–like grace. (Hey, even directors have an inner show-off!) That quelled the troops and got the rehearsal right back on track.

Stage Parents

When working with young actors, you also have to deal with their parents. The overwhelming majority of these moms and dads will be sane and supportive, but I fear a few will insist on making Mama Rose in *Gypsy* look like a beginner. The troublemakers almost always seem harmless at first, hanging around rehearsals and making occasional suggestions on better ways to put their darlings in the spotlight. But without warning, they can mutate into living, breathing headaches.

Such parents plague children's sports as well as the theatre. Unlike Little League coaches, you have the advantage of practicing in enclosed spaces. Use that advantage, and have a strict "No Parents Allowed" policy for all rehearsals. Set definite drop-off and pick-up times and abide by them, giving no one the chance to invade the main rehearsal space. If parents habitually arrive late for pick-ups, charge them a baby-sitting fee—it is not acceptable to have anyone abuse your limited free time.

Of course, this policy won't help much if a child's parents are members of your troupe. People you have known for years can surprise you when it comes to their kids. Even if you make it clear from the outset that no child will get special treatment, you will eventually hear something to the effect of, "Do you mind telling me why my Rory is stuck up left, while that Anderson kid is taking up space down center?" If you can appease someone without harming the show or setting off any chain reactions ("Why is *her* kid getting moved up front?"), make it clear that this is a one-shot deal and that you are not playing favorites. Of course, if you *are* playing favorites, you deserve whatever abuse you get.

Whenever you are working with a child who is related to a ranking member of the creative team or is (heaven help you) your own, tread with caution. There is sometimes no way to avoid such family connections in amateur theatre. No matter how qualified a child may be, the little green-eyed monster called jealousy will lead others to think envious thoughts. Everything you do with that child will be scrutinized and misinterpreted. There is no easy solution to this situation. Just do your best to treat all company members with a fair hand, and make every effort to avoid the appearance of favoritism.

The Least You Need to Know

- ◆ Only criticize or correct actors in private.

- ◆ Method acting has developed various techniques that amateurs can use to improve their performances.

- ◆ By knowing a character's history, an actor can understand what motivates that character's words and actions.

- ◆ All acting techniques aim to make it as easy as possible for audiences to hear and understand the action onstage.

- ◆ Memorization allows actors to set aside their scripts and begin the process of listening and reacting to each other.

- ◆ Actors and directors must treat each other with respect, thereby preventing the kind of arguments and tantrums that can ruin rehearsals.

- ◆ Actors' egos and stage parents can be disruptive and must be kept firmly in check.

15

Rehearsals: "One Mo' Time!"

In This Chapter

♦ Taking charge from the first rehearsal onward

♦ Important paperwork for cast and crew

♦ Making every rehearsal count

♦ Setting workable policies and procedures

The planning, organizing, and designing have laid the groundwork. With rehearsals, the cast begins the physical process of creating a performance. Lines are learned, words are mined for deeper understanding, and the director's production concept gradually becomes a workable reality.

From the very first day, the director's attitude and ability set the tone. Don't you prefer to have a boss who knows his business and doesn't waste your time? This chapter helps you offer that kind of leadership to your amateur theatre group.

First Rehearsal: "Getting to Know You"

Rehearsals are where a show comes together. They can be tremendous fun, as long as they are organized and productive. Such effective rehearsals give amateur casts and crews tangible proof that their efforts are getting somewhere, building a sense of accomplishment that can energize every aspect of a production.

Treat the first rehearsal as a serious working session where cast members begin to interact with the material and each other. Avoid the all-too-common mistake of allowing this session to morph into a social occasion. Permit no refreshments other than water. You cannot afford to waste rehearsal time, least of all the first few hours. From the moment the director calls everyone to order, the sole focus should be the show.

You will see a lot about rules in this chapter. Theatre cannot exist without discipline, and true discipline is based on respect. In Chapter 5, I mentioned that the first rule of writing is "Show, don't tell." Well, it's also the first rule of theatrical discipline. Talking about rules is just so much hot air. Nobody will pay much attention until they see the folks in charge live by and implement those rules. The best way to start is from the very first rehearsal.

Beginning on Time

To make it clear that promptness is essential, have your first rehearsal begin on time—okay, a five-minute grace period if the weather turns vicious, but that's it. At the appointed hour, post a notice saying, "Be on time, or you're not here," and then lock the doors. No matter who they may be, latecomers are left out.

Severe? Sure. Rude? No. Lateness is rude. I've seen too much rehearsal time wasted because people trickled in "a teeny bit late." The very first time someone is locked out, everyone in the company will get the message. Lay down the law on day one, and I'm willing to bet you won't have to contend with many late arrivals in the months to come.

By the same token, the director has an obligation to finish rehearsals on time, including this first session. You may be in the middle of a great scene or on a creative roll. No problem—you can pick up from the same place next time. If you want company members to respect your time, you have to show respect for theirs. Everyone in the production is making major sacrifices to be part of your show. They need to know that rehearsals will not take further bites from their other commitments.

Taking Charge

Actors at first rehearsals are like students on the first day of school, watching to see just how capable and organized the person in charge is. The director should do most of the talking at the first rehearsal. If you decide to go the traditional route and use this opportunity to give the cast its first look at the set and costume designs, let the director provide all explanations and descriptions. Keep these opening comments brief. There will be plenty of time to discuss insights and theories in future sessions.

Opening Paperwork

After the director offers a few words of welcome, the PSM can distribute the basic paperwork.

Contact List Information

This form can be a sheet or index card requesting the following information from all company members:

- Name
- Address
- Home, business, and cell phone numbers
- E-mail address
- Emergency contact (name and phone numbers)
- Special information (allergies, medical conditions)
- For company members under 18 years of age, full contact information for their parents or guardians

The PSM should gather and alphabetize these sheets in an emergency file and then use them to create a contact list with phone numbers and e-mail for all company members. In school productions, this list can be made available to the executive team; for all-adult companies, you may prefer distributing the contact list to everyone.

Please note: if you plan to distribute the contact list to the full company, the form should include a line granting permission for the distribution of this information.

Emergency Treatment Authorization

No matter how careful you are, accidents and unexpected illnesses can happen. When working with any cast or crew under the age of 18, you must have an emergency treatment authorization form signed by a parent or guardian.

Volunteer Letters of Agreement

Along with the information forms, the PSM can pass out contracts to all cast and crew. Some people find the idea of contracts for volunteers radical, but I think it makes perfect sense. In our society, we signify commitments with a signature. All you are doing is asking your company members to do the same. The wording can be quite brief and to the point:

Letter of Agreement

I _____ hereby volunteer my time, energy, and talent to Hammerstein High School's Spring 2008 production of *Show Boat*. In exchange for an opportunity to be part of this production, I agree to:

   ◆ Be on time for and offer my undivided attention during all rehearsals and performances.

   ◆ Abide by all the rules set down by the director.

I also understand that the director has the right to alter or suspend my involvement in this production and that missing rehearsals or engaging in inappropriate behavior can lead to my being excluded from specific scenes or removed from the production altogether.

Name: _____

Job: _____

With performers and crew under the age of 18, send these letters home for parents or guardians to co-sign. You want parents aware and supportive of this commitment.

Rehearsal Rules

Post a list of rehearsal ground rules, or better yet, distribute the list to all company members. Here are some rules worth considering for your list:

   ◆ **Be here, and be on time.** Nothing short of a serious illness or weather emergency should keep you away from rehearsals. (It is best to encourage those with contagious conditions to stay home and get well. If the flu or some other epidemic lays a large part of your team low for a time, be ready to adjust the rehearsal schedule.)

◆ In case of illness or emergency, please call and leave a message at _____. (Insert the name and number of a production team contact, such as the PSM.)

◆ Please be prepared. Review all relevant materials before rehearsal.

◆ Guests are not permitted. All rehearsals are closed to the public, including friends, family, and significant others. No *kibbitzers* allowed!

def•i•ni•tion

Kibbitzer, the Yiddish term for a bystander offering unwanted advice, is widely used in theatrical circles.

◆ All problems and questions must be channeled through the PSM.

◆ "Take five" means to take a five-minute break, not longer.

◆ Cast members should have pencils and erasers to notate scripts and/or vocal scores. Retractable lead pencils are best. (The PSM should have a few spares on hand but must not be turned into a human pencil dispenser.)

◆ Silence is required during all rehearsals, except during breaks. (Chatter is inevitable, but it must be discouraged.)

◆ Eating is not permitted during rehearsals.

◆ Water is the only beverage permitted in the theatre. (It is a good idea to allow bottled water, but anything else can become both a mess and a distraction.)

◆ Smoking of any kind is always prohibited in the rehearsal and performance spaces, including dressing rooms.

◆ No electronic gadgets may be used during rehearsals, including cell phones, text messaging, MP3 players, and video games. Turn them off and put them away. (Laptops and other expensive hi-tech items can easily "disappear," so you may want to discourage their presence altogether.)

◆ During down time, students are permitted to do homework. (School productions should make it a requirement for all cast and crew to maintain good grades.)

◆ Illegal activity and the possession of illegal items (including drugs, guns, etc.) are grounds for immediate dismissal from the company.

Types of Rehearsals

There are various types of rehearsal sessions, particularly where musicals are concerned. While all should be considered equally important, each has different requirements:

◆ *Scene rehearsals:* The director and PSM run through dialogue with leading and featured performers. No other company members are required. For nonmusical productions, these can make up most of the rehearsal process.

◆ *Music rehearsals:* The music director (sometimes a separate rehearsals pianist) runs through songs, sometimes with the full ensemble, sometimes with soloists.

◆ *Dance rehearsals:* The choreographer runs through dances, sometimes with the full ensemble, sometimes with soloists. With proper scheduling and enough space, you can run scene, music, and dance rehearsals at the same time.

◆ *Full company rehearsals:* Everybody into the pool! All cast and crew (and sometimes production staff) are required.

The PSM and director must consider the availability of facilities, cast, and crew when planning the various types of rehearsals.

Cast and Crew Research

To deepen the cast and crew's involvement in a show, consider assigning a little research homework. School productions have been doing this for years, but even adult groups are now using this informative technique. If your show involves a particular period, have the cast and crew create brief reports, with costume crew reporting on fashions, actors on specific characters, and so on. A knowledgeable cast and crew will be more likely to detect and correct little details that might distract audiences. Research can keep 1950s greasers in the right kind of jeans and 1930s hoodlums standing under the right kind of streetlight.

Could you just give the company all this information in a workshop or a handout? Sure, but knowledge gained through effort is more likely to be remembered.

> **Backstage Whispers**
>
> To minimize confusion backstage, have the PSM or ASM create a flow sheet, a large wall chart listing all entrances, exits, and the order of scenes. Posted backstage, this is especially helpful for members of the chorus, who often get confused about where specific numbers fall in the order of a show.

Giving Notes

In the first weeks, performers and the director will interact on an almost constant basis, interrupting rehearsals with frequent questions and suggestions. Over time, you want actors to prepare for the challenges of a live performance by playing through scenes and even full acts without stopping.

That is when it is customary for the director to take notes in the course of each session and go over them verbally with the full cast for 5 or 10 minutes just before everyone heads home. Known as *giving notes*, this process is a hallowed theatrical tradition.

def•i•ni•tion

Giving notes is when a director gives verbal or written feedback to the cast and crew regarding a rehearsal or performance.

The notes you jot down can be general ("Kitchen scene sagged") or specific ("Harold made late entrance in dance"). Like all directorial comments, giving notes requires a balance between frankness and discretion. I've already noted that it is never appropriate to publicly embarrass anyone in the cast or crew. Reserve any harsh or pointed comments for a private discussion. Leave long or detailed commentary for future rehearsals. Giving notes is the time for quick fine-tuning, for praising strong points while shoring up weaknesses. In fact, giving a cast well-earned praise can do a lot to boost company morale during the exhausting process of putting on a show. And it is not unusual for reliable performers to feel ignored when their good work in rehearsals goes unmentioned.

For example, let's say you have just finished rehearsing the Harmonia Gardens restaurant scene in *Hello Dolly*. Giving notes might sound something like this:

> "Okay, I'll try to make this as quick as possible. The overall energy was great tonight. A few waiters had some problems with the gallop. We will go over that routine again day after tomorrow, so go over your routine in your heads a few times before then. Dolly's entrance is coming along, as is the title tune. Be very careful during those jumps on the runway, please! We don't want anyone landing in the orchestra pit or the audience. I'm delighted everyone has his lines memorized ahead of schedule—thank you! Dolly and Vandergelder, great work tonight. If you could slow down your dinner dialogue just a bit, it will be even stronger. We want the audience to get every joke. Crew and chorus, talking offstage was a real problem more than once this evening. That has got to stop. That said, I think we're making good overall progress. See you all tomorrow!"

When rehearsing musicals, it is also customary for the musical director to give notes regarding singing and the choreographer to give notes on dance. They should follow similar guidelines for brevity and tone. And what if a rehearsal was terrible and the cast's effort halfhearted? Then by all means say so! Even the best company can get into a rut or find itself distracted by outside events. A good finger wag at the full company can do wonders, but keep the criticism general—avoid taking out any frustration on individuals. And while anger can be appropriate, tantrums never are, so always keep your criticism within reasonable bounds.

On Stage

The director at my college was known for his positive, encouraging manner. After a lifeless rehearsal, he gathered the full cast onstage and simply glared them into silence. After a long, awful minute, the director said in a quiet but clear voice, "I don't want to see anything like this … ever again. We'll start over … tomorrow." Without another word, and looking profoundly disappointed, he walked off the stage and out of the auditorium. The next evening's rehearsal overflowed with energy, and the director confided to me with a wink, "The quiet approach gets them every time."

Record with Care

When your cast is off book and has learned the basic blocking, you may find that the chemistry or pacing of a particular scene is not quite what you had hoped for. If your coaching is not enough to remedy this, consider videotaping a rehearsal. Most actors are their own harshest critics, and seeing themselves on-screen sets those inner critics to work. This is not a technique to use with the insecure or sensitive, but most performers find it irresistible. Sports coaches have been taping practice sessions for years, so it makes sense for us theatre folk to follow suit.

While videotaping performances without written consent is illegal, licensing companies understand the need to record scenes in rehearsal. (As a precaution, you will want to erase these tapes after the cast has viewed them.) Set up a camera where it can have a full view of the stage and let it run. If a camera operator can provide close-ups, by all means do so. This technique can help performers who are having problems with anything visual, such as posture, positioning, or hand movements. You won't have to encourage cast members to watch such tapes. In most cases, they will leap at the chance to see how their performances look. Some will be shocked ("Oh no, do I do that?"), but most everyone will find opportunities for some kind of improvement.

Surprise Problems

In the course of rehearsals, the director will learn quite a bit about human behavior. Those who have never been teachers or managers will also learn about group dynamics. Let's discuss several behaviors that are regular features in theatrical life. Although not malicious, these activities can disrupt rehearsals and distract people from the business at hand. With proper handling, these potential problems can be rendered harmless.

Giggling

Performers react to pressure in all sorts of different ways, and giggling is one of them. This tends to happen after the cast is off book, when the reality of performing before an audience starts to become tangible. If it happens, it will seem to strike out of nowhere and can stop a rehearsal dead in its tracks. It may involve one actor or several, a comic scene or a serious one. With any luck, it is an aberration and will pass, but every now and then it becomes a recurring problem requiring special attention.

The musical *Camelot* includes a resurrection scene where Sir Lancelot proves his spiritual purity by bringing another knight back from the dead. During rehearsals for a college production of this show, the ensemble developed a nagging case of the giggles. Part of it was the obvious improbability of the material, but mostly it was a manifestation of preopening nerves. When it became clear that the problem was growing, the director had us run through the scene in slow motion. Those who giggled or even smiled had to explain why. Within 10 minutes we were back on track and were able to move on to the next scene.

If one actor is the giggling culprit, try running a rehearsal where everyone else in the cast goes out of their way to make that performer crack up—with quiet asides, pointed looks, even bizarre offstage noises. Noel Coward used this technique to rid young Sir Laurence Olivier of his chronic giggles in the original production of the comedy *Private Lives*. If it was good enough for those theatrical legends, it just might be good enough for the future legends in your cast.

Practical Jokes

To alleviate an uneasy combination of nerves and boredom, some members of the cast and crew will resort to playing practical jokes on each other. One of your leads may get locked in a backstage room during tech rehearsal, or a body mike will "accidentally" turn on while the wearer is using the bathroom. You can shrug off one or two of these incidents, but always take a stern "we don't need this waste of time" attitude. If pranks become a pattern, tell those responsible that they face removal from the troupe. If necessary, follow through. The atmosphere of mutual trust that is essential to any theatrical production can be shattered by such nonsense.

Too Many Cooks?

Every now and then a glitch or unexpected problem turns everyone within earshot into an expert consultant. Whenever that happens, you can insist that people stick to their specialties. Let the lighting crew handle the lights, actors their dialogue, and so on. This prevents people stepping on each other's toes and keeps egos from clashing over trifles.

Memory Lapses

It's a horrible moment. You're moving into the final weeks of rehearsal, and a key player who has up until now been the model of preparation starts forgetting lines. It's as if whole sections of memorized material have somehow been erased. In most cases, this will be a pure and simple case of nerves. Instead of making a big fuss, treat such events with a "business as usual" approach. Have the prompter feed lines as needed. When a troublesome scene is over, take a moment to reassure embarrassed performers that such lapses are natural. Encourage a thorough review of the script before the next rehearsal, and say a silent prayer that this will do the trick.

On rare but unavoidable occasions, this particular problem becomes chronic and lasts right into performances. One way to avoid that—or worse come to worst, prepare for it—is to have the cast run a rehearsal or two with no prompting. When anyone drops lines, have the actors improvise around the problem. It is what they will have to do in performance, so they might as well get a taste of it ahead of time.

Private Lives: Where to Draw the Line

Remember that your cast, crew, and administrative team are human beings sharing the exciting and sometimes emotional experience of putting on a show. As the weeks roll by, friendships and rivalries will develop, and odds are that any number of romances will blossom backstage. Making friends is one of the perks of doing amateur theatre, and I for one am all for romance between consenting single adults. But rivalries and inappropriate relationships can grow into major headaches that land in the director's lap.

Rivalries

Battles between co-stars may happen, but they are rare. Those with major roles to play know that they must rely on each other to get through performances, so goodwill between actors is far more common than bad. It is more likely that rivalries will crop up in the ensemble or between people in the cast and one of the crews. If it never gets beyond snide comments and deadly looks, no problem. However, if emotions run high enough (as emotions often do in theatre), heated arguments can break out and even turn physical.

Pull the warring parties aside, let each state his grievance, and then tell them to bury it then and there or you will have to throw both of them out of the production. (Of course, if it's obvious that just one person was out of line, limit the warning to that one.) If appropriate, have them apologize to the rest of the company for disrupting rehearsals. While you never want to humiliate anyone, it is quite fair to let those who publicly act like babies face some degree of public censure.

Romances

Backstage romance is even more prevalent than the stereotypes suggest. I have seen it thrive among all age groups, from preteens to those in their golden years. As long as both parties are of legal age and their behavior backstage is reasonable, consider it a nonissue. "Reasonable" means that a gentle peck on the cheek is always okay, but heavy necking is not. Make it clear that anything beyond necking is unacceptable during rehearsals or performances. This can be a particular problem with teens. Use a wary eye (and if needed, additional adult supervisors) to prevent young Romeos and Juliets from running off into unsupervised areas.

Romance becomes a problem when at least one of the participants is already in a committed relationship. In the heat of production, libidos can override common sense. Many find it impossible to resist a fellow company member, regardless of who may be waiting at home. Such situations will set tongues wagging, even if neither party has done anything more than smile at one another. As long as the people in question do nothing inappropriate, tell the gossips to mind their own business.

However, if an extramarital relationship does flourish in your cast, it may pose a challenge, particularly if your production is affiliated with or housed in a religious institution. In private, let the amorous parties know that your group does not want any scandal or adverse publicity and that they must keep their private lives a private matter until the production ends. Such romances have a tendency to fizzle out a few weeks past closing night.

When to Hold, When to Fold

The director's instinct is to solve problems. By showing determination and by delegating jobs to the right people, you will be able to set the overwhelming majority of these issues right in the course of rehearsals. Determination is particularly important when dealing with issues like building an overall performance. It takes time and ongoing effort to teach amateurs how to feel and appear to be at home on a stage, and progress most often comes in the form of baby steps. Instead of getting frustrated, embrace the process. There is something wonderful about watching a performance come together—a new inflection here, a more effective gesture there. Encourage, nudge, and cajole it along. Now and then, a real breakthrough may occur, and you'll feel like Henry Higgins after Eliza Doolittle first mastered "The rain in Spain stays mainly in the plain."

Then again, some things will refuse to come together despite everyone's best efforts. When you've tried every available option and it becomes clear that an obstacle is immovable, admit defeat and say "Next!" If a few things are not quite what you had aimed for, so what?

The Point of Despair

There comes a time in almost every production when everyone is just about ready to give up, the director included. Weeks have gone by, the effort seems unending, and just about everything seems to be going wrong. There is only one cure: take a deep breath and carry on. This unsettling moment is actually a good sign. As they say in *Anything Goes*, "It's always darkest just before they turn on the lights."

The Least You Need to Know

- Make attendance requirements for all rehearsals clear in advance.

- Videotaping rehearsals is a great way to let a cast see its strengths and weaknesses.

- Such problems as onstage giggling, practical jokes, and memory lapses must be resolved during the rehearsal process.

- When you are ready to give up, don't. It's a sure sign that the production is coming together.

Chapter 16

Sets: "Take Me to the World"

In This Chapter

- The real purpose of stage sets
- The dangers of TMS syndrome
- Basic set elements, materials, and construction techniques
- Getting by with minimal sets
- The paramount importance of safety

From birthday parties to school dances to political conventions, decorations are a big part of any celebration, visually establishing a special sense of time and place. Stage sets do the same for theatrical presentations. Inexpensive materials like plywood, canvas, and paint are used to create dream worlds where songs and stories come to life. This chapter is a quick primer on the basics—the people, materials, and techniques involved in giving amateur productions a visible physical context.

A Quick History

The ancient Greeks used a small building called the "skene" as the central backdrop for theatrical performances. It housed props and dressing rooms, and painted panels could be attached to it depicting specific locations.

It was not until the Italian Renaissance that most of the scenic conventions familiar to us today came into use. That is when the newly invented art of perspective drawing made it possible to depict distance and depth in the confines of a stage by using a decorated backdrop surrounded by a series of side panels (called "wings"). To make the transition between scenes smoother, Italian theatres introduced an elaborate system of pulleys and ropes to lift and drop scenery as needed. Because this was the same type of rigging used on ships, unemployed sailors provided the expertise needed to work the ropes. As stage settings became the equivalent of gigantic paintings, Italians took the natural step of putting their stages in a gigantic frame: the proscenium.

Although most theatres still use the same basic technology, the introduction of electricity and computers has done much to change stagecraft. Electric lighting allows greater subtlety in set design. More three-dimensional elements enhance simple flats and painted backdrops. Mechanical power now augments manpower, so heavy sets can fly at the push of a button or be whisked away on a turntable. Professional productions now invest a major part of their budgets in complex sets and heavy hydraulic equipment. One of the greatest mistakes amateur groups can make is to try matching the pros at this high-priced game. Instead, amateurs must rethink material in terms of their existing production resources.

What Does the Material Require?

Thanks to the overproduced spectacles that have played Broadway in recent years, many people have the mistaken idea that stage sets are there to make audiences "ooh" and "ahh." Baloney! The main purpose of stage sets is to suggest a world where the story and/or songs can seem at home—and that means serving the dramatic needs of the material.

In most plays and musicals, particular elements are either specified in scene descriptions ("an elegant Victorian parlor") or implied by stage directions ("she sits" suggests the presence of something to sit on). In revues, songs and skits give similar pointers. Aside from such practical considerations, a set gives audiences something to look at besides the actors and their costumes. Just what kind of set do you need? That depends on various factors:

- The script and/or songs. These may require or at least suggest the need for certain elements.

- The director's concept. Is it realistic, abstract, or somewhere in between? The set must embody whatever approach the director takes.

◆ The performance space. The presence or lack of fly and wing space must be considered, and an arena/in the round stage would require set pieces that do not block audience sight lines. Whatever the staging format, the sets must leave enough room for the cast to maneuver both onstage and behind the scenes.

For multiple-set shows, determine which scenes require detailed settings and which can be suggested with a few props or a simple lighting effect. Why construct a set for a brief crossover scene on a cold winter street, when all the audience needs to see is an actor hunching her shoulders and rubbing her hands together?

This art deco Anything Goes *set is a great example of a handsome setting that serves the dramatic needs of the play and the physical requirements of a production.*

(Design by D.V. Panessa; photo by Tim Dingman, used with permission of NVOT High School Music Department)

TMS Syndrome

It is the saddest and most widespread phenomenon in amateur theatre, and it has ruined countless productions. The idea may be new to you, but I guarantee that you have seen TMS syndrome in action. It happens whenever you're sitting at an amateur production and a scene change takes several minutes or more. The orchestra plays the cover music over and over, and chatter breaks out across the audience as the stage crew struggles with a dizzying array of walls, staircases, and furniture. The audience is forced to sit there, wondering what could be wrong and wishing they could be anywhere else. By the time the lights come back up, the cast has to win back the audience's attention—until the next endless scene change stops everything dead again.

In case you haven't already guessed, TMS stands for "too much set"! I've heard many designers blame slow scene changes on lazy stage crews, but that's pure poppycock. Odds are that there is simply "too much set" flying around on that stage! In my experience, this problem is caused by one of the following:

♦ **A set designer forgets that sets are not the central issue.** In any amateur production, the central issue is the show. Sets are just one useful element in the whole picture.

♦ **The producer and director don't say "no."** If the set designer loses perspective (no pun intended), the producer and director must have the guts to call a halt.

♦ **The stage crew lacks proper training.** If possible, sets should be completed in time for the stage crew to have several run-throughs both with and without the cast before the first tech rehearsal.

Like all other production elements, sets are there to serve the show, not the other way around. So good set design begins with a look at the material the set in question must serve.

Basic Set Elements

Amateur theatre troupes use a battery of basic set elements to create their stage illusions. Even Broadway still uses them, with a few million dollars' worth of hydraulics and three-dimensional ornamentation thrown in. Basic set elements include the following:

♦ *Platforms* are tablelike structures that have legs (of any height) covered by a solid top or "skin." Theatrical platforms can be almost any size, but the industry standard is 4 by 8 feet. Heights vary. Separate platforms can be bolted together to create a freestanding stage. Low platforms can be placed on casters to simplify moving them (and objects placed on them) around.

♦ *Stairs* must be built at a comfortable angle, with all steps at an equal height to prevent stumbles. Any staircase with more than three steps should have a safety handrail.

♦ *Flats* are wooden frames covered with plywood or canvas. They can be painted to simulate walls or backgrounds in a stage set. To stand securely, flats must be supported—either by braces on the back or by connecting them to other flats on an angle.

♦ Sturdy *wooden cubes*, with or without hinged lids, are among the most versatile set elements, useful in minimalist or realistic settings.

◆ *Backdrops* are large muslin or canvas cloths suspended from *battens* over the stage. Plain or painted to resemble any setting, they can be "dropped" in from the fly space as needed.

def•i•ni•tion

A **batten** is a metal pipe suspended over a stage, used to hang lights and scenery.

◆ *Drapes* can be used for more than masking! They add a glamorous look to any production. The long-running Broadway revue *Black and Blue* used drapes as settings, reviving the lush look of a lost age.

◆ *Doors and windows* are useful accessories but complicated to build. With creative staging, most amateur productions can get by without either of these items.

Use these basics in various combinations to create all kinds of environments, from forests to tenements to ballrooms.

Simple set changes can be elegant and effective. For the same production of Anything Goes, *the main set was covered with metallic cloth, and a few painted wooden cubes and pyramids were added to turn the ship's bridge into the ship's lounge.*

(Design by D.V. Panessa; photo by Tim Dingman, used with permission of NVOT High School Music Department)

Construction Needs

Building stage sets requires a small army's worth of resources—and a small but crucial army of talent.

People

In Chapter 9, we considered the qualities to look for in a set designer, and in Chapter 8 I discussed what to expect from a stage crew. Your production will need at least one person with basic scene shop construction skills to act as head carpenter. If additional experienced hands are available, by all means use them. Otherwise, the designer and head carpenter will have to train as they go along—which can be very rewarding, if a bit more work-intensive.

In many amateur performing arts companies, the volunteers who help build the sets also serve as stage crew. Some love to build, some want to be part of the theatre without appearing onstage, some are there because loved ones are in the show, and others are there for the sheer fun of it. These hard-working souls are among the most dedicated and unsung people in amateur theatre. Be sure to give them a designer and head carpenter who know what they are doing. As a rule, stage crews have a low tolerance for bull but respond with genuine devotion to intelligent leadership.

Space

Set construction must be timed to fit your talent and the availability of facilities. A few theatres have a scene shop on the premises, and some lucky high school and college groups have access to a school shop. However, most amateur companies must handle at least some of their set construction off premises, either in professional carpentry shops or in the homes/garages of volunteers. If your performance space is available for only a limited period, you will have to store set elements in a secure, dry place until the load-in date. Some set elements may be too big to fit in a neighbor's garage, so plan ahead for any special storage and transportation needs.

Plans

Coming up with an effective set design won't mean much unless the designer sets it down in terms a carpenter and stage crew can work with. Many designers pride themselves on turning out handsome scale models. These can be useful as teaching tools for the cast and crew, but more formal written plans are needed before actual set construction can take place. A set design can be laid out on paper in various ways, all of which are done to scale, proportionally reducing each foot of design to an inch or less. This makes it possible to fit a full set design on a manageable piece of paper.

Most stage designers create two basic types of drawings for every set:

- *Designer's drawings* are scaled two-dimensional depictions of a full set or any of its components. These drawings specify dimensions, materials to be used, and special assembly instructions.

- The *ground plan* illustrates how all the elements of a set will be positioned onstage. This should include all set elements as well as the placement of any large props, *masks*, and anything else that might take up room in the performance area.

def•i•ni•tion

Masks are dark curtains used to hide production elements that are not in use.

Both of these plans utilize the same sort of drafting symbols used by architects and contractors to indicate doors, types of windows, stairs, draperies, etc. Each drawing should also include a boxed identification label that gives the show's title, designer, scene number, date, and the scale of the drawing.

Solid Materials

Sets are not the real world! They have to be affordable, moveable, and ready to withstand the rigors of live performances. The materials listed here are dependable, relatively affordable, and used by many amateur groups.

- Board lumber. The most affordable and practical choice for visible surfaces is white pine, grade C or better. Grade D is acceptable if it is to be painted, while grades 1 and 2 can be used for framing that is not seen by the audience. Lower grades are not reliable. Sold by the board foot, lumber comes in varying lengths and thicknesses. Use only two-inch-thick boards in weight-bearing structures.

- Plywood. Several thin layers of wood are bonded together with adhesive to form these strong, lightweight boards.

- Particle board. Made from woodchips, sawdust, and glue, this stuff is heavy, hard to work with, and too brittle for most stage applications. Avoid it.

- Styrofoam. Cheap and versatile, styrofoam is a great choice for decorative elements such as rocks and bricks. Just keep in mind that it is also very lightweight and easy to damage, so it is not practical for items that must carry weight or stand up to substantial wear and tear.

◆ Beadboard. Polystyrene sheets normally used as insulation, this substance is lightweight but easy to damage. It is useful as a low-wear surface covering.

> **Backstage Whispers**
>
> You can now purchase wood products at various locations, ranging from traditional lumber-yards to hardware superstores. Quality and price can vary, so the set designer and head carpenter should survey all local options. Most of the nonwood materials listed here are available at any large hardware center.

◆ Lexan. A tough, transparent polycarbonate, this can be used in weight-bearing set elements.

◆ Masonite. Made from pressed wood pulp, these sheets are used for flooring and facing. But it is slippery, so it must be sanded or painted before it can be walked on safely.

◆ PVC. Polyvinyl chloride, used in plumbing, is a great, lightweight option for use in set elements. With limited weight-bearing ability, it is available in pipes, sheets, and solid rods.

Accessories

Set elements can involve a number of standard accessory parts:

◆ Casters. Can be rigid (fixed position) or swivel (freely rotating) and used as needed on moving platforms. Synthetic caster wheels are quieter, while metal or rubber wheels handle heavier loads.

◆ Latches. Used in doors, windows, and kitchen cabinets, these come in a wide variety of sizes and styles.

◆ Hinges. Used to hang doors and join scenic units, these also come in a wide variety of sizes and styles.

Most of these items are inexpensive and can be found in standard hardware stores. Knowledgeable store staff should be able to help you select the right hardware for specific applications.

Fabrics

There is a short, time-tested list of fabrics that are strong enough to use in actual set construction:

◆ Canvas. This dense cotton fabric can be used to cover flats that must withstand heavy-duty use and to provide a paint surface for stairs and flooring.

- Muslin. This light cotton fabric can be used for backdrops, to cover flats, and as a paint surface for hard faced set elements.

- Sharkstooth *scrim*. This strong cotton weave fabric turns transparent when lit from behind—even if painted.

- Scenic netting. This wide weave net is used to support "cut-out" drop elements.

- Burlap. This coarse, heavy fabric is used to provide surface texture.

def•i•ni•tion

Scrim is sheer, gauzelike material used for drops or flats; it can be a plain color or painted like a backdrop. When lit from the front, it appears opaque; when objects behind it are lit, it becomes see-through.

All these materials are available from most fabric suppliers. Almost any kind of fabric can be used in set decoration, but use some judgment. Fragile fabrics may not be up to the job, and anything white can become a magnet for hard-to-clean splashes and scuffs.

Ropes

For centuries, Manila fiber rope was the theatrical standard. Still common, it is now augmented by a variety of synthetic fiber and metallic wire ropes. These newer ropes are more resistant to abrasion and mildew, and all have multiple theatrical applications. Consider all the options before making a major purchase.

Tools

Stage construction involves the same power and hand tools used in construction and the average home workshop. Be sure volunteers who bring their own tools mark them clearly—things like hammers and screwdrivers look an awful lot alike. If the production is buying tools, buy the best you can afford for each job—but keep in mind that the most expensive is not always the optimal choice. For example, lightweight hammers make more sense for certain uses, and disposable brushes can be more practical than pricey models that may just get tossed after the set is finished.

Backstage Whispers

A stagehand's secret: you can remove pine resin buildup on saws and drill bits with spray oven cleaner. In a well-ventilated area, spray the item, leave it enclosed in a box or paper bag for 15 to 20 minutes, and then clean it with soapy water and dry thoroughly. During this process, be sure to wear protective waterproof gloves.

Construction Techniques

The techniques used to construct most items used onstage (platforms, boxes, etc.) will be familiar to any experienced carpenter, but two elements are unusual and worth explaining here.

Drops

These large expanses of material (usually either muslin or scrim) can be tailored to whatever width and height are required to provide a full or partial backdrop. The top can either have small metal hole guards called grommets installed to simplify hanging or can be secured between two wooden battens. Hem the bottom to form a pocket, and insert into it a ½-inch PVC pipe or metal chain to provide better stability. There are usually 1-inch hems on the vertical sides. Scrim drops designed for backlighting effects should be seamless.

Flats

Flats come in various sizes and shapes. The standard rectangle frame is built from 1×3 pine, with a toggle bar across the middle and diagonal braces for the top and bottom halves. This light but sturdy frame is then covered with muslin or canvas, which is secured using nails or heavy-duty staples.

The Bare Minimum

When it comes to sets, less can be the strongest creative choice. There is no need to hit audiences over the head with lavish detail. All they need is enough to please the eye and get their imaginations going. No one in their right mind expects amateur groups to match Broadway's multimillion-dollar realism. Instead of wasting precious resources mimicking the pros, get creative! Thornton Wilder's moving comedy *Our Town* was the first modern production to prove that powerful theatre can take place on a bare stage with nothing more than a few pieces of furniture. Since then, countless amateur and professional productions have delighted audiences without presenting a single flat or drop.

When circumstances or a director's taste require it, a play can be staged with the barest minimum of a set. A few sturdy wooden cubes can become anything from a classroom to a dining table to a hilltop. Intimate shows like *The Fantasticks* and *You're a Good Man, Charlie Brown* were created with minimal sets in mind, but this approach can work with many plays and musicals that usually get elaborate stagings. My college production of *Camelot* used a unit set to excellent effect, surrounding the playing area with the gray walls and battlements of a fantasy castle. With small items (tables, chairs, etc.) used as accessories, the scene changes flowed with professional speed, and the colorful medieval costumes (in which most of the budget was invested) looked all the more dazzling against an understated background.

My advice to the inexperienced is to go with the simplest possible sets your first time out, graduating to more ambitious elements as your troupe learns the ins and outs of building and managing scenery. Simple, efficient settings always make more sense than unattractive time-eaters.

> **Gremlins**
>
> Masking tape and electrical tape are standard stage crew equipment, but most professionals forbid the presence of duct tape backstage, and so should you. It is no good for use on wiring or electrical connections and leaves a messy residue.

Safety

A designer who has been working in amateur theatre for years keeps large signs posted in his scene shop and backstage areas with the following reminder:

PUTTING ON A GOOD SHOW IS JOB #2—
SAFETY IS JOB #1!

Truer words were never written! The entire production team—especially those involved in set construction and installation—should always take every reasonable safety precaution.

One of the most important factors in crew safety is enforcing strict policies, such as the following:

◆ Proper attire is required during work sessions. Allow no floppy sleeves, long hair worn loose, or dangling jewelry that could become caught in equipment.

◆ Everyone must wear the right protective gear (goggles, gloves, ear protectors, etc.).

◆ Everyone must have the proper training and experience before using any tool, particularly power tools.

◆ Great care must always be taken when using ladders—teams only, no solo climbers!

Backstage Whispers

To dispose of leftover paint safely, save a bag of sawdust from set construction. Stir this into the paint can, which should be left open for several hours. Then toss the dried residue. (Note: be sure this meets with local disposal standards—every community has its own rules on this!)

◆ Smoking, eating, loud music, and distracting behavior are prohibited during work sessions.

◆ A basic first-aid kit must be on hand whenever and wherever set construction is taking place, along with emergency contact information; signed parental consent forms (if minors are involved); a fire extinguisher; and phone numbers for the fire department, ambulance service, etc.

Make these rules serious business by sticking to a strict "three strikes and you're out" policy.

As I mentioned in an earlier chapter, the catch with any set of rules is that the folks in charge must abide by them, too. A rule about protective gear won't mean much if the set designer never bothers to wear it. And anyone who thinks experience ensures that they won't get hurt clearly needs more experience!

The Least You Need to Know

◆ The main purpose of stage sets is to suggest a world where the story and/or songs can seem at home—and that means serving the dramatic needs of the material.

◆ Many amateur groups make the mistake of trying to copy Broadway's lavish stage sets, leading to what I call TMS syndrome—"too much set"!

◆ Simplicity is the best set choice for newcomers. Keep sets minimal until your team develops expertise.

◆ Sets must fit the needs of the material, the director's production concept, and the physical limitations of the performance space and still leave room (onstage and off) for the cast.

◆ Putting on a good show is job #2—safety is always job #1!

Chapter 17

Costumes and Props: "Give Me My Colored Coat"

In This Chapter

- ◆ Ways costumes and props serve the material and reinforce character
- ◆ The importance of color, durability, and safety
- ◆ Making, borrowing, and renting costumes
- ◆ Proper costume care and storage
- ◆ Creating and managing props
- ◆ Changing the time and place of a play
- ◆ Making do with the minimum

Since ancient witch doctors donned facemasks and covered their bodies with feathers and animal hide to impersonate gods and forest creatures, costumes and props have been a vital part of public performance and make-believe. Elaborate or simple, stage costumes are important tools in an actor's dramatic arsenal. Plenty of books are available that tell how to build costumes and achieve specific period looks. This chapter discusses basic approaches to using props and costumes in amateur productions, from design and rental to management and care—and including some ideas on innovative and minimalist approaches.

The Why and Wherefore

Despite the admonitions of religion and philosophy to never pass judgment on others, let's be honest—we do it every day, quietly (and sometimes not so quietly) forming opinions of others based on a few seconds of observation. Like a silent Sherlock Holmes, the unconscious mind equates dress with social standing, taste, even character. The clothes and accessories people wear form those first impressions. Half a dozen teenage boys in penny loafers, chinos, and letter sweaters carrying book bags would cause little fuss walking down Main Street. Put the same group in scuffed army boots, tattered jeans, and ratty biker jackets, and fellow pedestrians will cross the street to avoid trouble—especially if those boys are carrying 2×4s. It's an instinctive, self-preservative reaction that probably dates back to a time when our prehistoric ancestors depended on first impressions for survival.

> **Backstage Whispers**
>
> Classical musicians wear formal attire for concerts to give an immediate impression of elegance and sophistication. Rock musicians take the opposite approach, giving the most informal, even irreverent impression possible. Like the lawyer says in the musical *Chicago*, it's all show business.

Stage costumes and props take advantage of this instinct, giving audiences an almost instantaneous visual key to character, time, and place. Think of how costumes and props help to define such characters as …

- The 1950s street gangs in *West Side Story* (jeans, switchblades).

- The upper-crust Victorians in *The Importance of Being Earnest* (formal attire, cucumber sandwiches).

- The gossiping 1912 Iowa housewives in *The Music Man* (feathered hats, colorful handbags).

- The aging vaudevillians in *The Sunshine Boys* (scruffy 1930s-style suits, comic vaudeville props).

It is impossible to picture distinctive fictional characters without envisioning their attire. Actors have to make those characters three-dimensional through the power of their performances, but effective costuming gives actors and audiences a head start.

Start with the Script

As with every other creative aspect of a production, costume and prop design begin with a detailed look at the material being performed. This means the designers must read the script—not once, but several times, becoming familiar with every character and the overall shape of the play. Then they must work in close concert with fellow designers and the director so all the visual elements harmonize.

Costumes and props must express character in a manner consistent with the director's overall creative concept. A production of *Hamlet* set in medieval Denmark will have one look; re-set the action in contemporary Manhattan, and the costumes and props will need radical rethinking. Regardless of the overall concept, the costumes must help define the brooding title character, the fragile Ophelia, the babbling bureaucrat Polonius, and the ruthless usurper Claudius.

This high school production of Mame *made a point of not copying the original Broadway designs, but anyone who knows the musical will recognize prep school escapee Patrick Dennis and his charismatic aunt, thanks to their character-specific costuming.*

(Costume design by Debbie Trainor; set by D.V. Panessa; photo used with permission of NVOT High School Music Department)

If the director and designers have a disagreement, there should always be room for private discussion. However, the director has the final say in all creative issues, so if an impasse occurs, designers must adjust their vision to fit the director's concept.

Consistency

Once the production concept is defined, all costumes and props must be planned to fit that concept and, at the same time, reflect the social and financial status of each character. This kind of consistency is essential if audiences are to suspend disbelief and accept your production's storytelling approach.

Let's say your group has decided to do a traditional staging of *The Music Man*. The costume designer should research the fashions worn in the midwestern United States in 1912. Every costume seen onstage must fit the styles of that era and the character wearing it. The men may all wear period suits, but each should have distinctive features that help visually set each character apart. For example …

◆ A traveling salesman might wear a loud, colorful checked suit, carry a well-worn suitcase of samples, and wear shoes that show signs of constant travel.

◆ A shopkeeper could add a white apron, sleeve guards, visor, or other accessories unique to his business.

◆ Mayor Shinn's formal coat and high hat mark his station as a prosperous business owner and community leader.

All these outfits must be appropriate for an Iowa gentleman of that time. Throwing in fashion ideas from a different era would distract viewers and weaken the overall effect of the production.

Props must also be consistent with the production concept and the characters involved. The appearance of common items like guns or telephones can change quite a bit from one era to another. Putting the wrong phone in a character's hand is like arming a medieval knight with a machine gun.

Color

Much has been said and written on the physical and psychological effects of color. Costume designers and coordinators must pay careful attention to the colors worn on stage. Here are some basic examples:

◆ Black can tire the eyes if used heavily, but it is a great accent color—and yes, as a costume color, black most definitely *is* slimming.

◆ White and bright red are powerful colors that can overwhelm the viewer. Use them with discretion.

- Cream or light beige are attractive under harsh lights and can be used in place of white, especially in costumes.

- Cool colors like green, blue, purple, and darker shades of red suggest class, elegance, and wealth.

- Warm colors like orange, yellow, and the brighter reds suggest joy, celebration, and high energy.

- Shades of gray have a neutral effect and can be used to make people or objects blend into their surroundings.

Color can also be used to set important characters apart from their surroundings. Consider the now-classic effect designer Cecil Beaton used in *My Fair Lady*'s Ascot scene. The ensemble was dressed in eye-popping combinations of black, white, and gray, all seen against a striped black and white backdrop. By putting Henry Higgins in brown tweed and Eliza Doolittle in lavender chiffon, these two characters stood out from the crowd.

Aside from conferring with the set designer to coordinate the use of color, the costume designer must use such color contrasts to set key players apart from the set and the ensemble:

- In a group dressed in formal black and white attire, anyone in a bright color stands out.

- In a group dressed in varied colors, anyone in a pure white or black outfit catches the viewer's eye.

- White and black each provide the ultimate contrast to the other.

Gremlins

When more than one principal character wears the same color in a given scene, it can be confusing to the audience, especially in large performance spaces. Of course, if the material calls for confused identities, same-color costuming can be used to reinforce the effect.

At the same time, the colors of every element in a costume must blend to form a pleasing appearance—unless the designer is trying to achieve a particular effect.

Color can also be used as an indicator of social status. Bright colors have always been more expensive to create and are, therefore, often reserved for wealthier or more powerful members of society. (In ancient Rome, only the emperor and members of his immediate family were allowed to wear purple garments.) Characters in the lower classes are usually marked by earthier tones and faded colors. Mark Twain's classic story *The Prince and the Pauper* doesn't mean much if the look-alike title characters do not have radical differences in costume to set them apart. And you don't need three guesses to tell which of the two is going to wear the more colorful wardrobe.

Durability, Comfort, and Safety

Stage costumes are not just street clothes. A short-lived amateur production does not involve the wear and tear caused by a prolonged professional run, but even a few days of makeup and heavy perspiration will take a toll. Seams and collars should be reinforced, and sturdy fabrics are needed to withstand strains, stains, and cleanings. Of course, store-bought street clothes can be used in shows with contemporary or recent settings, but it is important to avoid using delicate or valuable items.

> **Backstage Whispers**
>
> When the original Broadway production of *Kiss Me Kate* faced a tight budget, designer (and co-producer) Lemuel Ayers used drapery fabric to construct the colorful period costumes. This relatively inexpensive material gave the Shakespearean scenes a rich, distinctive look—and they stood up to the strain of eight performances a week.

> **Gremlins**
>
> One costume designer suggests that actors wear newly constructed costume pieces inside out at the first fitting. This makes it easy to trim away spare material or other obvious sources of irritation.

Aside from withstanding the rigors of performance, stage costumes and props must be comfortable to wear and use or, at the very least, endurable. Actors have to contend with memorization, characterization, timing, audibility, and tech cues. They do not need the added burden of costumes that leave them in pain or props that defy graceful handling. A jacket that's too tight can make it impossible to execute even the simplest gesture. Costumes should be built out of durable fabrics that "breathe," with natural fibers like cotton being the most obvious choices. Nonporous substances like rubber, vinyl, or plastic suffocate the skin and should be avoided. And all props must be as easy to handle as possible.

Safety concerns must get top priority, surpassing any artistic considerations. Be sure any dragging hems or long sleeves are re-tailored to prevent accidents. Potentially harmful items like real knives, hatchets, and guns should never appear on any amateur stage—ever! Spare me any malarkey about blank bullets and blunted blades being "harmless." Under the pressure of a live performance, even the steadiest hand can make mistakes. Be certain that none of those mistakes involve objects that could cause anything worse than a paper cut. Theatre is a place for make-believe, and that includes using make-believe weapons.

This community theatre production of The Music Man *is another example of costumes helping define character.*

(Photo courtesy of the Gingerbread Players, Forest Hills, NY)

Creating Costumes

While it helps to have a seasoned team building your costumes, previous experience is not a necessity. What matters most is knowing how to sew and how to interpret a dress pattern. Anyone with those basic skills can learn how to build and maintain stage costumes. There are a number of good books on the technical aspects of costume creation, and Appendix B suggests several worthwhile titles. You can find these and more at your local library or through any major bookseller. Encourage your costume team to read as many of these books as they can get their hands on, looking for any techniques that may serve your production's needs.

Capable volunteer seamsters and seamstresses are becoming harder to find today. Luckily, you can also rent or borrow costumes—most productions wind up doing a bit of each.

Costume Rentals

A quick web search will lead to several companies that specialize in costume rentals. Aside from putting your cast in professional costumes, these firms offer package deals for established shows, especially major musicals. Just tell them the title of the show, provide cast measurements, and you'll receive a full *costume plot* tailored and shipped to order. Mind you, the costumes may have been in use for some time and may not jibe with the rest of your production concept. The tailoring will need fine-tuning, and all this "convenience" comes at a price. Aside from the initial rental fees, rented costumes must be dry cleaned and shipped back when your show is done, adding to the overall expense.

def•i•ni•tion

A **costume plot** is a full list of all the costumes used in a production, broken down by scene and by character.

Many amateur groups limit their costume rentals to items that are too difficult for their costume crew to create, such as hoop skirts, armor, or royal court robes. If at all possible, arrange for a preinspection of any rental items, or at least review accurate photos. This can help prevent serious misunderstandings regarding style and color.

Purchases

Second-hand shops and rummage sales are a great source of costumes. A designer can transform inexpensive used items into wonderful creations. This can be more cost-effective than rentals, and your group can keep these items for future use. In some cases, inexpensive items such as shirts and minor accessories may be bought new. Whenever performers purchase anything to be worn onstage, be sure they understand that these items may be subject to damage in the course of production.

Borrowed Glory

In some cases, you can assemble simple costumes from existing clothing and accessories. Plays set in the present or recent past can often be dressed, at least in part, from the closets of your cast. Always warn actors that any personal items worn on stage must be expendable. Perspiration and makeup can permanently ruin clothing, as can the rips and tears that often occur in the adrenaline-fueled heat of performance. If clothing has financial or sentimental value, actors should leave it safe at home.

You can often borrow costumes from other theatre groups or individuals. While theatre groups usually understand that borrowed costumes will suffer somewhat, you must remind individuals that anything loaned or donated for stage use is liable to come back the worse for wear. A letter of agreement should accompany all loans, spelling out the following:

- The item (or items) borrowed.

- The time frame of the loan.

- An assurance that the item will be cleaned before it is returned.

- A statement of mutual understanding that the items may suffer a reasonable degree of wear and tear.

- How any irreparably damaged items will be replaced or paid for.

Authorized representatives of the production and of the individual or organization making the loan should sign this letter, with each keeping a signed copy.

Care and Storage

Costumes that survive the dangers of live performance can still be ruined by mishandling backstage. Performers must be trained to treat all costumes and accessories with care, putting them on hangers and/or returning them to the costume team when not in use. The simple act of properly hanging a costume on a hangar can prevent wrinkles, soiling, and other unsightly damage. The pressures of performing can distract even the most fastidious actors, so the costume team should check dressing rooms frequently for stray items.

Iron or steam costumes as needed. If the production is to run for more than one week, either launder or dry clean important costumes between sets of performances. If nothing else, this will keep costumes smelling fresh.

Backstage Whispers

When superstitious actor John Barrymore enjoyed the greatest success of his stage career playing the title role in *Hamlet,* he refused to let anyone launder his custom-padded black tights. As the months rolled by, Barrymore's fellow actors found the resulting odor increasingly offensive. Although carefully preserved in a museum archive, those tights have partially crumbled away due to the corrosive effects of the great actor's perspiration.

Be sure all costumes and accessories are stored securely when not in use, preferably under lock and key. While it is preferable for storage areas to be well ventilated, this is not always a practical option. Rolling clothing racks provide effective centralized costume storage, moving easily from locked storage areas to a hallway or common room accessible to the entire cast. Use sturdy racks with heavy-duty casters that can withstand the weight and maintain mobility.

Wardrobe Inventory

In the whirlwind of activity surrounding dress rehearsals and performances, backstage areas can turn into "black holes" where costumes and accessories disappear. Whether stolen, borrowed, or lost, a missing item can leave the entire production in the lurch. The remedy is for the costume team to take a quick inventory before and after every rehearsal and performance. They can do this in a matter of minutes if they have a thorough wardrobe checklist.

Despite a limited budget, this community theatre production of Shakespeare's Much Ado About Nothing *boasts simple, attractive, and character-specific costuming.*

(Photo courtesy of the Gingerbread Players, Forest Hills, NY)

Your costume team can create such a checklist using any word processing program. Organize both the checklist and the costume racks according to character, with every costume and accessory listed and hung in the order of use. This makes it a simple process to go through the rack and verify the presence of every item. Track down any missing costume pieces immediately. In my experience, the sooner a search begins, the more likely it is that a lost item will be located. Immediately remove anyone who maliciously steals or hides items from the production team. Such "practical jokes" are not funny and waste a lot of valuable time.

Props

There are two types of stage properties—more commonly referred to as "props":

- **Hand props:** Objects that are carried or handled by actors while onstage.

- **Set dressing:** Objects used to furnish or decorate a set, ranging from artificial flowers to sofas.

All props must fit the characters using them and reflect the time and place of the play. Unless your production concept is abstract, a contemporary hi-tech kitchen chair does not belong in Henry VIII's Hampton Court throne room.

Maneuverability and safety are more important than authenticity. Audiences know that what happens onstage is make-believe and will accept props that appear artificial—as long as there is a reasonable attempt at imitating the real thing.

In the budget-conscious world of amateur theatre, obtaining or building the "perfect" prop is not always possible. If your team winds up unable to find or create the exact piece your designer has in mind, make do with the best option available. As long as the prop in question gets the job done, audiences won't care. The goal is to avoid glaring anachronisms, such as seeing a plastic princess telephone in a 1930s office. (Yes, I've seen that actually happen, and it was not intended as a joke.)

Backstage Whispers

The acting editions of scripts often include detailed prop lists. Based on the original professional production, these lists can be useful references, but do not feel obligated to follow them. Depending on the director and set designer's approach, your production may have very different needs. Set up your actual prop list accordingly.

Building or Buying

Several simple rules govern the process of buying or building stage properties:

- Props must be strong enough to withstand more than the expected strain of performance. Tables and chairs that are going to be stood or danced upon must be reinforced to handle two times the weight expected. This prevents embarrassing and dangerous mishaps.

- Backups of inexpensive disposable props (drinking glasses, cigars, lipstick, etc.) should be kept on hand for all performances.

♦ The most expensive option is not always the most appropriate one. Meet the needs of the production, not those of a designer's ego.

♦ Wood props that come in contact with actors should be checked before each performance for splinters, rough spots, or protruding nails.

As with costumes, the primary concern in prop selection or manufacture is safety. Actors cannot give their best if they are not confident in the props they have to use.

Managing

In Chapter 24, I discuss the importance of a well-organized prop table and the need for secure storage of props. The prop team should also have a checklist of all properties, organized by scene or act. While setting up this system takes some time and effort, nothing compares with the time and effort it saves.

Changing Time and/or Place

Audiences demand to see certain shows in lavish period costuming, usually because the cultural setting is crucial to the effectiveness of the piece. It would be hard to imagine an effective attempt to re-set *My Fair Lady* anywhere but Edwardian London or move *The King and I* to someplace other than Bangkok in the 1860s. Any amateur group staging these or similar shows must be prepared to costume them in a traditional manner.

But many plays and musicals with less exacting requirements can thrive in the face of fresh, creative thinking. The only requirement for re-setting a show is that the new time and location must not detract or distract from the material's original meaning. I have seen these examples successfully staged over the years:

def•i•ni•tion

Commedia dell'arte was the improvisatory theatre of the Italian Renaissance, featuring clownish characters and broad physical comedy.

♦ Shakespeare's comedy *The Taming of the Shrew* has been staged as a knockabout *commedia dell'arte* spectacle or a confrontation between twentieth-century mafia dons.

♦ Gilbert and Sullivan's *The Mikado* has been reset in modern corporate Japan and in an African American ghetto.

- Gilbert and Sullivan's *Iolanthe* can be moved to any nation with a parliamentary system of government (Canada, India, etc.), or rewritten to poke fun at America's system.

- Wilde's *The Importance of Being Earnest* can be timed to spoof any class-conscious social circle.

- Shakespeare's tragedy *Richard III* can be a British monarch, a fascist dictator, or a U.S. president.

- Fairy tales that embody timeless truths and archetypes can be re-set in any number of historical periods, including the present. Rodgers and Hammerstein's *Cinderella* has undergone numerous rewrites since its debut in 1957, with three different TV versions and several major stage adaptations—the most recent featuring multiracial casting and hip-hop street lingo.

It is not just a question of creativity. To the extent that a costume plan serves the script, fits the director's concept, and makes sense to audiences, it will be successful.

The Not-So-Bare Necessities

Before going out on the road or beginning previews in New York, many Broadway productions hold a "gypsy run-through," allowing the cast and crew to invite other industry professionals to a special rehearsal. The show is performed in a legitimate theatre with no sets, costumes, or props—just the cast in street clothes, with rarely more than a small instrumental ensemble in the orchestra pit. These bare-bones performances are a wonderful opportunity to judge the material and cast on their own merits. While it is impossible to deny the importance of sets, costumes, and props, theatre is still primarily a question of the material and the performers.

Don't be afraid to keep your physical production simple. When the budget is non-existent, what is the least you can get by with? That depends on the material in question and the talent of your cast. At all times, costumes and props must help clarify identity. In a show featuring a small cast (six or fewer performers), generic costumes like black jeans and T-shirts accented with colorful accessories may make sense, but this approach can become visually confusing with larger casts. Unless the play is a mystery in which identities have to be muddled, audiences must always be crystal clear as to who is who.

The Least You Need to Know

- Well-designed costumes and props give audiences an almost instantaneous visual key to character, time, and place.

- Use color to help establish character and to set performers apart from their surroundings.

- You can create, rent, or borrow costumes and props; most productions do a bit of all three.

- Costumes and props must be properly stored when not in use and cleaned as necessary. This is especially true for items that are to be returned to others after the production ends.

- Costumes and props must be comfortable and durable, but at the risk of repetition, safety is always the first priority. Never use any costume or prop that poses a safety risk.

- Don't be afraid to keep your physical production simple. Let the material and ability of your team determine what is essential.

Chapter 18

Makeup: "Put On a Happy Face"

In This Chapter

- The main purposes of stage makeup
- Facial features and essential tools of the trade
- Basic stage makeup techniques
- False features, facial hair, and wigs

From Shakespeare to Hugh Jackman, actors have relied on makeup, hairstyles, and wigs to help create the illusion of character. While makeup cannot make a performance great, it can give amateurs an increased sense of self-confidence when facing an audience. This chapter gives various ways you can use makeup to enhance your production.

Changing Faces

People used makeup to enhance their appearance in the ancient empires of Egypt and Persia, but it took many centuries for makeup to reach the stage. The earliest actors worked behind elaborate masks, making the appearance of their faces irrelevant. Not until Elizabethan times did actors begin using their faces as dramatic tools, mixing animal fats with different colored dyes to create pastes that altered their features. The derogatory phrase "ham" actor comes from a time when struggling performers used cheap but pungent pork fat as a makeup base.

As theatre moved indoors, the switchover from candles to harsher, yellow-tinted gaslight led actors to wear thick layers of makeup, until Victorian audiences became accustomed to seeing almost clownlike faces on the stage.

The introduction of high-powered electric lighting in the twentieth century changed the performing arts forever. Brighter and more stable than gas flames, it forced actors to rethink their use of makeup. Experts like Hollywood legend Max Factor developed more naturalistic cosmetics, and stage actors soon adopted them. Aside from being gentler to the skin, these new products allowed for greater subtlety in performances.

The Stage Is Not the Big Screen

Motion pictures have done much to redefine the art of makeup, particularly when it comes to fantasy, horror, and science-fiction films. From Frankenstein's monster to J.R.R. Tolkein's hobbits and wizards, Hollywood has spared no expense turning actors into all sorts of fantastic creatures that look believable during even the most detailed close-ups. They have also perfected the art of adding or subtracting years from an actor's face.

Stage makeup is a very different art form with its own set of priorities. Onstage, the goal is to accent features so they can be seen from a distance. The heavy prosthetic attachments common on-screen have no place onstage where they obliterate the facial features that are so vital to any actor's performance. Now and then, stage makeup is used to turn an actor into something he is not, but this is done in limited ways that leave the face readable. For example, the felines in the musical *Cats* were clearly human beings with catlike features added to accent their still-recognizable faces.

In general, stage makeup should …

- Reinforce facial features, which can flatten under light.

- Counteract the way strong lighting drains skin color.

- Suggest a character's general state of health, ranging from a ruddy glow to an icy pallor.

- Indicate personality, using anything from glamorous color to gory scars.

- Empower (rather than encumber) an actor's performance.

- Instill confidence in performers, who appreciate the assistance makeup gives in creating a character.

The last reason cannot be overstated. When I directed a circus-themed children's musical, the kids playing clowns did not really come to life until they wore their makeup for the first time. And the character roles I played in my college years all got a great lift from effective makeup.

Backstage Whispers

While makeup is an important theatrical tool, it is not always a necessity. All-child productions, including elementary school plays, can be done without makeup, as can most concerts by performers of any age group. And in intimate theatres with less-powerful lighting, there is little if any need to reinforce facial features the audience can easily see.

Facial Features

We look at faces every day, often giving little thought to them. We know people on sight because of their distinctive facial features, and the topography formed by those features is what makeup must work with. Makeup coordinators and actors who will be expected to apply their own makeup should take some time to stand in front of a mirror and study the face in detail. Bones and cartilage beneath the skin create a moonscape of ridges, hollows, puffs, and prominences. Every feature contributes to our perception of a person's age, lifestyle, and character. Consider ...

- The bloated red nose of a heavy drinker.

- The bleary, hollow eyes of a drug addict.

- The thin, pursed lips of a righteous spinster.

- The cauliflower ears of a washed-up boxer.

We have seen these real-life stereotypes onstage time and again, created by talented writers and actors with a definite assist from makeup.

Gremlins

In the excitement before performances, amateur actors tend to rush through makeup application. Professionals do the opposite, using makeup time as a Zenlike opportunity to focus their mind and body before show time. Encourage all cast members to give themselves ample application time.

Makeup must always be custom designed to fit the actor and the role involved, allowing clear and easy emotional expression—so be wary of "one size fits all" solutions. In the musical *Man of La Mancha*, the lead must apply complex makeup in full view of the audience, changing from Cervantes into his eccentric fictional hero Don Quixote with few smears of paint, false eyelashes, and a long moustache. Many great actors have played this role over the years, but no two have worn the distinctive makeup in exactly the same way. This was in part due to different facial shapes and sizes, but also to the way each actor used his face in his performance. It's not just a case of having the right moustache, but of setting it at the right angle.

Assistance and Training

Women may be under the impression that they need no help working with makeup, but the stage makes different demands than everyday life. It is a good idea to provide some kind of training for anyone who will be applying stage makeup for your production, particularly beginners. See if any professional theatre companies or other organizations in your area offer workshops on the subject. Other amateur theatre companies may be able to steer you toward local experts who would be able to give classes to your team. If a cosmetician offers to help, be sure he or she has experience working on stage productions.

If you are not able to find experienced help, your team members will have to get some experience of their own. Have them read whatever they can find on the subject. Books on stage makeup are available for purchase (see Appendix B for some suggestions), and your local library can probably dig up several useful titles. With or without expert assistance, all cast and makeup crew should hold several practice sessions to learn basic application and removal techniques. If anyone plans to use special accessories like prosthetics, try to arrange some training for them.

Essential Tools

Most amateur groups provide any unusual requirements (false noses, wigs, etc.), but require actors to provide their own basic makeup kit. The items required are mostly inexpensive and easy to find. Some groups are lucky enough to find a local cosmetician or store that will put together a basic kit and make it available to cast members at a reasonable price.

A basic makeup kit should include the following:

- A mirror large enough to reflect an actor's full face
- Several small plastic foam sponges with small pores for applying foundation
- One coarser stippling sponge for applying 5 o'clock shadow and other rough textures
- Several brushes, ranging from a fine flat eyeliner to a fluffy rouge mop
- Two or more velour powder puffs
- One fluffy down-type powder puff
- A generous supply of cotton balls and swabs
- Foundation in various shades (more on this later)
- Cake or dry powder rouge
- Lining color in various shades for highlights and details
- Translucent face powder
- Lipstick, various shades
- Eye shadow, various shades
- Mascara in black, brown, and navy blue
- Eyebrow and eyeliner pencils
- Small scissors
- Makeup remover
- Towels, paper towels, and facial tissue
- Moisturizer for use after makeup removal

Backstage Whispers

Special stage eye makeup is no longer necessary. Current over-the-counter brands are safe and quite attractive under theatrical lighting.

The tool kit boxes found in any hardware store are natural choices for organizing these items.

Basic Techniques

To prepare for makeup application, all performers should wash their faces and hands thoroughly. Men should be freshly shaven, with any real facial hair trimmed and groomed as needed.

Foundation

Makeup begins with foundation, which provides the basic skin tone. Foundation comes in two basic types:

◆ Greasepaint comes in cream form. Easy to blend, it requires powder to fix it in place.

◆ Pancake is more difficult to blend but has an attractive matte finish that does not require powdering. It tends to be gentler to the skin.

Foundation is applied to the face using a slightly damp sponge, in as thin a layer as possible. The actor's natural coloring and gender determine which shade of foundation to use, as well as the character being created. Use …

> **Gremlins**
>
> A little makeup can go a long way. Never allow creative makeup to prevent an actor's face from communicating clearly with the audience.

◆ Shades of slight to medium brown for men.

◆ Pinkish brown to neutral for women and children.

◆ Ivory and other pale shades for older characters.

◆ Reddish brown for Arabs, Indians, and Native Americans.

◆ Yellow brown for Asians.

Clear, healthy skin needs only a light application of foundation, with perhaps a touch of blush on the cheeks. Unevenly colored or blemished skin will need more.

Rouge and Highlights

After the foundation is applied, dot rouge onto the cheeks and blend in. Then use a brush to apply dark makeup wherever folds or shadows are required to highlight the structure of the face. Use a finger to merge these smears into the foundation, turning them into gentle shadows. Then apply light highlights with a brush immediately adjacent, making those shadows stand out—again gently smooth these shadows into the mix using a finger. To create an older look, add additional dark lines and light highlights to create or accent existing wrinkles. You can apply freckles by using a cotton swab and medium brown makeup in an irregular pattern.

Facial Structure

Makeup can have a substantial visual effect on the shape of the face. Horizontal lines, shadows, and facial hair (moustache, beard) broaden the face, while vertical accents (long sideburns) can lengthen it. Strengthen a weak jaw line by placing a slight blended shadow just below the natural jawbone line right up to the ear.

Eyes

Eyebrows are tricky and can make or break a good makeup design. Heavily drawn eyebrows can look cartoonish, so I suggest filling in the natural eyebrow using hair-like strokes with an eyebrow pencil. Whenever changing the shape of an existing eye-brow, be sure all lines are sharp to clearly indicate the new edges and overall shape. Use eyeliner pencil to outline the eyes. The upper and lower lines should not meet to make the eyes look bigger. To eliminate dark circles below the eyes, apply a small dab of light colored foundation or cover cream and blend it into the surrounding foundation by hand.

> **Gremlins**
>
> Makeup acts like a magnet for cigarette smoke, holding onto the stench for hours. For the sake of everyone onstage and off, prohibit smoking during and after the application process.

Lips

Lip color is the last step. Leave men's lips in as natural a shade as possible, such as a brownish red. Overpaint women's lips to suggest plumpness, or cover the outer edges with foundation to make the mouth look smaller. You must finish off greasepaint with a fine neutral powder that is patted (never rubbed!) onto the finished product. The finer the powder, the more invisible its effects will be, and it should always be a slightly lighter color than the foundation. Use a brush to ever so gently remove any excess powder.

> **Gremlins**
>
> Makeup and applicators can carry germs and viruses, so sharing is forbidden—no exceptions!

Hands

Don't forget the hands! The same foundation used on the face goes on the back of each hand and up the arms if they will be visible in performance. To "age" hands, use a brush to apply dark makeup on natural lines and along the sides of fingers and then use fingertips to blend these lines into the foundation. To finish, lightly apply and blend in a lighter color to the knuckles.

Makeup and Children

Children can pose a special challenge. Young ladies usually leap at the chance to work with and wear makeup, but boys can bridle at wearing such a "girl thing." The good news is that children do not need to wear any makeup onstage. Most boys playing clowns or fantasy characters are willing to deal with makeup as part of the make-believe process. However, children sharing the stage with made-up adults may wind up looking washed out. In such cases, a light coat of foundation and (if you can get the kids to sit still long enough) a small amount of blush are all that is necessary.

> **Backstage Whispers**
>
> If a boy complains about wearing makeup, point out that his favorite he-man movie and sports stars wear it each time they step in front of a camera—even to appear on talk shows!

Makeup Removal

Amateur actors blame all sorts of skin problems on stage makeup, but in many cases, the real issue is incomplete makeup removal. In the rush to meet with friends and family after a performance, many do a less-than-thorough job of getting the goop off. This is particularly true of men and youngsters, who are not accustomed to dealing with makeup. Encourage cast members to take this part of the process seriously.

Various cream and liquid removers are available today. Cold cream can be a bit greasy but has been a reliable standby for generations. Baby oil is the cheapest option but can be hard on complexions. Water-soluble products cost more but are much easier on the skin and well worth it. Skin tonics are great for removing any remnants of makeup or oily removers left behind by soap and water. Apply makeup remover manually to all relevant parts of the face, neck, and hands; then wipe it off with soft cloths, paper towels, facial tissue, or cotton balls. Cotton swabs are great for detailed removal around sensitive areas like the eyes.

False Additions

Paints, creams, and powders can only do so much to change the face. For extreme character features, you must add false pieces to reshape noses, cheeks, and ears. In such cases, the primary choice is between ready-made latex and homemade putty.

Latex

Lightweight, comfortable to wear, and reusable, latex pieces are great for almost any facial feature, including noses, double chins, fantasy ears, and so on. They usually move with the face, allowing the actor's expressions to come through without interference. You can buy these ready made, or check in advanced makeup instruction books for directions on custom making your own.

Always secure latex items in place before you apply any other makeup to facilitate color blending. Trim away excess edges (irregular cuts, please—straight lines are harder to hide), apply *spirit gum* to the skin, and allow it to dry to a gummy stage. Place the piece in the exact position required. If you must adjust, remove the spirit gum and start over, or you risk unsightly wrinkled edges. Use a finger wrapped in a damp towel to press the edges into place. Because standard greasepaint eats into latex, use a special variety designed for such pieces.

def•i•ni•tion

Spirit gum is a quick-drying liquid adhesive used to attach synthetic whiskers, wig edges, false noses, and other prosthetics to the face. It can be removed with acetone.

Putty

Putty can be shaped on the spot as needed, works well for small accents (noses, ears, moles), and is far less expensive than latex. On the downside, it rarely matches the look of professional latex pieces and requires an investment of fresh time and effort for every application. However, with practice, you can learn how to achieve some great effects. Practice is essential because most novices are surprised by how little putty it takes to change the appearance of noses, chins, or ears.

Putty must be applied before any other makeup is used. Knead a small piece of putty with your fingers until it softens, forming a ball. Apply it to thoroughly cleaned skin, shaping it as needed and smoothing the edges as you go along. Add more pieces as needed until you achieve the desired effect. While the putty is still moist, cover it with a thin layer of foundation and finish with some powder. Because putty tends to be lighter than skin tones, you may need to use a slightly darker shade than you are planning to use on the rest of the face.

Beards, Sideburns, and Moustaches

Real facial hair may require the same treatment as eyebrows, using hairlike strokes of a matching colored makeup pencil to more clearly indicate the overall shape and edges. The majority of beards seen onstage are artificial, in part because it is not hard to create realistic whiskers.

The best false facial hair comes premade from professional suppliers. These items can be reused for a number of performances, which makes the price reasonable. Secure prefabricated facial hair with spirit gum, unless the manufacturer indicates otherwise. Apply artificial whiskers over a well-powdered foundation, which helps buffer the skin from possible irritation. Brush a thin film of spirit gum on the face, let it dry, and then apply a second coat. Gently press the hairpiece into place, using a damp, lint-free cloth to work the edges into the gum. Use matching eyebrow pencil strokes to blend beards and sideburns into natural hair. After use, thoroughly clean any hairpiece webbing with acetone and carefully store each piece to preserve its shape.

Wool crepe hair may be less realistic, but it is also far cheaper and can get basic jobs done. It comes in various colors and needs a bit of processing before it can be used. Cut it into workable lengths (six to eight inches), soak them in warm water until the curl begins to relax, and then lay them out on towels to dry. This hair can be cut and applied to the face. Brush an initial coat of spirit gum over the area to be covered and then work in small patches by adding a second coat and pressing in the crepe hair, using a damp, lint-free cloth to help set the hairs in place. Build beards and goatees from the center outward, but build sideburns and other whiskers from the top downward. Instead of a comb, use fingers to gently brush out any loose hairs.

> **Backstage Whispers**
>
> Spirit gum grabs onto dirt, so be sure your hands are spotless before working with it. And never apply it any closer to the eyes than the upper edge of the eyebrows.

Toppers

The stuff on top of our heads is a multibillion-dollar industry in America, so it is no surprise that so much attention is paid to the hair's appearance and presence (or lack thereof) onstage. Here is a quick primer on some of the most common uses and abuses of hair.

Natural Hair

In my opinion, whenever possible, actors should use their natural hair, which can be styled as needed. The most common issue is when young actors have to play older characters. Color sprays available at any cosmetics counter make it easy to "tip in" gray wherever it is needed—from sideburns and streaks to an overall cover. The main drawback with natural hair is that it can become matted from excessive perspiration.

In plays and book musicals, unless your production concept aims for a farcical mix of styles, hairstyles should fit the period and culture being depicted. A bit of research at your local library will help avoid any distracting errors. If members of the ensemble are expected to prep their own hair, be sure they are briefed on what looks are acceptable.

Wigs

There is a contemporary mania for using wigs onstage, whether or not it is necessary. However, few amateur groups can afford high-quality wigs. Under those merciless stage lights, cheap wigs can make performers look like bad Harpo Marx impersonators. However, when issues of length or style make it necessary, a good wig is a worthwhile investment. Be sure to buy wigs only from genuine theatrical suppliers. Some websites offer cheap prices on what they call "theatrical" wigs, but anything under $100 is not going to stand up to the physical demands of multiple rehearsals and performances.

Before donning a wig, an actor's natural hair must be flattened by wearing a tight hair net or a cap made from the top of a lady's nylon stocking (cut to length with a knot tied in one end). After this is secured using hairpins and slides as needed, the wig is put on from the front to the back, stuck on as snugly as possible and secured with several hairpins. If the wig has a fabric strip that reaches onto the forehead, it should be worn while facial makeup is applied so the strip can be spirit gummed, covered, and blended in.

Always store a wig on a wig block or Styrofoam head form to keep its shape and allow for easy styling. When styling, comb and roll it gently; use gentle hair dryer settings and only a light coating of hair spray to set it. After use, remove any spirit gum with acetone and store the wig on a form. Wash the wig after approximately a dozen uses (see the following sidebar). With proper care, a quality wig can last through several amateur productions.

Gremlins

Never use regular shampoo on a wig! Special wig shampoos are available through salons and cosmetics shops. Add the shampoo and a teaspoon of baking soda (to help remove odors) to a sink filled with cool water, soak for 15 minutes, rinse in more cool water, and leave the wig on a towel to air dry overnight—no wringing! When completely dry, gently restyle and store the wig on a form or wig stand.

Bald Heads

Certain roles call for actors to go bald, such as Daddy Warbucks in *Annie* and the monarch in *The King and I*. Some actors opt to keep their hair and wear a bald pate cap. Even the finest makeup artists have trouble making one of these things look good. Frankly, I have never seen one of these bald pates look less than ridiculous onstage. Professional actors from Yul Brynner onward have known that the only effective way to portray baldness onstage is to take the plunge and shave it all off. (Aw, stop fussing—it grows back!) Thanks to recent fashion trends, this look is now common among all age groups. For stage purposes, the scalp requires the same treatment as any other facial skin—a light coating of foundation and a bit of powder usually do the trick. If an actor refuses to shave off his hair, you can find instructions on creating and wearing bald pates in full-length makeup books.

On the other hand, some male actors with receding or nonexistent hairlines may want to wear wigs for certain roles. Most audiences have reached a point where baldness is no longer a barrier to acceptance. Men often find wigs hot and uncomfortable to wear, so directors may encourage actors to show their domes and let their talents do the rest!

The Least You Need to Know

- Stage makeup must always be designed to enhance a performance, leaving the actor's face unencumbered and expressive.

- Every performer should have his or her own basic makeup kit.

- A variety of basic stage makeup techniques should be taught and practiced well in advance of opening night.

- Thorough removal can prevent most of the skin problems commonly blamed on theatrical makeup.

- False noses and facial hair must be applied properly to create an effective stage illusion.

- When wigs are necessary, invest in quality pieces designed for stage use.

Chapter 19

Light: "Show Me!"

In This Chapter

- The development of stage lighting
- The main purposes of stage lighting
- Key lighting equipment defined
- Light placement, shaping, and color
- Ways to make do with less
- Safety is the only option

Noel Coward once remarked on "the modern delusion that sex is a question of lighting," but he was enough of a stage pro to realize that theatre as we know it could not exist without lighting. All the other visual elements of a production won't amount to much if the audience can't see them. There are few resources available to give nonprofessionals a basic introduction to lighting. This chapter attempts to fill that gap, giving a first-time director or producer enough basic information to work with lighting designers and crewmembers.

A Quick History

The ancient Greeks staged theatrical performances in broad daylight, leaving lighting in the hands of the gods. Artificial stage illumination began during the Italian Renaissance, when the first indoor theatres used candlelight and oil lamps. The flames were filtered through glass containers filled with colored water, and mechanical devices were soon invented to simultaneously raise or dim the flames, making the first light cues possible.

Gaslight came into general use in the early 1800s. While gaslight may sound romantic, it made poorly ventilated theatres unbearably hot and stuffy at most any time of year. So audiences were delighted when theatres began installing electricity in the 1880s. Aside from allowing fresher air, electric lights were far brighter than gas flames and made it possible to focus powerful beams of light on specific areas of the stage. Tinted gelatin filters were placed over lamps to add color and variety. In the 1890s, theatres began dimming the *house lights* during performances, forcing audiences to keep their attention focused on the stage.

def•i•ni•tion

House lights refers to general lighting in the audience area of an auditorium.

By the 1930s, stage lighting began to gain serious recognition as a dramatic tool, and playwrights and directors began turning to lighting designers for effects that could contribute to the theatrical experience. The introduction of computerized controls revolutionized the field from the 1980s onward. Thanks to a constant stream of new techniques and inventions, lighting is now one of the most dynamic stage arts.

The Purposes of Stage Lighting

Stage lighting fulfills five crucial functions:

◆ To illuminate. This is the primary purpose of stage lighting. The action onstage only matters if an audience can see it.

◆ To define action. Marking the beginning or ending of a scene; showing the weather or time of day.

◆ To focus audience attention. Either on a full scene or particular performers.

◆ To set mood. Creating or altering the visual context of stage action.

◆ To decorate. Light can imitate dappled leaves or a full moon.

Lighting has become a basic theatrical tool. For example, a quick blackout can denote the end of a scene, and a slow fade-in of light adds drama to the start of a scene. Although productions can get very creative with the use of light, a clear line exists between serving a production's needs and feeding a designer's ego. Lighting should complement or enhance a production without calling attention to itself. The short-lived Broadway production of *Dance of the Vampires* began by raking the seating area with hundreds of blinding lights—twice. This annoyed the audience and set the show off on the worst possible start, from which it never really recovered.

> **Backstage Whispers**
>
> One line in the musical *Dirty Rotten Scoundrels* says it all: "Breeding is important, but lighting is *everything*."

Every lighting effect and change of color or intensity must serve a specific dramatic purpose, such as signifying a change of time or location or calling attention to an altered mood. Arbitrary changes in the midst of a scene or song may show off what your equipment can do, but they also distract audiences from the material and the performance.

Lighting Instruments

So what are all those black metal fixtures aimed at the stage? In the United States, they are generically referred to as lighting *instruments*, and some lighting crews also refer to them as fixtures.

Most theatrical lamps hang on battens using heavy-duty C-clamps to guarantee secure placement. Whenever possible, safety cables should be attached to each fixture as an added precaution against falling.

There are two basic types of lighting instruments: hard and soft edged.

Hard Edged

Hard-edged instruments create a crisp, clear beam of light. They are most useful as *specials*. These beams can be adjusted in various ways:

- *Ellipsoidal.* These versatile units use an elliptical reflector to create either a sharp or softly focused beam of light.

- *Follow spot.* A manually controlled lighting unit used to follow a performer onstage. These are traditionally used in musical productions where fluidity of motion is a necessity. If you have a quality follow spot or can afford to get one, by all means use it. However, musicals can be done without them.

Left: an ellipsoidal—one of the most popular and versatile lighting instruments. Right: a follow spot, useful for musicals, dance recitals, and concerts.

(Courtesy of Altman Lighting)

def•i•ni•tion

A **flood** is an unfocused instrument that fills an area with general light.

Fresnel (pronounced *fren-ELL*) spots are named for the Frenchman who invented concentrically marked circular lenses to strengthen lighthouse beams.

A **special** is a unit reserved to light important people or objects or to run a special effect.

Soft Edged

Soft-edged beams are unfocused and can blend imperceptibly, creating a warm, gentle, even romantic atmosphere onstage:

♦ **Fresnel.** Using a *fresnel* lens with distinct concentric rings, these units provide a soft-edged beam that can be adjusted to serve as a *flood* or a spot.

♦ **PAR can** (Parabolic Aluminized Reflector). A bright, intense spot, great for basic applications of strong light.

♦ **Scoop.** A scoop-shaped reflector that floods light in one direction.

♦ **Strip or border lights.** A strip of lights in one common housing either hung above the stage or placed at floor level for up lighting.

Left: a fresnel, one of the most commonly used stage lighting instruments. Right: a PAR can, sometimes compared with a "car headlight in a can."

(Courtesy of Altman Lighting)

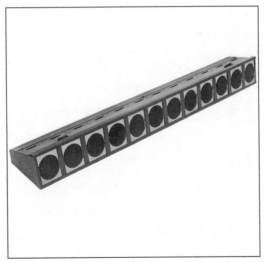

Left: a scoop, used to flood the stage with coverage light. Right: strip or border lights are great for providing general illumination or for highlighting a cyclorama or backdrop.

(Courtesy of Altman Lighting)

Soft-edged lighting creates a warm, gentle, even romantic atmosphere. The edges of soft-edged beams can blend.

Special Lighting

A number of special lighting elements can be used as special accents. Two kinds are commonly used in amateur productions:

◆ Strobes create quick flashes of bright light, simulating photographic flashes, explosions, lightning, and the flicker of silent movie projectors. Because strobes can affect certain medical conditions, post a notice warning audiences when these lights are being used. Purchase or rental of these units can be expensive.

◆ Ropelights, strings of small bulbs encased in lengths of flexible plastic tubing, create lines of light around set elements, prosceniums, and runways. Some models allow a chase effect that gives the glamorous impression of twinkling movement.

These elements were once priced beyond the means of amateur groups, but affordable strobes and ropelights are available today. A designer should treat both much as a chef treats a fiery spice—a little goes a long way.

Lighting Positions

Standing onstage in a fully equipped auditorium, you can find lights facing you from various directions. Each location has its own name:

◆ Electric—hanging directly over the stage.

◆ Beam—hanging directly over the audience.

◆ Boom—vertical battens beside the stage or in the auditorium.

◆ Box boom—vertical battens inside wall boxes in the audience area, usually found to either side of the stage.

◆ Balcony rail—along the front edge of the balcony.

◆ Footlights—floor-level lights lined up along the apron. Once a staple, footlights are rarely seen today.

All the equipment discussed here is used to bathe stage action in light that varies between naturalistic daylight and blatantly theatrical effects. Depending on the size and complexity of your production, you may not need instruments in all or even most of these positions. For example, a cabaret-style concert or simple one-set play can be effectively lit from two booms set in front of the performance area.

Angles, Shaping, and Coverage

Aside from providing enough illumination for the audience to see the activity onstage, lighting can be used to enhance dramatic effects. This requires lighting instruments to be placed at various angles, shaping the light and selecting the right sort of coverage for every part of the playing area. This process involves the following features:

◆ **Front lighting** is the traditional source of lighting, used primarily to create general illumination and color, also known as *washes*.

◆ **Side lighting** comes from a low angle stage left, stage right, or both. It dramatically accentuates movement, particularly dance. If placed at floor level, these lights are known as "shin busters."

◆ **Cross lighting** comes completely from a high angle stage left, stage right, or both. Less dramatic than side lighting, it is more naturalistic.

◆ **Back lighting** leaves people and objects in silhouette, surrounding them with a halo. Three-quarter back light (coming over the shoulder of a performer) can have a pleasantly naturalistic effect.

◆ **Up lighting** shines from below the front of a person or object, creating an eerie, almost surreal effect.

◆ **Down lighting** shines from directly above a person or object and is used to create an illusion of depth or add a color wash.

If this sounds like a lot of equipment, it can be. Many productions use just a few of these angles. It all depends on the effect a designer is aiming for and the company's resources.

Lighting designers aiming for a naturalistic look tend to use instruments aimed at a 45-degree angle. The ideal approach is for a designer to divide the stage into several acting areas, providing each with coverage from multiple directions—at least one of which is front and one back. This formula can be varied for each section of the performance space as needed, with colors and special effects added as required. Your lighting plans should include some general wash light to blend these acting areas, achieving an attractive general cover for the entire stage.

Gremlins

Watch the angle of your backlighting! Audiences in dark theatres loathe a bright light shining or flashing into their eyes. That is why back lighting is almost always angled up from floor level.

Control Boards

The simplest light control is a standard wall switch that turns on and off. Many home light switches now include dimmers, allowing users to set a fixture at varying light levels as mood or necessity dictate. A dining room chandelier can be set to full power for a child working on homework and reduced to a gentle glow for a dinner party.

Theatrical lighting operates on the same principle but on a larger scale, following a clear chain of control:

◆ Each instrument is part of a circuit.

◆ Each circuit is controlled by a *dimmer*.

◆ Each dimmer is controlled by one channel on a *control board*.

◆ All channels are controlled by the *crossfader* switch.

def•i•ni•tion

A **dimmer** is an electronic device that raises or lowers the level of illumination provided by lighting instruments. All dimmers are managed by a control board.

A **control board** controls the dimmers for all lighting instruments. It can be either computer operated or manual.

A **crossfader** is a lighting board control that fades all channels at once, which is very useful for quick, full-stage effects such as blackouts.

Dimmers are electronic devices that adjust the power supplied to stage lights. They usually sit somewhere backstage and are managed from a control board. Control boards allow lighting designers to preset and adjust every light with the touch of a botton.

In older performance spaces, you may still find an old-style lighting board sitting backstage. These gigantic metal boxes covered with dials and bulky levers look like something out of Frankenstein's laboratory. Elegant tabletop control boards have long since supplanted these beloved relics.

There are two types of control boards in common use today:

◆ *Manual boards* allow the lighting operator to control all lights by hand. These boards have two or sometimes more sets of control levers, each known as a preset. While one preset is in use, the other can be adjusted for the next light cue. The crossfader is a master control button that allows you to fade from one preset to another.

◆ *Computerized boards* use computers to set, time, and run light cues. Light cues for an entire production can be preprogrammed, including special light effects. These boards usually include manual controls to allow the operator some flexibility during performances.

Although computerized boards are more expensive, they are standard equipment for many amateur groups today. Expensive to buy, these boards can be leased. Make the best choice your group can afford.

Color

Bare electric stage lamps can shed a harsh and unattractive light. Color is added by inserting tinted gels that come in varying sizes and hundreds of shades, allowing an almost infinite number of variations and combinations. Designers and directors pay careful attention to this process because the colors they choose can glorify or devastate the appearance of sets, costumes, and even performers. The intelligent use of color in stage lightning separates the amateur from the amateurish.

Strong colors are most effective when used sparingly. The richer and more aggressive a color is, the stronger the statement it makes. It is possible for color to become a distraction. For example, lighting a full-length scene in deep red or blue not only looks melodramatic, but it can become painful to look at as well. That is why powerful colors are best reserved for outstanding emotional effects, backgrounds, and special highlights.

Most stage lighting involves pale gels, which are easier on the eyes and have an attractive effect on skin tones. Pale amber, pink, and straw gels are gentle, naturalistic colors that allow actors to move an audience with their text and talents.

Lamps can use one stationary gel or can be fitted with remote control *color changers* that can change gels between scenes or make gradual color shifts during a scene. The latter is particularly useful when simulating changes in daylight or aiming for a shift in mood.

Lighting designers must select gels for each

Backstage Whispers

Yul Brynner starred in many productions of *The King and I* and always insisted that pink gels be used wherever possible "because they make women look so beautiful." His motives weren't totally selfless, because pink gels also did wonders for his famous shaved head.

def•i•ni•tion

Color changers include color wheels (disks with up to five colored gels) and scrollers (a rolling sheet of color gels).

scene in close consultation with the set and costume designers, and all three must defer to the director's judgment as to what combinations best serve the production. No one can be sure which gels to use until late in the rehearsal process when all the various production elements come together for the first time. Anyone can understand that strong gels can make set, makeup, or costume elements of the same color appear washed out. But it is impossible to know in advance which shade and intensity of light will have the best effect on a particular blend of physical colors and textures.

Backstage Whispers

At times, lighting can contribute a show-stopping effect. In particular, two lighting effects invariably win a heartwarming "Oooooh!" One is the lighting of a large Christmas tree. The other is the unveiling of a star drop, a black cloth backdrop with small lights or fiber-optic pinpoints sewn in to create the illusion of a starry night sky. When a show calls for these effects, by all means indulge, but there is a catch—they must be presented with flawless polish. If wires show or the timing is off, the "Oooooh!" effect will be ruined.

Making Do

Lighting designers working with professional budgets can utilize hundreds of lights for a single production. Most amateur productions, especially first-time efforts, have to make do with far less. An experienced lighting designer can't be expected to work outright miracles, but it is possible to create general coverage—and even some artistic effects—with a small number of lights.

Until you can get what you want, use what you've got. Even if you've got nothing, remember this book's mantra: get inventive. Most hardware stores carry clip-on household flood bulbs set in inexpensive aluminum casings. These may be crude, but at a few bucks apiece, they are useful problem solvers that can be clamped on to various structural elements.

If you don't have most of the equipment discussed in this chapter, don't sweat it. Over time, your organization may be able to invest in more ambitious lighting equipment. Until then, make the best possible use of whatever equipment you have. I produced several school musicals with a handful of small fresnels and PAR can lights that turned on and off. We had no dimmer, no follow spot, and no special effects, but we got standing ovations every time. For concerts, cabarets, one-person shows, and simple plays, general coverage can be enough. As long as there is basic illumination, audiences are willing to let their imaginations fill in whenever technology falls short.

Safety Issues

Always have a licensed electrician inspect and approve your lighting installation. If you cannot find one willing to volunteer his services, go ahead and pay. When you blend high voltage with volunteers, you cannot afford to economize. Remember: safety is always job #1.

In case you are not working with an experienced lighting designer on hand at all times, every director and producer should keep in mind a few basic safety pointers:

- Always have qualified supervision when volunteers change bulbs or otherwise risk high-voltage contact.

- Only use gaffer's tape on any instruments or wiring. Standard masking tape and even duct tape can melt near hot lights.

- If those lights can melt duct tape, they can do far worse to skin. Handle instruments that are on (or that were recently lit) with extreme caution.

- Stage instruments use two types of plugs. Stage plugs (three round pins in a square plug) need taping; twist-lock plugs (three L-shaped curved blades that lock when twisted into a matching socket) do not.

- Only use extension cords that are calibrated for the wattage involved.

- Dispose of any frayed or worn-out wiring immediately.

In short, when it comes to safety, always, always, always err on the side of caution. Sure, you may have to spend a few bucks, but it is worth whatever it costs.

Whenever you are in doubt about electrical issues, find out! At the very least, unsafe wiring can ruin your performances. And the worst? Let's put it this way: lighting-related theatre fires are rare these days. Keep it that way.

The Least You Need to Know

- Like all production elements, lighting must be designed to serve the material.

- Control boards can simultaneously adjust all of a production's lighting instruments, either manually or by computer.

- Use color and angle to make lighting more attractive and naturalistic.

- Be ready to make do with what you've got. A lighting plot with only a few instruments can be enough for simple productions.

- A licensed electrician should install or at least inspect all lighting setups.

- When it comes to electrical safety, never skimp!

Chapter 20

Sound: "Make Them Hear You"

In This Chapter

- ◆ The dramatic possibilities of sound effects, live and prerecorded
- ◆ Different types of amplification equipment
- ◆ Creating a sound plot
- ◆ Vocal projection, the natural option to amplification
- ◆ The secret sound system audiences never hear

Many amateur directors and producers remain clueless about sound. They are intimidated, and it's easy to see why. Mixer boards can have hundreds of dials and buttons, and those masses of cables, microphones, and battery packs … who has the time to learn about it all? You do! The next few pages give you the basic vocabulary you will need to have a constructive conversation with a sound expert and show you how to handle performances where the only sound equipment in use is the human voice.

Sound Effects

Drama is brought to life through sound. That is why a good production concept often includes the creative use of sound effects. The gentle chirping of birds can make a bucolic hillside visible before the lights go up, and the chaos of a city street can be depicted by the cacophony of car horns, jackhammers, and sirens.

Sounds can define environments and help ignite an audience's imagination. Let's say a scene is set in a forest, at night. Ambient sounds can invoke a wide variety of emotions. The gentle croak of a frog and the rhythmic calls of katydids make your forest feel peaceful, even romantic. If the wind whips up a rustle of leaves as an owl hoots nearby, a note of expectancy is added. A clap of thunder or the howl of a wolf can build tension or even spoof convention and be played for laughs. Throwing in an unexpected sound, like a mooing cow, strikes an absurd note. All of these can be valid options.

Thanks in part to the wonders achieved by digitalized film soundtracks, today's audiences take high-quality sound effects for granted. They expect theatrical sound effects to be clear and believable. This is nothing new. Sound effects have been part of stage performances for thousands of years.

In ancient Greece (500 B.C.E.), actors wore masks with built-in megaphones that made them more audible in massive amphitheatres. Shakespeare and his contemporaries (1600s) relied on various sound effects to heighten dramatic atmosphere. Some Elizabethan theatres had angled troughs built into the ceiling where they could unleash cannon balls to simulate the sound of rolling thunder. Victorian theatres used various wind and rain machines. Large metal sheets were given a vigorous shake to imitate thunder, and members of the ensemble would pitch in to provide offstage chatter or even imitate animal noises.

Prerecorded sound effects were introduced in the 1930s, but the practice did not become widespread until about two decades later. As the technology evolved, records were replaced by tape decks, reel-to-reel tapes by cassettes, and CDs by computer-controlled digital samplers. Professional and amateur productions now rely on prerecorded effects equipment to create *ambience*. A number of recent plays have even used prerecorded voices for unseen minor characters. This keeps casts smaller and physical productions simpler but can only work if high-quality sound reproduction is used.

def•i•ni•tion

Use sound cues to establish or enhance the **ambience**, or atmosphere, of a scene.

Amplification

Broadway musicals began using electronic amplification sometime in the late 1930s, installing a few microphones among the footlights.

The introduction of rock music required more complicated amplification—*Hair* (1969) and *Jesus Christ Superstar* (1971) were among the first Broadway productions to use sound designers. *Cats* (1982) is believed to have been the first production to give every performer a wireless body mike. Today, every performer in a Broadway musical is wired for sound, and sound design has become a major line item in every professional theatre budget.

For many years, amateur theatre groups would not even consider using sound systems. Such equipment was far too expensive, and purists felt that amplification placed an unwanted layer between actors and audiences. Performers were told to project their voices, and those with proper training had no trouble being heard in spaces that sat a thousand or more spectators. But as audiences and performers began demanding amplification, even in intimate venues, many amateur groups were forced to invest in sound equipment.

On Broadway, the best sound designers strive to make effects, voices, and instruments sound as natural as possible. Sound is spatial—we sense where it comes from. Over-amplification can make a sound feel as if it is coming from all over the room rather than from the stage. That is why speakers are usually placed in close proximity to the performance area, so everything audiences hear feels as if it is emanating from the stage.

On Stage

The Broadway revival of *The Music Man* (2000) made inventive use of its sound system. As the lights came down, the digital sound of marching drummers was fed through speakers at the back of the theatre. It was so realistic that audience members often turned to see where the musicians were. That sound moved through the auditorium, reaching the stage as the curtain rose to reveal the orchestra onstage, performing the overture.

Basic Sound Equipment

The use of amplification depends on the material, the space, and the availability of equipment. While I prefer the unaided human voice, amplification has become a fact of theatrical life. Some performance spaces have poor acoustics, and some are so large that untrained voices have no hope of filling them. But the main reason for amplification during live stage performances is that many people have become lazy listeners. Accustomed to movie houses, home theatres, and iPod earphones that can reproduce the slightest whisper with digital clarity, some listeners expect the same at live performances. Most amateur groups cannot match Broadway's resources, but good equipment is accessible.

Sound systems transmit sound through a progression of electronic devices:

Gremlins

Be sure your amplifier is the last element of the sound system turned on and the first element turned off. This will prevent obnoxious noises that could damage your sound equipment.

- A *mixer* blends incoming signals from various sources and passes them on to …

- An *amplifier*, which boosts the signal to audible levels and passes it on to …

- An equalizer and/or effects processor, which shapes and colors a signal and then passes it on to …

- A speaker or headphone, which reproduces the signal as sound.

A theatrical sound system includes such items as these:

- Speakers. Be sure your speakers match the resistance specified by your amplifier, usually either 4 or 8 ohms.

- Standard microphones. Mikes come in all price ranges, but anything below a hundred dollars won't be up to the demands of live performances. To avoid electromagnetic interference from other equipment, stick to dynamic, low-impedance mikes and wires, the kind that use XLR (three pin) plugs.

- Wireless microphones and power packs. These can be hidden in costumes or wigs, but are easily damaged by physical activity and perspiration. They must be checked before every performance.

- Auxiliary equipment (headsets, monitors, etc.). Stage and lighting crews may need these to communicate during the performance, particularly in large auditoriums and/or for technically complicated productions. (More on this later in this chapter, under "The Secret Sound System.")

Playback Equipment

In planning sound cues, you must know what sort of equipment will be used for playback. Because of the rapid changes in sound technology in recent years, a variety of options are currently in use:

◆ Reel-to-reel. For many years, these tape players were the highest standard in sound. Sound and music tracks would be edited and then spliced together by hand with leaders. The leaders were numbered for each cue. Some of these units are still used in theatres and, if properly handled, can give excellent results.

◆ Cassette decks. Although easy to use, these were always seen as reel-to-reel's poor cousins. DATs have eclipsed them.

◆ DAT players. Digital audio tapes (DATs) are sonically superior to other forms of tape, and, consequently, the required equipment is more expensive.

◆ Compact disc and minidisc players. As the least expensive form of digital sound, these discs are a popular option. Now home computers can burn CDs for pennies apiece, letting you create separate cue-able tracks and provide performers with rehearsal discs—either with vocals or karaoke style.

◆ Digital samplers. *MIDI* keyboards are designed to play computer sound files at the touch of a button. These high-quality digital files require large amounts of computer memory, making this an expensive option.

def•i•ni•tion

MIDI (Musical Instrument Digital Interface) is a technology that allows computers and electronic keyboard instruments to interact.

Go with the best equipment your group can afford. Avoid outdated technology such as long-playing LPs on turntables, which can be very unreliable during performances.

Gremlins

We've all cringed at the deafening howl of sound system feedback. It occurs when a microphone wanders into the path of a speaker, literally feeding back sound into the system. The simple answer is to keep speakers and microphones pointed away from each other—not always easy in a staged performance. By rehearsing at least once with your sound system, you can identify and eliminate unexpected feedback situations.

Budget

The sound designer's first priority is to inspect the performance space and any existing sound equipment, including all tape decks, soundboards, cables, microphones, and speakers. As producer or director, it is in your best interest to have some working knowledge of these items. If the materials on hand do not meet the needs of a particular production, you will have to purchase, rent, or borrow additional equipment. The sound designer also determines if auxiliary items have to be purchased or borrowed to create live effects—doorbells, metal sheets, etc.

Some businesses are willing to offer items to schools or nonprofit groups at a reduced rate, and neighboring theatre troupes have been known to loan out or even co-purchase equipment. If the production's sound budget will not cover what you need, it is up to the sound designer to let this be known. When there is no way to increase the sound allotment, you will have to scale back plans to use amplification. The object is to do the best you can with the money available.

Sound Effects

If you are going to use sound effects, select every effect with care. Know the specific purpose of each sound. Is it there to provide subtle background, or does it play a role in the plot (a gunshot, an explosion, etc.)? Once the sound designer hunts down several likely options, the director can hold one or more sound auditions, running all potential effects by the director. This fuss is necessary because contemporary audiences know that a blunderbuss does not sound like a Magnum handgun and a pick-up truck does not sound like a sports car.

Copyrighted Materials

Like all other kinds of recordings, sound effects can be copyrighted. Hundreds of sound effects CDs are available. Some sound collections consider the purchase price as granting you full rights, but not always. Be sure your production clears the rights to any recorded material you use. If you want more details on this, your local library keeps current copyright laws on file.

To use existing musical recordings as part of a sound plot, you must have the written permission of the performing artist or his estate. This involves contacting the artist's manager, producer, or recording company and will probably entail the services of an attorney with experience in performing arts contracts. Even with the performer's okay, you will also need permission from the songwriters. ASCAP and BMI handle the rights to most songs that are not in the public domain (see Appendix B for contact information).

Some popular plays indicate the use of specific songs as background music. Paying for the rights to a play may not automatically give you the right to use these tunes. Double-check to see if anyone still controls the song rights. They may be in the public domain. My earlier list of suggested plays includes two examples:

◆ *Ah, Wilderness!* suggests using specific period songs to reinforce the 1906 atmosphere. All these are now in public domain.

◆ *The Dark of the Moon* calls for live performances of several classic folk songs, all long since in the public domain.

How much will the rights to a recording cost? That varies according to the whims of the rights owners. Such factors as the number of performances, the size of the theatre, and the specific way in which a song is used tend to affect the final amount. There is no average figure to offer you.

Your Own Recordings

If your team makes its own sound recordings, copyrights are not an issue as long as your recordings do not incorporate copyrighted material (pop songs, film soundtracks, etc.). If you record a kettle whistling in your own kitchen, that effect is yours to use free and clear. The same is true if you record songs that are in the public domain. For example, songs of the 1800s used as background for your Civil War drama are rights free, as long as all the vocalists and musicians on the recording have consented.

Live Effects

Those of us with a passion for theatre want it to be as "live" as possible, but live sound effects can be tricky. Like all other sound effects, they must be audible. In some cases, nothing beats a live effect. But safety is another concern. For gunshots, it is always best to use a quality prop gun. It is difficult to coordinate recorded shots with stage action, and recorded shots cannot match the physical impact of a live blast. However, under no circumstances should real guns be used anywhere in a theatre. Firing a real gun will rattle your audience, but it is not worth the risk.

Other effects have a special impact when created live. At the end of the wedding scene in *Fiddler on the Roof*, Tsarist soldiers wreak havoc on the town of Anatevka. The audience does not see this pogrom—we only hear it. Some productions opt for recorded chaos, but I find that a live effect has far more impact. Backstage, the crew drops one or two large, sturdy wooden boxes filled with old dishes, glassware, and a few pieces of metal. The sound of live breaking glass is unmistakable and chilling, especially when it is augmented by the shouts and cries of the offstage ensemble. In a large performance space, some amplification may be needed, but the more physically direct the sound of such an effect is, the greater the impact.

Gremlins

Every theatre group has its share of stories about microphones accidentally left on. When an entire audience listens in on a trip to the ladies room, the value of a detailed sound plot—and an alert sound engineer—becomes clear, albeit a bit too late.

The director should audition all live effects long before tech rehearsals to be sure they will have the proper volume and dramatic impact. This includes all door and phone bells, doors, footsteps, and so on you plan on performing live. Experimentation is crucial. You may have to try a few doors before you find just the right slam!

The Sound Plot

For simple productions using a few stationary microphones, your sound team may not need to do much more than set up the equipment, run a brief sound check with the performers, and make a few mid-performance volume adjustments. But for most plays and musicals, sound designers create a *sound plot*, a detailed list of every sound cue in a particular production. The sound plot serves as the sound engineer's performance bible.

def•i•ni•tion

A **sound plot** is a detailed list of every sound cue in a production.

When reading through the script for the first time, the sound designer creates the sound plot by noting all likely sound effects, musical sequences, and song cues. The designer then goes over this list with the director, noting where the use of equipment and/or recordings will be required. These notes should be translated into a formal sound plot, which must be constantly updated and revised right through tech rehearsals.

The sound plot should break down sound cues by act, scene, and script page number. Here is a sample preliminary cue sheet for the first act of *Cyrano de Bergerac*.

Act/Scene	Page	Effect	Notes
Act I, Scene i	7	Precurtain music	Recording
		Background music—flute	LIVE cue
	19	Montfleury fanfare	Recording
	34	Flute	LIVE cue
	44	Harp	Recording
	45	Exit march	Recording
Act I, Scene ii	46	Background music—flute	LIVE cue
	60	Cadets entrance music	Recording
	63	Drum	LIVE cue
	79	Curtain music	Recording
		Intermission music	Microphones on MUTE; cue recording

Once the sound designer has all potential cues listed, adding any special equipment cues will be easy. The sound plot does not have to make sense to the casual observer, but it must be clear to the designer and to anyone else who will run the sound system during performances.

It used to be common for a sound plot to use recordings from various sources—a CD track here, a cassette track there. While this can still happen in theatres equipped with multiple decks, it is now far more common to find all the sound effects and music burned onto CDs or placed in well-organized computer sound files. This saves a lot of time and minimizes the chances of misplacing a recording. It is vital to have back-up copies of all CDs or sound files on hand in case of an unexpected problem.

By the time you reach final dress rehearsal, the sound plot should be far more detailed, including sound sources, track numbers, and any other information the sound team finds useful. Here is an expanded version of the sound plot for *Cyrano de Bergerac*.

Act/Scene	Cue	Page	Effect	Deck/Mic	Tracks	Notes
I, i	1	7	Pre-curtain music	D1	1	5 minute call
	2	7	Background music—flute	M11		LIVE cue

continues

continued

Act/Scene	Cue	Page	Effect	Deck/Mic	Tracks	Notes
	3	34	Flute	M11		LIVE cue
	4	44	Harp	D1	2	
	5	45	Exit march	D1	3	
I, ii	6	46	Background music—flute	M11		LIVE cue
	7	60	Cadets entrance music	D1	4	
	8	63	Drum	M12		LIVE cue
	9	79	Curtain music	D1	5	
	10	79	MUTE mikes			
	11	79	Intermission music	D2	6	

Your sound team may find additional information useful, such as equipment settings or specific microphone assignments (e.g., body mikes or headsets).

Some productions place the sound operator in the auditorium, where he or she can hear if anything needs adjusting. However, if your operator has to change cassettes or hold urgent conversations, drama at the mixer can eclipse what is happening onstage. It may be more practical to place your sound techies in a booth or backstage area, but they must be able to see and hear the performance. Be sure ample power is available, avoid overloaded outlets at all costs, and prohibit food or liquids anywhere near valuable sound equipment.

Gremlins

Lighting dimmers give off an electromagnetic field that can wreak havoc with sound equipment, so keep your sound mixer and lighting controls as far away from each other as possible. If you have any doubts, run a test of both systems before tech rehearsals.

Set up sound controls so the operator can handle every task while sitting or standing in one fixed position—running around in mid-performance is not an option. The mixer should get central placement, followed by the main tape deck or computer console being used for sound effects. All sound cables must be laid neatly and marked to prevent confusing them with other electrical connections. It takes serious expertise to hook up sound equipment, so no matter how good your crew may be, have the sound designer supervise this process.

The sound team should run a thorough sound check before all tech rehearsals and performances, testing every piece of sound equipment. Check each microphone, speaker, playback device, and channel, with someone in the performance space to verify that sound is getting through clearly. Also check any production monitors (speakers placed in backstage areas).

Projection

When I started in amateur theatre, sound systems were not part of the scene. Even the youngest casts were expected to project their voices. The orchestrations of most musicals were designed to support the unamplified voice, not drown it out. If a recorded song or sound effect was required, some budding techies would set up a tape deck and a speaker or two.

But times have changed! Musicals now utilize rock and other contemporary forms that are written with amplification in mind. It would be impossible to perform *Rent*, *Footloose*, or *Jekyll & Hyde* without miking the singers. Even with more traditional music, you cannot expect unamplified amateurs to be heard singing over an orchestra. Most drummers today are trained for contemporary music and have no clue how to accompany unamplified singers. In the brief time it took to write this chapter, I attended unamplified productions where lyrics by Coward and Sondheim were lost in a relentless hail of drumfire.

However, if your performance space holds 400 or fewer people and the cast is not competing with a full orchestra, natural projection is a viable option. There is no secret to it, other than practice. Performers must accustom themselves to talking and singing full-out without shouting. A famous voice teacher used to explain projection this way: "There is someone standing on the roof of a four-story building across the street. Make sure he can hear you!" The best practical test of your cast's projection ability is to sit in one of the seats farthest from the stage. If you can hear them clearly from there, you have no need for a sound system.

Sustained shouting is not the answer. Performers must learn to project without taxing their voices. The voice box is a few small pieces of fragile vibrating tissue, and frequent strain can cause nodes and other lasting damage. If the rehearsal process leaves performers struggling with laryngitis, find the money for some kind of sound system to assist them.

The Secret Sound System

Completely separate from any public sound system, a secret intercom headset system allows the stage managers and crews to communicate during a performance. Such a system may cost a bit to rent or buy, but it can be a real show-saver, used for everything from giving cues to avoiding emergencies. An intercom system is particularly useful for large-scale musicals. Once limited to professional productions, these are now standard equipment in many amateur theatres. Invest in the best you can afford to buy or lease.

The Least You Need to Know

- The use of amplification and sound effects in theatre dates back to ancient times.

- A wide range of sound equipment is available. Go with the best your group can afford.

- If sound equipment is not available, consider using natural voice projection. But be realistic—few performers today can be heard over a sizeable orchestra.

- An intercom headset system makes it possible for stage managers and crew to communicate during performances.

Part 5

Marketing— "Sing Out, Louise!"

Performances are community celebrations, and it's up to you to make sure your community knows your production is there. Anyone who has ever owned a business will tell you that the Hollywood-spawned proverb "If you build it, they will come" is a lot of hogwash. Unless you're playing to a guaranteed institutional or corporate event audience, you have to get the word out! Your message must be loud and clear, making your show the local must-see event of the year. Part 5 deals with reaching out to the public, drawing them in to see your performances, and providing them with a program that is polished and (if you plan it right) even profitable.

21

Publicity: "I Gotta Crow!"

In This Chapter

◆ Designing and implementing a publicity campaign for your production

◆ Creating the best advertising you can afford

◆ Great publicity money can't buy!

◆ A detailed list of publicity basics

Producers have shared one nightmare since the first theatre ticket went on sale—having the curtain rise on opening night to reveal 42 actors onstage and 11 people in the audience. I would love to tell you that such things never happen in real life, but they do. "Build it and they will come" may be great dialogue for a fantasy film, but it's a formula for disaster in amateur entertainment. You have to get the word out!

Creating a Publicity Plan

Early on in the production process, the producer, publicity director, and a few intrepid volunteers must sit down for one or more serious brainstorming sessions. I prefer to have this happen well ahead of auditions, giving the PR team plenty of time to have its plans in place and ready to roll as soon as production starts. At this meeting, begin by asking yourselves some basic questions.

What Audience Are We Trying to Reach?

The basic principal behind theatrical publicity is simple: when you put on a show, you want audiences to show up. Believe it or not, plenty of people in your community will be interested in attending your show. The challenge is to be sure they hear about your show and keep on hearing about it as often as possible. This will require an ongoing, multi-faceted campaign, limited only by your imagination and the resources at your disposal.

How Can We Best Focus Our Efforts to Reach That Audience?

Are you trying to sell tickets to a closed group (students, employees) or to the community at large? The size of your target audience will have a profound effect on what sort of publicity efforts your group should focus on.

What Local Media Can We Focus On?

List all local media outlets that might provide coverage. Your production should get whatever it can, from a featured article to a listing in the community calendar. Be as inclusive as possible. When the news is slow, you never know what might catch a reporter's or editor's interest.

What Aspects of Our Production Are Press Worthy?

Determine which events might be of interest to the local media: auditions, first rehearsal, dress rehearsal, etc. Does your company include a local celebrity or someone with a great background story (a showbiz family connection, long career in amateur theatre, etc.)?

Where Can We Obtain Relevant Mailing Lists?

Consider which local organizations or companies might be willing to share or sell mailing lists that cover your target audience. Because mailings cost money and tend to be very labor intensive, only send flyers, postcards, and other items to potentially interested recipients.

What Is Our Likely Advertising Budget?

If your advertising funds are limited, don't sweat it. While money is a useful publicity resource, it is not the most important one. A good publicity campaign requires time, creativity, and energy. With those, you can reach out and find almost any target audience.

Do We Have Any Special Publicity Goals?

Are you looking to sell a one-time-only performance or to build an ongoing reputation as a performing arts organization? Is your show just out to sell itself, or is it designed to build your organization's reputation in the community at large? These legitimate goals can help shape your plans.

The "Final" Plan

Once you define your publicity goals and resources, your production's PR plan can begin to take shape. Your meeting should result in the creation of the following:

◆ A detailed publicity calendar you can incorporate into your overall production schedule. This includes likely dates for any planned press releases and media events.

◆ A media contact list covering all local media outlets, including newspapers, magazines, local websites, TV (broadcast and cable), and radio stations. Get street addresses, phone and fax numbers, and e-mail addresses, as well as specific contact names so every press release and invitation lands in interested hands—rather than some anonymous slush pile.

◆ A posting place list of all public bulletin boards, store windows, and Internet outlets where your group will be able to post information.

Once in place, these cornerstones of your publicity campaign must be open to constant adjustment and reassessment—consider your plans "set in marshmallow," ready to change as events require. The best publicity plan is a flexible one that can take advantage of unexpected options.

Many options are open to you, perhaps far more than you realize. The suggestions that fill the next few pages are no more than starting points. There are plenty of good books on publicity, some of which are mentioned in the suggested reading list (see Appendix B), and new ones are appearing all the time. Publicity, which I call the "art of reaching out," is an ever-developing field and by no means an exact science. What works in one town may not work in another, and this year's great new technique can become old hat before the seasons change. By all means, come up with new approaches of your own—and if they work, be sure to let me know about them for future editions of this book.

Maintain a Professional Appearance

Every piece of publicity material generated by your production must look as polished and professional as possible. Back in Chapter 1, I explained that *amateur* does not mean "amateurish." Well, few things scream "amateurish" as loudly as unreadable window cards or a sloppily reproduced press release. To make your materials look good takes only a tad more effort and expense. Must you use the most expensive paper? Of course not—but the cheapest is not the best alternative either. When a few additional dollars or minutes are all that stands between you and a polished product, go for it.

If you see publicity for a local production that looks half-baked and cheaply reproduced, does it inspire your confidence, or do you instinctively tell yourself to stay far away? Your neighbors, whether they are media pros or the folks next door, are no different. To entice them into your show, you will have to put your message out in an attractive, well-prepared manner. No one expects you to spend millions of dollars, but they do want to see that you give a darn about the impression you make.

Pick a Logo and Use It Everywhere

In our visually oriented society, a *logo* is an excellent way to establish an identity in the public's mind, especially for a play or book musical. Your sponsoring organization (if any) may have a familiar logo, and if so, consider including it in your publicity materials. But it's important for your show to have a logo of its own, a simple combination of text and image that people can instantly identify with your production.

def•i•ni•tion

A **logo** is a graphic design that incorporates the name of a production or organization.

Gremlins

Sexist images, such as those focusing on intimate details of the female anatomy, can be offensive and should always be avoided.

Broadway productions spend thousands developing arresting images for their logos. Remember the dancing yellow eyes and scratchy lettering used by *Cats*, the white half-mask and elegant font of *The Phantom of the Opera*, or the helpless waif and period lettering that represented *Les Misérables?* If you do, that's in part because they were distinct and memorable—and in part because they were emblazoned on every ad, poster, T-shirt, mug, and program those shows turned out. While you may have the option of paying for the right to use an existing logo, in my opinion, you're better off creating a new one that is your group's own.

You may be lucky enough to have access to a professional graphic artist willing to work for little or no cost. If not, turn to your production team. Productions affiliated with a school can also consider inviting the student body to take part in an open logo competition. Stress the need for a simple, striking combination of graphic art and the show's name—in a form that will fascinate most and offend no one. While it is permissible to use a design that echoes a show's original logo, a blatant copy would be illegal.

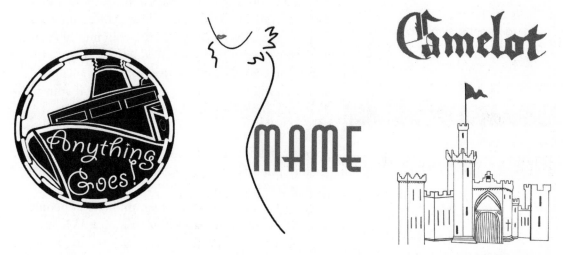

Here are three sample logos designed for various school productions of classic musicals. Each one is simple and instantly recognizable.

(Courtesy of the author's collection and NVOT High School)

Once you have a logo, put it on everything—including window cards, flyers, tickets, audition and casting announcements, press releases, promotional T-shirts, lapel buttons and caps, programs, production ID tags ... drum it into your community's consciousness!

Advertising: Aim Every Dollar

As with all the other aspects of amateur production, the challenge with publicity is to get the maximum effect out of every dollar you spend. And spend you will. Absolutely cost-free publicity is impossible. Someone will have to pay for phone calls, Internet access, paper, copying, printing, postage, and the like. If you can get all or part of these expenses covered by some generous donor, that's great. No matter who foots the bill, there is no point in wasted effort. A well-focused publicity campaign is essential.

def•i•ni•tion

Window cards are small posters, traditionally 22×14 inches, designed to be posted in shop windows and on bulletin boards.

Flyers are handbills publicizing a production, with all necessary performance and ticket purchase information.

On Stage

A little well-aimed publicity can go a long way. For a sing-along concert series at a local community center, I designed flyers on my home computer, and used the center's equipment to make several hundred photocopies that were distributed at all their events. That, plus an e-mailed press release that led to coverage in several local newspapers, led to packed audiences.

Most amateur productions do some sort of formal advertising, placing at least one ad in local newspapers, *window cards* in as many local shop windows as possible, and *flyers* throughout the area. These involve some expense but are very effective publicity tools, and their appearance is always a major morale booster for everyone involved in the show. More important, your formal advertising gives the community at large its first impression of your production. Potential ticket buyers will not fault you for being amateurs, but they will think twice about attending if your publicity materials look amateurish or sloppy.

There was a time when it was necessary to find a local professional to design, typeset, and print high-quality publicity materials, but the age of personal computers has changed all that. A wide variety of easy-to-use programs has given millions of people the ability to create handsome graphics. While your groups may need professional assistance to print large quantities or to turn out a multi-page booklet, now your group can do much on its own.

Any window cards, flyers, or advertisements designed for publication in local newspapers or magazines should include all the following:

- The show's title
- Any information required by your license agreement (author's name, etc.)
- Performance dates, times, and location
- Ticket prices
- Times and places to purchase tickets

Use a clear, decently sized font for all text, and be sure the overall design is not so jam-packed that the text becomes difficult to read.

"No Money" Is No Excuse!

Sometimes there is no budget for formal advertising. That does not mean you can afford to overlook publicity! As you read through these pages, note how many of these PR options require no real financial investment. Printing up a good-looking press release costs next to nothing, and getting it distributed in a timely manner requires little more than a bit of advanced planning.

Even the most economically strapped group can find someone willing to design and run off a few hundred flyers. Cheap photocopy centers can often handle projects for pennies per item, and some may be willing to donate or discount their services for a worthy cause. Just be sure the results always look as good as possible—and that means good enough to impress you if they were coming from another group.

PR Basics

Certain elements are part of almost every publicity campaign. You will want to plan on including these in your production's efforts.

Contact Person

Make someone available to the press as an official contact person, an adult who has some experience dealing with the media. This job usually falls to the publicity director, but not always—especially if your PR director is a student. The official contact person must be willing to provide a phone number and e-mail address on press releases and other media materials and should be ready to field questions from the press.

In most cases, this is a simple enough task, but in the case of unexpected controversy, your contact person will have to handle media flack. It is usually impossible to foresee what may cause tempests in the local teapot. So your contact must always be ready to respond to the media with calm integrity.

Press Releases

Every day, newspaper and magazine editors are inundated with bogus press releases, thinly veiled attempts to get free publicity. Be sure your group only issues releases for events or developments that are newsworthy. Anything that might be of interest to the general public merits a press release. That would include auditions, first rehearsals, any unusual talent or equipment you bring in, and, of course, the opening of your show.

To write an effective press release, you must …

- **Capture the five w's in your opening paragraph.** The five w's are the who, what, where, when, and why of your story.

- **Use clear, simple sentences throughout.** Make every point clear.

- **Include quotes to enliven the text.** Quotes add interest.

- **Be brief.** Keep your release to a single page whenever possible.

- **Use a closing paragraph.** Wrap up the message.

- **Always include contact information.** This info helps for possible follow-ups.

- **Include photos whenever possible.** Photos increase usability.

- **Revise, revise, revise.** Leave no extraneous verbiage.

Keep your message as straightforward as possible. It is not unheard of for editors to put press releases into local newspapers with little if any revision, so always be sure yours are print worthy.

Here is a fictional model press release that follows the eight rules listed earlier:

FOR IMMEDIATE RELEASE

ANDERSONVILLE HIGH SCHOOL TO PRESENT *THE KING AND I*

Continuing a 35-year tradition of spring musicals, Andersonville High School is staging a new production of Rodgers and Hammerstein's classic *The King and I* on May 5th through May 7th. With more than 100 students in the cast and crew, this production promises to be one of the most lavish and ambitious theatrical presentations our town has ever seen.

Director Ann Canfield, who worked as a professional actress before coming to work in Andersonville High's Drama Department, says, "Everyone knows *The King and I* for its wonderful songs and exotic atmosphere, but its call for personal freedom and interracial understanding is as powerful as ever. Our students have gotten a lot out of working on this show, and I know the entire community will be proud of their efforts."

Students held a series of fund-raising events, including car washes and bake and candy sales, to help raise funds for this production. Any profits will go toward the school's library fund, which was almost completely wiped out by recent county Board of Education budget cuts. As Canfield put it, "We are happy to use the performing arts to help support the Humanities at Andersonville High!"

Tickets are priced at $10 for general admission, $5 for children and seniors, and are available through the school office at 333-444-5555. Last year's production of *The Secret Garden* sold out weeks in advance, so advance reservations are strongly suggested. Photos from recent rehearsals are attached; more are available upon request.

Contact: Mr. George Grodon, 333-444-5555

Note that the *where* (Andersonville High), *what* (*The King and I*), *when* (May 5th through 7th), *who* (more than 100 students), and *why* ("most ambitious ever") are all included in the opening paragraph.

Aside from brevity, editors also appreciate timely submissions. If your press release arrives the day before a publication goes to press, it won't do your event any good. Find out when submission deadlines are, and get your material in well ahead of time.

Media Advisories

Issue media advisories to inform the press of any events they might be interested in attending, such as a first rehearsal or opening night. These can use much the same format as press releases, with the addition of an RSVP so space can be reserved. It is customary for press to receive complimentary admission—the coverage they provide is worth far more than the value of a pair of tickets.

Feature Stories

If you have a story that is particularly newsworthy, ask local newspapers and magazines if they would be interested in publishing a feature-length story. In some cases, publications that are short of staff will welcome a prewritten feature—otherwise, they may be willing to send in a journalist. Keep in mind that it is impossible to control what most publications will finally put into print.

> **Backstage Whispers**
>
> If press coverage takes a negative turn, shrug it off—coverage is coverage. As playwright Oscar Wilde once quipped: "The only thing worse than being talked about is *not* being talked about."

Calendar Listings

Here is a great example of accessible, free publicity. Many companies, newspapers, newsletters, and a fair number of local TV and radio stations maintain active community calendars. A surprising number of people pay attention to these listings of local events, so it makes sense to get your production into as many of these calendars as possible. There is usually no charge, so even if you only reach a few people, it is well worth the effort. Most community calendars require that information be submitted a month or more in advance, so do your homework, and get your submissions in ahead of time.

Promotional Photographs

Thanks to digital photography, it is now easy to print your own photos for a nominal cost. Until recently, most publications preferred black and white photos, but that standard is no longer universal. Find out what sort of photos each of your local papers and magazines would prefer (a simple phone call will clarify this), and include the proper format with your press releases and other submissions. An increasing number of publications prefer to receive photos via e-mail in digital form as jpegs or bitmaps. Be sure to know what resolution these publications require—300 dpi is usually sufficient. Be sure to obtain a written release from anyone included in released photos. Here is a sample photo release form.

Photo Release Form

I, (photo subject's name), hereby authorize (name of organization), its successors, legal representatives, and assigns, to use and reproduce my name and photographs, and circulate the same for any and all purposes, including public information of every description. I will make no further claims of whatsoever nature, and have made no representations.

_____

Signature and address (if legal age)

_____

Signature and address (parent or guardian)

In-House Coverage

Any sponsoring organization or school is bound to have an in-house newspaper, magazine, or website you can use to publicize your production to employees, students, etc. Such coverage is usually free, so make the fullest possible use of it.

Advanced PR

Ready to move beyond traditional print media? Consider these exciting publicity angles that most amateur productions fail to take full advantage of.

Internet Promotion

It costs very little to set up a website, especially if volunteers do the actual site construction. A few pages will do the trick, providing basic information and some cast photos. Setting up secure web-based ticket sales can be tricky—so consider hiring a professional service to handle this for you, or just tell web surfers to call a phone number or stop by a ticket sale location.

At a time when many people have turned themselves off to traditional advertising, your production may benefit from a little anti-advertising. If people enjoy the show or even if they are having a blast working on the production, encourage them to talk it up on Internet chat rooms. Be sure the postings are legitimate—"phony" e-postings are easy to detect and can backfire.

TV and Radio Coverage

As with print media, local TV and radio journalists may be interested in covering your event, especially if there is a twist. Is the star of your show a leading player on the school football team? Is a physically challenged member of the company making a special contribution of time and/or talent?

Public Service Announcements

Many radio and TV stations make free public service announcements. You cannot always be sure when they will be broadcast, but no matter—it's no-cost coverage. If your production is affiliated with a school or nonprofit organization, it may qualify for such announcements.

Media Sponsorship

Local radio stations are sometimes interested in providing sponsorship for local productions. They may not contribute much cash, but the free coverage can be more than worth the difference.

Tie-Ins and Ticket Giveaways

Ticket giveaways, either through local organizations, special events, or local media, can be a great source of low-cost publicity. The tickets can be contest awards or lotto-style prizes—again, use your imagination.

The Least You Need to Know

- The whole point of theatrical publicity is to get the word out and bring the public in to your performances.
- Carefully work out a publicity plan for your production, but be ready to adjust it as events require.
- Be sure all your publicity materials look good.
- Design a catchy logo, and use it everywhere you can.
- Make every advertising dollar count, reaching your target audience.
- Low- or no-cost techniques should make up the bulk of any publicity plan.
- Remember the mantra of amateur theatre—get creative! Use your imagination to find inventive publicity ideas.

22

Tickets and Seating: "Join Us! Sit Where Everybody Can See"

In This Chapter

- Various types of seating plans
- Planning and printing tickets
- Setting up a ticket sales system
- Locations and times to sell tickets
- The skinny on house seats, group sales, and complimentary tickets
- Preparing ushers

Theatre tickets are such common items in our lives that people take them for granted—you buy one, hand it to a ticket taker, get a seat, and enjoy a performance. However, a tremendous amount of thought and planning goes into those little slips of paper, and the next few pages will lead you through a subject that until now has been rarely discussed in print. So be forewarned: after reading this chapter, you may never be able to buy a ticket to a movie or live performance without at least a momentary realization of what goes into creating one.

Open vs. Assigned Seating

I'm not sure when theatre tickets were invented. Theatrical performances used *open seating* ("first come, first seated") from ancient times through the 1700s. Then someone got the idea of selling the right to sit in specific seats, and by the mid-1800s, assigned seating and tickets were in use on both sides of the Atlantic. Open seating never disappeared, but it is now used primarily at events where no admission is charged.

While open seating does save a great deal of advance effort, it has major drawbacks, too. Crowds of theatregoers start gathering long before curtain time, all clamoring to land the best seats. Tempers flare as early arrivals try to hold entire rows of seats "for people who are coming." Latecomers have to scrounge for leftover seats. If a performance sells out, arguments can occur. Ushers turn into ringmasters, and the house manager winds up playing lion tamer. It's not pretty. My advice is that open seating is acceptable if an event is admission free, but amateur productions that sell tickets should provide assigned seating.

Seating Plans

The first step is to have a seating plan that gives each seat in your audience space a unique number. Most auditoriums have seating schemes already in place. But if you are working with a new space or one where folding chairs give flexibility in seat planning, this section is for you. Several basic seating plans have evolved over the years. They will work for your amateur group just as efficiently as they do everywhere from Broadway to the Bolshoi.

Standard Seating

Most proscenium auditoriums have a central seating section surrounded by two side aisles and additional seating off to either side. If you are facing the stage, seats to the left get odd numbers, while those to the right get even numbers—the center section uses 100s (101, 102, etc.), numbered from left to right. Letters of the alphabet are used to signify the rows. If a theatre has a mezzanine or balcony, the same system is usually repeated in each area.

Note: large theatres usually switch over to double letters after the twenty-sixth row (AA, BB, etc.). In some cases, double-letter rows indicate special seats placed near the stage when no orchestra is needed.

	STAGE		
9 7 5 3 1	A	101 102 103 104 105 106 107 108 109 110	A 2 4 6 8 10
9 7 5 3 1	B	101 102 103 104 105 106 107 108 109 110	B 2 4 6 8 10
9 7 5 3 1	C	101 102 103 104 105 106 107 108 109 110	C 2 4 6 8 10
9 7 5 3 1	D	101 102 103 104 105 106 107 108 109 110	D 2 4 6 8 10

Most traditional auditoriums use variations of this standard seating chart—100s for the center section, odd numbers on the left side of the house, and even on the right.

Some theatres have unbroken rows that stretch from wall to wall of the auditorium. This cumbersome arrangement usually adapts the same system used in traditional center sections—numbering seats from left to right using 100s and lettering the rows.

> **Backstage Whispers**
>
> Extra-wide auditoriums with four seating sections use a cross between the standard and center aisle charts—the two central sections use 100s (odds to the left, evens to the right), and the two outer sections use simple numbers (again, odds to the left, evens to the right).

Center Aisle Seating

Smaller theatres sometimes have a center aisle dividing the seats into two sections. When this happens, the seats on the left-hand side of the house get odd numbers, while those on the right get evens.

	STAGE		
13 11 9 7 5 3 1	A	2 4 6 8 10 12 14
13 11 9 7 5 3 1	B	2 4 6 8 10 12 14
13 11 9 7 5 3 1	C	2 4 6 8 10 12 14
13 11 9 7 5 3 1	D	2 4 6 8 10 12 14

Theatres with a center aisle break the seats up with odd numbers on the left side of the house and even on the right.

Arena, In-the-Round, and Thrust Seating

When seats surround a stage on three or four sides, the numbering system mutates to give each section of seats one set of 100s (200s, 300s, etc.). Very large in-the-round theatres copy sports arenas by giving each section a letter, but that can cause confusion in smaller seating plans.

When seats surround a stage, each section is designated by a different set of 100s.

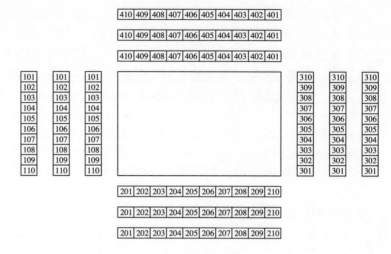

Pricing

Oh, how amateur producers sweat over ticket prices! Plenty of pricing formulas are bouncing around these days, but here is one taught to me by a Tony-winning producer—and it works for amateurs as well as professionals: find a price that will cover all your costs if you sell no more than half of your available seats.

Let's say you're presenting a play. The scholastic and community theatre groups in your region sell tickets at anywhere from $15 to $20—a wide but realistic range for the first decade of this century. Break out your calculator and start crunching numbers. If you're giving four performances in a 300-seat house, your total sales potential is 1,200 seats. Figure out what you would have to charge for 600 tickets to pay your bills. For example, at $15 a seat, half-filled houses would bring in $9,000. If your expenditures came to a mere $8,500, you have your ticket price. If you've spent $12,000, you'll have to consider the $20 option.

Plenty of pressure will be put on you to keep your price low, but you have to charge a figure that gives your production a serious hope of at least breaking even.

Planning and Printing

Once you've settled on your seating plan, I recommend creating a chart to illustrate it. Aside from formalizing the plan, a chart becomes a valuable tool for the sales team, allowing customers to see where their seats will be. You can create such a chart using any number of widely available computer programs. I used Microsoft Excel to create the samples in this chapter. It's a good idea to run off separate copies of the chart for each performance—then, using a light colored pencil (erasable, in case of changes), fill in each seat as it is sold. This gives you a clear visual depiction of how sales are going.

Let's take a look at the anatomy of a theatre ticket. Each one embodies a complete business transaction. In exchange for a set amount of money, the bearer is entitled to attend an event and sit in a particular seat at a specified date and time. Most theatre tickets range in size, but the ideal is to have something that fits into a wallet or a standard mailing envelope. With so much to spell out, there is no room on tickets for extraneous information. Every word matters and must be planned with care.

This theatre ticket is a great example of how to include all the required information (and a tad more) in a clear, easy-to-read format.

Anatomy of a Ticket

Theatre tickets should include the following:

◆ Name and address of the venue.

◆ Name of the event.

◆ Performance day, date, and time.

◆ Seat number (for reserved seating) or ticket number (for general admission). If you opt for general admission, number the tickets to correlate to the number of available seats.

◆ Admission price.

◆ The notation "No Refund—No Exchange." Ticket holders often change their minds, asking if they can exchange for other performances or demanding their money back. The box office manager can make exceptions for those who have suffered an unexpected emergency (illness, death in the family, etc.), but having a "no refund—no exchange" policy printed right on the ticket helps keep such requests to a minimum.

◆ A tear-off tab that restates the date, time, and seat number. This allows both the ticket taker and ticket holder to retain proof of attendance. Broadway tickets still have these appendages, but some theatres no longer tear tickets, using laser scanners to pop the information straight into a computer. While this technology may one day reach the amateur level, currently it is too expensive.

Any additional information is optional. Just don't overcrowd a ticket with text! As the sample illustration shows, the judicious use of font sizes can create enough clear space to make everything easy to read.

If your sponsoring organization has in-house printing facilities, your group can turn out its own tickets. Most professional printers know how to create these as a matter of course, and several companies now market special ticket printing services on the Internet. While I always prefer to encourage local businesses, it is hard to deny the obvious advantages of dealing with firms that know the ins and outs of theatre tickets. Shop around and identify your best option.

Color Coding

As an usher and house manager, I have sometimes found people holding tickets to the same seat. The reason was always the same—one of those tickets was for a different performance. To minimize confusion, use different colored stock for each performance. This usually requires no more than a minor additional cost and can make it easier for ticket takers to spot gaffes before they become major embarrassments.

Ticket Sales: Coordination Is Crucial

Few if any amateur companies can afford the luxury of a formal, fully equipped box office. Ticket sales are usually run out of the homes and/or businesses of volunteers—or better yet, one volunteer. However many people may be on your box office staff, it is vital that only one person serve as the box office/ticket sales manager, handling all sales and maintaining one clear, centralized record of all transactions.

Where and When to Sell Tickets

Before tickets go on sale to the general public, it is customary to give cast and crew an opportunity to purchase seats for family and friends. You can usually handle this in the course of one or two rehearsal sessions—more if you have a large company.

Productions affiliated with a church or other organization may allow that group's office to host preperformance ticket sales. School productions often set up a ticket sales table during a convenient time of day—say before or after classes or during lunch. Be sure to provide sufficient change for the ticket seller.

Establish a secure place to leave both the cash and tickets during classes and overnight. Some community-based groups make tickets available at local retail businesses or offices—with the full consent of the proprietor as well as any volunteers who may work there.

In our communication-obsessed age, it is no longer essential to have a physical box office. Any telephone with an answering machine can become a virtual box office, where people can leave their name and phone number to secure a reservation. The drawback to this is that there is no way to accept payment—credit card sales involve equipment and fees that most amateur groups cannot afford. Cost is also a factor in considering Internet ticket sales. Aside from credit processing, the time and expense of creating a web sales system is prohibitive. Some venues may offer their web sales services to your group at a price, but please think long and hard before paying top dollar for a service that capable volunteers could handle for little more than the cost of supplies. My advice is to keep it simple and post a web page giving the same information you put on your posters, with perhaps some additional photos—all guiding surfers to a phone number they can call to reserve seats.

Group Sales

Group sales are the bread and butter of professional theatre and are becoming a common factor in amateur ticket sales, too. Every community has large organizations that look for affordable group activities, including theatre. To encourage such group sales, offer a special reduced price to any group of 15 or more—anywhere from 25 to 30 percent off the standard cost. Your sales efforts should include a group sales mailing to such prospects as these:

- Senior centers
- Youth groups (for child-friendly shows)
- Scout troops
- Churches, synagogues, and other religious institutions
- Fraternal organizations (Elks, Shriners, etc.)
- Women's auxiliaries

No doubt you can add more possibilities to this list. If your show's theme relates to a particular group or organization, stress this connection in your cover letter.

House Seats

Every show on Broadway sets aside several dozen house seats for each performance. These prime locations are only available for sale through the producer's office and go to VIPs, certain members of the theatrical community, and those with ties to the production (investors, cast members, etc.). As a precaution, most productions try to hold onto some house seats until a few hours before curtain time, at which point the box office puts them up for general sale.

Following this lead, amateur producers may want to mark off a few pairs of good locations as house seats and make them unavailable through the box office. If the fates are kind and your show nears sell-out, local big shots and friends of the production will clamor for last-minute seats—and your team will be able to accommodate them. If unsold, they can be released to the general public a half-hour before curtain time.

If having house seats sounds unnecessary to you, consider this real-life scenario: the boss/principal/big kahuna calls on opening day. She knows you're sold out but wonders if you would "be a team player" and squeeze in her kids/in-laws/hair dresser. Would you rather be forced to say, "No can do, sorry!" and face thinly veiled animosity in weeks to come, or instead say, "Consider it done!" and get all kinds of brownie points for yourself and your troupe? The best part is that a house seat plan won't cost you a nickel and takes barely more than a nickel's worth of time to set up.

Complimentary Tickets

They go by various names—comps, paper, or freebies. Complimentary tickets are a fact of theatrical life. You don't want to know how often you paid good money to sit next to someone who got in to a show or concert for free. In the professional theatre, comps are distributed to investors, the press, and a limited number of people in the theatrical community. Comps are also distributed to community organizations to fill in large blocks of empty seats during previews, a process known as "papering the house." Amateur productions may use comps to get coverage in some local media, but beyond that, what use are comps to you?

Comps can be an asset to any amateur production. For starters, they are a great way to say "thank you" to corporate and private sponsors. Some productions offer a free pair of tickets to anyone buying a full-page program ad—not a bad perk! Comps are also a great way to encourage local VIPs who might otherwise miss your show to stop in and see your group in action. You also should invite local politicians and other community figures who might prove useful in obtaining funding for future productions. In such cases, it is best to send a formal letter of invitation, giving options for attendance dates and an easy way to RSVP.

Ushers

You've dealt with ushers all your theatregoing life and probably never paid much attention to them unless they did something wrong. A capable usher gets you where you have to go with painless ease. It is the ill-trained or uncaring ones who get noticed by planting ticket holders in the wrong seats or giving unclear directions to those in search of rest rooms. These little slip-ups wreak all kinds of minor chaos, leaving members of the audience ruffled and annoyed before the curtain ever opens. You can avoid all this with a quick and easy two-step process: planning and preparation.

Create a Plan

The producer and house manager must come up with a plan that deploys the house staff around the performance space as effectively as possible. Consider doing the following:

- Create signs, using a word processing program, giving directions to the auditorium, rest rooms, etc. Post them in the access hallways before the first performance.

- Place a ticket taker at the entrance—two for larger auditoriums. Unless you are performing in a stadium-sized space, there is no need for more.

- Position guides by every door to check tickets and send people to the correct aisle for seating.

- Plan for at least one usher for each aisle—two if there are more than 20 rows. These ushers see ticket holders to their exact seats, distribute programs, and give directions to rest rooms, concessions, and exits.

- Ask the entire house staff to lend a hand with folding and placing program inserts.

This is an ideal staff plan. If your performance space is small or your team is short-handed, you can combine the jobs of ticket taker and guide and limit the number of ushers to one per aisle.

Preperformance Prep

About one week before your production faces its first audience, have all ushers and other house staff attend a meeting to go over seating plans, review directions, and learn pointers on handling common audience problems (late arrivals, illness, ticket disputes, etc.). Establish guidelines for all staff on when to hand a problem over to the house manager. This get-together should take less than an hour, but it can save a lot of headaches.

Require house staff to be on hand an hour before every performance, making sure that all public areas are clean and ready, prepping programs, and briefing any ushers. As the "meet and greet" team, they help put audience members in a relaxed and receptive mood for the show.

The Least You Need to Know

- Standard seating plans can be adapted to fit any performance space.

- Group sales and house seats are part of professional ticket sales plans and can be part of yours, too.

- Complimentary tickets are a useful way to thank benefactors and reach out to influential people in the community.

- A well-prepared house staff helps put an audience in the right frame of mind for a performance.

Chapter 23

Programs: "Giving Credit Where It's Due"

In This Chapter

◆ Publishing a successful program

◆ Estimating a program ad income

◆ Pricing and selling ads

Every theatre lover has a collection of programs, providing a written record of the shows and performers he or she has enjoyed over the years. These programs were originally created to give participants in a production credit for their contributions. Today, programs can also provide some advertising income, and in this chapter, I discuss various ways to maximize that through effective sales efforts. But when it comes to programs, keep in mind that money is not the main issue. The goal is to give the people in your audiences and your company something worth reading and keeping.

Get with the Program

Believe it or not, first-time amateur producers often ask, "Do we really need to publish a program?" Of course you do! No theatrical experience is really complete unless you have a program to take home, telling who did what. When the final curtain closes, programs become prized mementoes for audiences and members of the company. I have been to performances where audience members expressed annoyance because no program was distributed.

No one is certain when and where programs were first distributed to audiences, but it was almost certainly sometime after the invention of the printing press in the 1450s. By the 1700s, troupes in Britain and the United States were expected to offer several plays per evening, so audiences were given simple printed sheets listing performers and the "order of play." Advertising was added in the mid-1800s, and Broadway programs gradually developed into the elaborate *Playbill* magazines now given out at professional performances. While professional theatre programs may reap a fine income from advertising, it's best for amateur theatre companies to keep their hopes for program ad income realistic.

Not Quite a Gold Mine

In an informal survey, I asked several amateur theatre producers if they made any major misjudgments during their first productions. All agreed that they seriously overestimated the income they would get from program ads.

Just what kind of program ad income can you expect? That depends on several factors:

- The current price for comparable advertising in your area. Find out how much local schools and other organizations are charging for space in programs, journals, and yearbooks. Ad space is far more enticing when it is offered at the prevailing rate.

- The program coordinator's sales skills. Having a responsible program coordinator with a "can do" attitude and a sense of dedication can make a world of difference in meeting your sales goals.

- The size and type of paper you use. While most theatre programs are small magazines about 8 inches in height, larger ones are not unknown. Glossy paper costs more than flat, and both can be used with equal effectiveness.

◆ The quality of your program package. A professional-looking product is always easier to sell. If you promise quality layouts, graphics, and printing to your advertisers, deliver on those promises.

◆ The size of your potential audience. The more people likely to see an ad, the more advertisers will be willing to pay for it. This selling point matters more after a group develops a proven attendance record.

Most amateur productions can count on program ads to bring in a few hundred extra bucks. ("What!?!") With luck and a lot of hard work, your team might even bring that up to a thousand or more ("That's more like it!"), but you cannot take that kind of figure as a given. Before we get to ad sales, we must consider a lot of preliminary work, beginning with some serious planning.

Required Content

Theatrical programs require the same careful preparation and dedicated effort that go into every other aspect of a successful production. A program serves the same basic function as the opening and closing credits of feature films, giving credit to all participants. An amateur program must include all of the following elements.

Front Cover

This should be an attractive combination of the show's logo, the name of any sponsoring school or organization, and performance dates. Use color if at all possible. One warning: some amateur productions use a facsimile of the professional *Playbill* or *Showbill* logo on their programs, not realizing that these are copyrighted properties that they cannot use without the express written consent of Playbill, Inc. The same is true of original logo artwork—some licensing companies can sell permission to use these familiar images.

Title Page

The very first page inside the booklet gives the title of the show and then lists the authors and major members of the production team. School productions tend to aim this particular print spotlight on student participants. Many licensing agreements spell out special requirements for program credits, such as prominently listing the name of a show's original director or producer. These can be so picayune as to require specific font sizes. (Hey, agents and show biz attorneys have to do *something* to impress their clients!) The producer and program coordinator must be sure the program meets all such obligations.

THE 42ND ANNUAL PRODUCTION
NORTHERN VALLEY REGIONAL HIGH SCHOOL AT OLD TAPPAN

MARCH 3, 4, & 5, 2005

The Dream On Community Players
Present

The Taming
of the Shrew
by William Shakespeare

starring
**Ewan McGregor – Kate Winslet
Ann Hathaway – Jake Gyllenhaal
Jim Broadbent – Joe Pesci – Victor Garber**

and
**Hilary Cohen – Bruce Levi
Mary Marotta – James Morgan – Cory Rochester**

Lighting by Jules Fisher
Set Design by Eugene Lee
Costumes by William Ivey Long

**Musical Direction by Paul Gemignani
Directed by Joe Mantello**

This high school program cover (left) and fictional title page (right) show exactly what is required—a clear, attractive presentation of information, free from clutter. Note the generous use of white space.

(Used with permission of NVOT High School Music Department)

Synopsis

Use the next page or two to list all scenes and/or musical numbers. Book musicals also list the characters in each song; revues list the real name of each song's performer.

Please do not stint on this feature. The synopsis helps theatregoers follow the action and identify who is doing what. It also gives them a sense of when the intermission and final curtain will occur—important information for anyone feeling the call of nature. If your show has no intermission, be sure to highlight that fact, and perhaps have ushers politely mention it to patrons as well.

Cast List

This is a complete list of all roles and performers. In the case of multiple casting, actors' names should appear next to every role they play. If your production uses understudies, a list detailing who covers each role should appear just below the cast list.

Orchestra List

Next comes a list of all musical personnel, specifying which instruments they play and mentioning any special production jobs they handle. Be sure to include mention of any additional musicians, such as an audition or rehearsal pianist.

Production Staff List

This roll call should include everyone from the producer to the lead carpenters. Many school productions provide separate lists for adult and student staff. Do not be surprised if this list runs for a full page or more.

Special Announcements

This is a great place to post the same announcements that are made verbally just before the curtain opens. Redundant? Perhaps, but some people "tune out" during precurtain speeches—and anything that gets more people to turn off their cell phones is worth doing.

Lists of All Crews and Production Committees

These lists should encompass every person who volunteered time and talent on this production. School productions should include a list of all parent volunteers. It is appropriate to conclude these lists with a brief but gracious statement of thanks.

List of Patrons and Donors

Include anyone who has offered financial support. If anyone has requested that his or her name not be used, it is customary to note him or her as "Anonymous."

Special Acknowledgments

Conclude with notes of thanks to those individuals, organizations, and businesses that assisted in the production. Be generous with your thanks because it will be noticed and appreciated. Include as many people and organizations as you wish here—it is not uncommon for this feature to fill an entire page.

Professional theatre programs include biographies of major participants, but in my opinion, this is not necessary at the amateur level. Bios take up a lot of page space, require a great deal of time to process, and do little more than stroke the egos of those involved. However, if such bios are a "must have" for your group, limit them to a few sentences each, and insist that all cast and crew have their information submitted during the first week of rehearsal. Make it a policy that those who miss this deadline get no program bio. Otherwise, your program coordinator will have to waste valuable time chasing people down.

While I have seen amateur productions cram production information into as few as 4 pages (i.e., one folded sheet), it usually takes 10 or more pages to set the basics out in a clear, readable format. Tiny fonts are not the answer. They are often hard to read and a real nuisance to older readers. Stick to a clear 12-point font, and allow plenty of white space—no cramming! After months of generous effort, the members of your company deserve to see their names in something better than fine print. Please limit the number of fonts to one or two, though. The age of the personal computer has encouraged the indiscriminate mixing of fonts, with eye-aching consequences.

Backstage Whispers

All program lists should conclude with the statement, "We apologize for the omission of any names that were added after our publication deadline." Some groups go a step further by posting a list of late volunteers and donors in the lobby. A note on spelling: the program coordinator must check and double-check the spelling of every name in the program. Even the most well-planned program can have a typo or two, but too many amateur theatre programs are awash in obvious misspells. Show your company members more respect than that!

Types of Advertising

Several types of ads appear in a typical amateur theatre program:

- ◆ Commercial ads—traditional advertising placed by local businesses and professionals.

- ◆ "Best wishes"—businesses, family, and friends place ads expressing best wishes or congratulations to the entire company.

- ◆ Family and friend ads—ads addressed to specific company members, usually placed by family or friends.

Encourage and treat all three types with equal care. You have no way of telling in advance how many of each to expect. From year to year, the mix will vary.

Break thy Leg,
Brian Francis!

Love and hugs,
Noni & Nono

Pinizzotto Construction
24-32 19th Street
Ourtown, USA

Musicals101.com

The Cyber Encyclopedia of Musical Theatre, Film & TV

Congratulates the Dream On cast and crew of *Taming of the Shrew*!!!

Best Wishes
to the cast & crew
from City Councilman

Gary Maresco

CONGRATULATIONS!

To
BRUCE
and the
Cast & Crew
of
SHREW!

**Love,
Joe & Barbara Gallo**

Thank You,
Frank Louis Quality Press

Printers for the
Dream Community Players
for 15 years!

Casa Mangia

Cozy Italian Bistro
"Taming" local appetites since 1957

207 Clara Paul Street
Reservations: 222-0000
Eleanor & Frank, your hosts

These fictional ads include some of the most popular types: local business ads, best wishes from loved ones, thank you to sponsors, etc. Any of these ads can be expanded to fill a full page or more if needed.

In recent years, advertising content has become an issue. Be sure to prohibit questionable language and political messages. Do not accept negative comments about competing troupes or schools—this is a place for praise only! Program ads should generate income, never controversy. In short, all program ads should be G-rated and universally user friendly.

Budgeting: How Much Will Your Program Cost?

The next step is to figure out how much printing your program is likely to cost. The cost of using a professional printer can be steep. One group I work with currently spends an average of $6,000 to turn out its programs. Their well-organized sales program usually sells more than $7,000 worth of ads, so it is no loss. If those figures terrify you, try to relax—depending on various factors, you can turn out a presentable program for far less.

Backstage Whispers

Many amateur companies find that printers from outside their immediate area offer the best bargains. If friends suggest such an arrangement, it may be worth investigating. Just be sure to consider the cost of shipping in your bottom line.

Sit down with whoever handles your printing needs and discuss such basic issues as …

♦ The number of pages. Be sure you have ample space for all required production credits.

♦ Type of paper. Glossy paper looks great but is far costlier than a flat finish.

♦ Color versus black and white. Most amateur groups limit any use of color to the cover. While you can charge more for color ads, printing them costs a lot more, too.

If you are farming this project out to outside professionals, do some comparison shopping and have this conversation with several competitors. Get price quotes, keeping in mind that the lowest price is not always the best—any figure that is "too good to be true" invariably turns out to be a pipe dream, if not an outright lie. If a printer offers to do the job for free, this is one "gift horse" you will want to look in the mouth. A polite request for samples of similar projects will give you some idea of what to expect. If you have any reason to doubt the quality of someone's product, look elsewhere.

When formalizing an agreement with a printer, be sure the contract includes a guaranteed delivery date well in advance of opening night and a flexibility option that allows you to add more advertising pages at a reasonable cost. With a firm written estimate, you now know the target cost of your program—which also serves as your minimum sales goal. Every dollar's worth of advertising you sell above this base cost spells profit for your production.

Ad Pricing

Aside from considering the rates charged by comparable organizations in your area, the overall size and cost of your program will affect your ad pricing. At the very least, you want advertising to cover all program-related expenses, but odds are you want several times that amount in profit.

For example, let's say your program requires 10 pages for production information. Plan on allowing at least as much room for ad space, giving you a total of 20 projected pages.

If printing a 20-page booklet costs you $1,000 (and that is a very conservative figure), you will have to charge $100 per ad page to break even. By kicking up your ad price to $200 per page, your total potential ad income becomes $2,000—a $1,000 profit. Not an astronomical sum, but a helpful one when the time comes to balance the production accounts. With a full-page ad going at $200, you can easily set half-page ads at $120, one-third page at $100, quarter-page ads at $60, and eighth-page ads at $30. The pricing of smaller ads is designed to make the full-page rate a better overall deal. Mind you, this is only an illustrative example of a pricing scale—set your prices as your circumstances demand.

While many businesses have predesigned ads ready and waiting to use, others (such as family and friends) will need to have a layout created for them. Always make it clear that your team will be happy to whip up ad layouts at no extra charge. Some groups offer a slightly reduced rate for ads placed by family and friends. I advise limiting this discount to full-page ads placed by an early submission deadline.

Selling Ads: Blow Your Horn!

Who buys program ads? All sorts of people! Most amateur productions can focus their sales efforts on a sizeable list of potential advertisers:

♦ Local businesses—both large and small companies are worth asking.

♦ Community leaders—public officials and politicians want to be identified with grass roots performing arts projects.

♦ Local professionals—doctors, lawyers, dentists, etc. look for inexpensive, positive opportunities to put their names before the public.

♦ Company members—ads are a great chance to congratulate colleagues.

♦ Families and friends—loved ones get to support the production and cheerlead all at the same time.

> **Backstage Whispers**
>
> A useful selling point: theatrical programs become keepsakes, treasured long after a performance takes place. An ad purchased today will remain in people's homes for years to come.

As you can see, this sort of sales program is very much a team effort, one that reaches out to every member of the company.

Sales can be left in the hands of an individual or a committee. Some theatre groups have a contest, offering a modest prize to whoever sells the most program ads.

People pay for ad space, but that does not mean you have to publish anything they tell you to. If someone submits ad copy that is in poor taste or that is likely to stir up a negative reaction, the program team has every right to courteously insist on revisions.

Seven Sales Pointers

Hundreds of books discuss the art of selling, and a quick browse of your local library, bookstore, or favorite Internet seller should yield some interesting options. However, a few basic suggestions are in order here:

◆ **Ask!** Instead of talking yourself into inaction ("Oh, they'll never go for it"), pick up the phone, send the letter, or do whatever it takes to ask that prospect to buy ad space. Many potential advertisers (and sponsors, for that matter) never get involved because no one bothers to ask.

◆ **Ask the right person.** Instead of getting an automatic turndown from an efficient receptionist, find out who makes the advertising decisions and address your inquiries directly.

◆ **Have the right person do the asking.** If someone in your troupe has connections to a potential advertiser, see if he or she would be willing to ask about buying ad space—or at least provide an introduction to the right decision maker.

◆ **Be prepared.** Have handsomely reproduced sample pages showing what ads will look like in your program. Your printer can usually provide samples, or you can present a sample program from a prior production.

◆ **Be upbeat.** You would not buy anything from a salesperson who looks or sounds desperate; why would anyone else? Make your sales approach relaxed and unworried.

◆ **Take "no" gracefully.** Always be courteous. Thank the prospect for his or her time and leave a card or flyer with contact information. Occasionally, people change their minds.

◆ **"No" does not always mean "no."** Ask politely why the answer is "no," and most prospects will give you a frank answer. If they need more information or might be interested at a later time, follow up as needed.

Those new to sales must learn that there is no point in taking a "no" personally. There can be all sorts of reasons why a business or individual does not buy an ad, so unless you and the prospect share some personal history, there is no reason to think you are the issue.

Bartering Ads

Most Americans have forgotten about bartering, the old and practical custom of exchanging one service for another. Amateur troupes don't have much to offer in such trades. A pair of tickets can be an enticement, but their face value is rather low. Free advertising is another matter! If there is a business or individual who can provide you with a useful product, service, or discount, see if they will accept a free program ad in lieu of cash. When an electrician or attorney gives you pro-bono assistance or a local business gives you free merchandise, ad space is a classy, tangible way to say thank you. Just don't give away too many ads, or your program might turn into a financial liability. Let the paid ads outnumber your freebies by at least four to one.

The most desirable (and high-priced) ad space in theatre programs is the back cover—with the inside front and back covers running a close second. If a business or individual sponsors the full cost for your production, it is appropriate to offer them the back cover ad at no charge. If they decline, be sure the program includes a prominent and gracious note of thanks.

> **Gremlins**
>
> One catch to bartering ad space—if you give away too many ads, the program can turn into a financial liability. So exercise moderation in your bartering!

The Least You Need to Know

- The main purpose of a theatrical program is to give every participant credit for his or her contribution.

- A successful theatre program requires careful planning and setting realistic ad sales goals.

- When looking for printers, comparison shop and get price quotes from several prospects.

- Ad prices are based on the cost of printing and the prevalent cost of similar advertising in your area.

- You must courteously prohibit potentially offensive or controversial ad content.

- You can barter a limited amount of ad space for goods, services, or discounts.

Part 6

Showtime and Afterward— "Another Opening, Another Show"

It's finally showtime! The combination of excitement, terror, and sheer energy on an opening night can be overwhelming. These final chapters tell you what to expect, how to ride out the thrilling final weeks of preparation, and how to get a head start on your next show. I know you may be swearing that you'll never put yourself through this madness again, but odds are you will. Crazy as it seems, putting on shows is addictive. Unlike most other addictions, this one will enrich your life and the lives of everyone who works in or attends one of your productions. Let's go on with the show!

Final Rehearsals: "Will It Ever Be Right?"

In This Chapter

- Keeping your priorities clear in the final weeks
- Avoiding overwork
- Organizing the backstage areas
- Security and backstage etiquette
- Running tech and dress rehearsals
- Giving the cast a night off

One day you are going to look at the calendar and realize that it's just two weeks to opening night. Places deep inside you will tighten, and just the teensiest bit of panic may smash its way into your consciousness. If you fail to stifle a small scream, it's understandable. Tumultuous days lie ahead. The avalanche of final rehearsals can easily overwhelm inexperienced troupes. This chapter offers ideas that can help you minimize the angst and pull your company's efforts together. Will it ever be right? You bet it will!

Priorities: You Want It *When?*

As your company enters the final two weeks before their first performance, do not be surprised if everyone's to-do lists swell to unnerving proportions. Along with the big last-minute challenges like finishing sets and stepping up publicity efforts, there are always a few chores to take care of that might have been dealt with earlier but somehow slipped through the cracks. As the sense of urgency grows, volunteers have a tendency to go into overdrive. Tempers may flare as lighting directors contend with jammed *gobos*, and designers lock horns over color combinations. Performers can suffer meltdowns with or without visible provocation. Even the most trivial issues can begin to take on disproportionate importance.

def•i•ni•tion

Gobos are silhouette patterns that turn a light fixture into an atmospheric projection unit. Depicting anything from a word or symbol to the outline of a window or leafy foliage, gobos can be used to add atmosphere or even take the place of a full stage set.

At this point, the producer and director have fulfilled the bulk of their production duties, but they still have to guide and encourage, keeping everyone's focus on the main goal: putting on a good show. Never allow petty problems ("The men's room is out of soap!") to eat up time and energy that the team leaders should invest in crucial production concerns. If you have built a sufficient production team, there should be people on hand to handle the details for you.

When the pressure is on, the attitude of the folks on top of any organization becomes very contagious. Rudyard Kipling once wrote, "Keep a cool head when everyone else around you is losing theirs." Wise amateur producers and directors make this phrase their mantra, and instead of just chanting it, they embody it, becoming the calm center of all theatrical storms. If the bosses appear calm and assured, it can inspire the same in the rest of the team.

When you are calm, you can opt for confidence. If by any chance you find yourself panicking, get over it immediately. Accept that you can only do so much. Once you have done all you can, let go. If you have no idea how everything will get done in time, that's okay! Most of the things that really matter will somehow be handled, and even if they are not, so what? Your getting an ulcer won't help one bit. Find a constructive way to dispel your fears. Meditate, exercise, knit, weave baskets—anything that will help keep you on an even keel.

Why are dress rehearsals so important? Consider this hapless fellow, photographed during a dress rehearsal of Camelot. *That rather un-medieval wristwatch was just one howling error that came to light that night—rushed stitching in this costume brought far more to light before the session was over. (And yes, the actor is yours truly in my college years.)*

Avoid Marathons

If you worked out a realistic production schedule and managed to stick to it, there should be no need for extreme effort at this point. However, as Shakespeare noted, "the best laid plans of mice and men oft go awry"; an influenza outbreak, a broken water pipe, or even a few messy snowstorms can gum up your schedule and leave everyone scrambling to make up for lost time. The altruistic instincts of cast and crew will kick into high gear, and with or without a director's urging, people will start pouring extra time into the production.

Most accidents and injuries occur during these final weeks. The reason is simple— fatigue. An exhausted cast and crew are more likely to make mistakes and far more susceptible to colds and other illnesses. The answer is to keep everyone working within reasonable limits. Resist the temptation to add extra evenings of rehearsal or to have crews work around the clock to install equipment. If your production team insists on working overtime, try to limit them to no more than one or two extra hours per day.

When Marathons Happen Anyway

Sometimes, even the best-organized effort will come up against forces that are beyond your control, such as weather emergencies or the availability of facilities. Your team can find itself with no choice but to pull one or more late-night sessions to finish the sets, install and adjust lights, or resolve other technical issues. Assuming your facility allows late access and that all members of your team are adults who are open to this idea, working into the wee hours might be doable. If you are dealing with anyone under the age of 18, parental consent notes are a must. Whatever the age group, take special care to get everyone home safely whenever the session ends. To have anyone stranded at a bus stop in the middle of the night is unacceptable.

Also, be sure to provide some creature comforts. Temporarily suspend the "no food" policy. Encourage participants to brown bag a snack, or (if your budget allows) provide a table of beverages and snacks in an adjacent break area. Keep all food and drink far from the sets, costumes, and equipment. And don't overdo it, or precious time will be wasted. If any cast members are among the late-night volunteers, send them home at a sane hour. A lack of sleep can ravage singing and speaking voices, something you cannot risk in the days leading up to the first performance.

Backstage Space

As the physical elements of the production fall into place, it will be necessary to start formally organizing all backstage areas. Established theatre groups may have the luxury of a formal workshop and storage closets, but others will have to improvise. It is wisest for the producer or director to oversee this process, sparing the PSM the onerous chore of trying to appease senior production staff.

You must set aside sufficient space adjacent to the performing area for …

- ◆ Sets.

- ◆ Costume racks.

- ◆ Technical equipment.

- ◆ The PSM's command station. Traditionally, the PSM's station was placed immediately to one side of the stage. With nontraditional performance spaces, the PSM may call the show from a booth. Prompters are rarely used today, but if you choose to have one, he or she will need a small podium in the wings.

◆ Prop tables. During final rehearsals and performances, all the production props are laid out backstage on tables. A life-simplifying technique: cover the tabletops with plain, heavy-duty paper, lay out all the props in the order they will be used, and then use a black felt-tipped pen to outline and label the space for each item. This makes it possible for the prop team to see at a glance if any props are missing.

Also, post a bulletin board backstage in an accessible, well-lit location. Known as the *callboard*, this is where you post company announcements as well as sign-in sheets for the cast and crew. These sheets allow crew chiefs to know at a glance if anyone is missing.

There can be a lot of electrical and sound wires backstage, and all of these must be placed overhead or along the walls. Do not leave any wires, ropes, or cables of any kind lying on the floors, where they would endanger people, sets, and anything else that moves. Even if taped down, floor-level wiring is an accident waiting to happen.

Dressing Rooms

The cast must have sufficient space to prepare for dress rehearsals and performances. These rooms must have mirrors (at least one full length), decent ventilation, good lighting, and reasonable access to rest rooms. Most amateur productions get by with two common dressing rooms—one for each gender. Anyone expecting private star dressing rooms will have to make do with communal facilities.

Dressing rooms need regular maintenance. In amateur theatres, these spaces are often allowed to become toxic hazards, littered with makeup-stained tissues, empty water bottles, dirty towels, and worse. It's not that actors are slobs—as performances near, they have many other things to worry about. Be sure someone steps in and either prods the cast into cleaning up after itself or does the cleanup for them.

For school or youth group productions, responsible adults should chaperone dressing rooms. High spirits and hormones can get the better of nervous young performers, beginning with final rehearsals. If possible, your sound system should include monitors in all dressing rooms. This makes it possible for the PSM to page performers and allows cast members to hear what is happening onstage.

Security Concerns

The final whirlwind of preproduction and performances can make it all too easy for people to let down their guard. Secure storage space must be provided for all the following items:

- Equipment

- Tools

- Costumes

- Props

- Makeup

- Musical scores

You will also need some kind of lockable or guarded place for cast and crew to store personal belongings. Take security seriously. As someone who has had his own wallet pilfered from backstage during a performance, I can assure you that these things happen. You may even want to put an ASM in charge of backstage security.

Backstage Behavior

From the dress rehearsal onward, everyone should observe certain rules backstage. Enforcing them now will give performers and crewmembers a chance to acclimate themselves to proper backstage behavior before performances begin. While every company has its special needs, a few rules are more or less universal:

- All cast and crew must sign in on arrival.

- Once the house opens to the public, complete silence is required backstage.

- Eating and smoking are not permitted anywhere backstage.

- Cell phones may not be used backstage during final rehearsals or performances.

- Bottled water is the only beverage permitted backstage.

- Costumes are not permitted in the makeup area.

- Performers in costume must remain backstage, avoiding all public areas.

- Damage to costumes must be reported immediately to the costume crew.

- All props must be returned to the prop table or prop crew.

- Only company members are permitted backstage.

Post copies of these policies on the callboard, and take a minute to go over them verbally with the full company before final rehearsals begin. This can prevent all sorts of annoyances, like seeing an expensive white ball gown covered with cranberry juice or stopping the dress rehearsal because someone's cell phone rings during a climactic scene.

Orchestra Rehearsal

Musicals open their final preperformance week with the orchestra rehearsal, bringing the full cast and orchestra together for the first time. If your production uses piano-only or a prerecorded score, you can skip this session altogether.

This is a music-only session, setting aside all dialogue and physical aspects of the production so the performers can become accustomed to singing with full accompaniment. Attendance is mandatory for the director, music director, PSM, orchestra, and all cast members. For a typical book musical, expect this session to run about three hours. If the performance space is available, by all means use it. If not, you will need another room large enough to accommodate the cast and all musicians. Traditionally, the cast gets assigned seats (either onstage or in the audience area), with leading players in the front row.

The music director helms this session, rehearsing the score in order from start to finish, overture included. When soloists perform, they stand front and center. The ensemble usually remains seated while singing. There will be plenty of interruptions, but maintaining silence is a must. Encourage everyone to bring a book and a bottle of water and to be ready to take notes on conducting cues.

Costume and Prop Parade: Pickled Eggs Are Not Pickles

Set aside the better part of one rehearsal session for the cast to try on their costumes, wigs, accessories, and props for the first time and parade around in them under full stage lights. All actors must have whatever footwear and undergarments they are expected to provide. If your production requires any elaborate makeup, this is a good opportunity to see it in use for the first time. The director and all members of the design team must be on hand to see the results.

This is a very exciting time for the cast and a moment of truth for the designers. The costume and prop designers will assess the fit, shape, and color balance of every item; the lighting and costume designers will consider how the costumes look against the sets and what color gels will be most effective from scene to scene. Some groups wait until dress rehearsal to stage the costume and prop parade, but in my opinion, it is best to have this event take place as early on as possible, giving your team a few extra crucial days to correct any glaring errors. There are almost always costumes that do not fit or turn out to be the wrong color.

On Stage

A friend of mine once directed a college production in which one of the required props was a jar of pickles. During the costume and prop parade, out came a jar of pickled eggs—not quite the same thing. Those "not quite" items can pop up when least expected. Scheduling your parade a few days in advance of the opening allows time for corrections to be made.

The full costume and prop teams must be on hand to make the inevitable adjustments and repairs and to handle postrehearsal storage. From this point on, these teams must attend all rehearsals where their materials are in use. Be sure someone from these teams with needle and thread expertise is on hand full-time. Count on seams, zippers, buttons, and bows to give way at the darnedest moments. Also have an iron and/or steamer available to deal with wrinkled costumes, backdrops, and set elements (such as tablecloths).

Tech Rehearsals: More Is Less

Over the decades, amateur theatre groups developed an unfortunate tradition of endless tech rehearsals. At one time, the technical aspects of a production could be covered in one rehearsal, but those tech needs increased over the decades, and it seems no amateur group wanted to admit that they required multiple tech sessions. So it became standard procedure for these mind-numbing sessions to drone on from midafternoon into the wee hours.

I am happy to tell you that tech marathons are going the way of gaslight, greasepaint, and other outmoded relics of the theatrical past. An increasing number of amateur companies have realized that two or three tech sessions make more sense than trying to cram it all into one exhausting night. So you are hereby released from any obligation to perpetuate this idiotic tradition.

Dry Tech

Also known as the cue-to-cue, the dry tech gives the crews a chance to run all technical cues in performance order. While the PSM calls the cues and the lighting and stage teams work their tails off, the director and all designers must be on hand to resolve any creative issues. The cast either gets a night off or runs through the show in a separate space. Crewmembers can take turns acting as stand-ins for the cast as needed. This session will resolve some of the worst technical issues, shaving hours off the wet tech.

Wet Tech

The wet tech is another primarily technical session, only with cast, costumes, and every other aspect of a performance thrown in—just no audience. All cast, crew, and designers must be on hand for this, with the PSM calling cues. Countless interruptions will occur. The brightness, color, and exact focus of lights will have to be adjusted and set positions must be fine-tuned, as well as sound system levels and the installation of any microphones. Even if you have a dry tech, this session can run about twice the length of an actual performance. I always advise inexperienced directors to consider dividing the wet tech into two sessions, especially for a complex, multi-set show. Either run one act per session, or divide the material approximately in half.

Forewarn the cast that this will be a tedious process as they will have to stand about while the tech crews work their magic. This is one time when all-out performing is not wanted. Let performers save their voices for the busy days ahead. Mind you, there will be plenty of talking. Even the best-behaved company will start chattering during long delays. Don't let this anger you. Just keep calling for quiet as needed.

Photo Opportunities

Production photos cannot be taken during public performances when camera flashes would prove a distraction, so most groups find it easier to take photos during the wet tech, where the presence of cameras gives performers a reason to perk up and stay attentive. Some groups arrange for a capable volunteer photographer to take these photos (including some casual offstage shots), which you can later sell separately or in packages to cast members and the general public. Aside from providing the company with a morale boost, these photos can become a small moneymaker for the production.

Curtain Calls

At the end of a performance, an audience (minus those who think getting to their cars 86 seconds sooner will improve their lives) wants to show its appreciation. Curtain calls give them an opportunity to do so. Wet tech is often the best time to stage this sequence because the cast will be eager to get home and ready to go along with whatever the director has planned.

Curtain calls do not have to be elaborate. In fact, this is one more area where simplicity rules. For small casts of 10 or fewer, the performers can take a common group bow or step forward for individual bows in reverse order of importance. Larger casts can be broken down in the following order:

◆ Ensemble (chorus or nonspeaking roles)—in large groups

◆ Small speaking roles—in groups of three to five

◆ Featured players—in duos or solo bows

◆ Leads (two to three largest roles)—solo bows

If two leads have more or less equal roles (Anna and the King, Higgins and Eliza, etc.), you may opt to have them bow together. Male performers should note that audiences love seeing a gentleman defer to his female co-star, giving her the last bow.

On occasion, an individual may feel slighted by his placement in curtain calls. Unless the director heartily agrees that there has been an unintentional oversight, meet such complaints with the following timeless truth: placement in curtain calls is meaningless! If the audience likes your performance, they will let you know it regardless of when you bow. I have often seen a featured player get a much louder and longer reception than a star.

Dress Rehearsal

Dress rehearsal brings together all the elements of a production for the first time, running the entire show as it will appear on opening night. The PSM runs the cues, freeing the director to watch for anything that still needs tweaking. Some gluttons for punishment plan multiple dress rehearsals, but in my opinion, one is quite sufficient for simple revues and small plays and two is plenty for large-cast musicals. Dress rehearsal should take place within a day or two of the wet tech, and all cast, crew, and designers must attend.

Crew Dress Codes

Beginning at the dress rehearsal, require all stage and lighting crews to wear plain, all-black clothing, including black rubber-soled footwear. Thanks to contemporary fashion trends, most will have no trouble meeting these requirements. This includes spotlight operators, who will be in full view of the audience throughout performances. If T-shirts are worn, do not permit colorful logos or vulgar sayings—these can become an unnecessary visual distraction. Some groups always have black or midnight blue production T-shirts so the crews can use them during performances.

It is also a good idea for ushers and concession staff to have a common dress code, making it easy for the public to identify them as members of the production team. Wearing an official production T-shirt or lapel button works well, but it is just as effective to have these folks wear inexpensive ID tags marked with the production logo.

Providing an Audience

To give cast and crew an opportunity to get used to audience reactions, many amateur companies recruit a nonpaying audience for the final dress rehearsal. As long as you charge no admission and attendance is by invitation only, licensing firms are not likely to complain that this counts as a public performance. Your dress rehearsal audience should consist of people who are not connected with the production and are not likely ticket buyers. Local senior community centers are on the lookout for such events. For children's theatre, make your dress rehearsal a daytime event and invite a youth group or a few classes from a local school. Depending on the material, these rehearsal audiences can generate favorable word of mouth for the production. They can also provide your team with valuable feedback, letting you know which elements of the show are working and which are falling short.

Before the curtain opens, the director should step onstage and take a few minutes to welcome everyone (if you have charm, prepare to use it now!) and explain that because this is a dress rehearsal, there is always the possibility of an interruption if unforeseen problems pop up. Then leave your cast and crew to give it their best shot. Even a subdued response will give the cast some indication of where to expect laughter and applause during actual performances. Be sure all attendees are safely on their way before gathering the cast for final notes.

Final Notes

Following the dress rehearsal, gather the full company in the main performance space for final notes. It is customary for the cast and crew to sit in the audience area during this process, while the director and anyone else making comments stands either on or just in front of the stage.

After dress rehearsal for A Midsummer Night's Dream, *waiting for the director to give final notes.*

Theatrical lore tells us that an abysmal dress rehearsal means a great opening night. There is some truth to this. It doesn't take a degree in psychology to understand that a poor dress rehearsal can keep everyone on edge, while a flawless one can leave people feeling overconfident. Whatever way the dress rehearsal goes, the director must keep the company focused on the first performance. While noting any major problems, be sure to give praise where it is due, keeping your overall tone honest and yet as positive as possible. Give the designers (and for musicals, the choreographer and music director) a chance to add their thoughts, but urge them all to temper criticism with encouragement. When all notes have been given, the director sends everyone home, telling the cast to enjoy their day off.

A Day Off: The Nonoptional Option

When planning your production schedule, I urge you to give the cast a full day off between the dress rehearsal and the opening night. For this one day, the performance space is off limits to the performers. The production team and crews only come in as needed. This idea may not be traditional, but it can be a real blessing for amateur companies.

The benefits are obvious:

◆ A much-needed rest for performers' voices. Even one day can make a real difference for voices and nerves strained during those grueling final rehearsals.

◆ An opportunity for stage, costume, and tech crews to make final adjustments. Most dress rehearsals reveal a host of little details that must be handled before the opening: seams that need re-sewing, lighting gels that must be replaced, etc.

◆ Time to prep the performance space and adjacent areas for use by the public. This includes general maintenance, decorating the lobby, setting up concession booths, etc.

Urge cast members to use their day off wisely. Encourage them to steer clear of sports events, rock concerts, alcohol, cigarettes, or anything else that might threaten the larynx with harm. Performers should also avoid participating in contact sports or other activities that could cause serious injury.

The Least You Need to Know

◆ Avoid marathon work sessions for the cast and crews, but if such a session proves unavoidable, arrange for meals and safe transportation home.

◆ The director and producer oversee the arrangement of backstage space, including dressing rooms and secure storage areas.

◆ Have a clear set of rules governing behavior backstage.

◆ Many amateur companies now break up tech rehearsal into two sessions—a dry tech (no actors) and a wet tech (full cast).

◆ Dress rehearsal shows how far your company has come and can reveal all sorts of details that must be fixed.

◆ Amateur casts should get a day off between dress rehearsal and the first performance. Tired voices can rest while crews make last-minute adjustments.

Showtime: "Cross Your Fingers and Hold Your Heart"

In This Chapter

- ◆ Making the transition from taskmaster to cheerleader
- ◆ An audience syndrome that may surprise you
- ◆ Opening-night traditions, superstitions, and procedures
- ◆ Problem solving at performances
- ◆ Getting your company through a brief run

Finally, it's opening night! The months of meetings, rehearsals, and dramas have all led up to this. Don't be surprised if a generous dose of bemused exhaustion blurs your sense of accomplishment. Like the lyric says, "you've been through the mill." But despite all the trials, you're still in one piece. If you've made it this far, take heart—the show is going to happen. The tough part is letting go.

From Taskmaster to Cheerleader

Performances can be traumatic for the producer, director, choreographer, and designers. After months of hard work, these dedicated people suddenly have to sit back and let go. Instincts will tell them that it's a time for action—and it is, but that action must now be taken by others. If the production team has done its job, the cast and crew are ready (well, as ready as they will ever be) to do this show on their own. As of the first official performance, the taskmasters must turn into cheerleaders.

First-time producers and directors may be a little amazed to see how the first performance day unfolds. You have created a team, which should now be ready to make things happen with little or no assistance from you. This is never an easy moment. Some say an opening night is similar to seeing a grown child head off to college or move out of the house. My advice is to embrace the cliché and "go with the flow." Dress up (you've earned it!), pin a corsage on your dress or a flower on your lapel, and slip into a relaxed, positive attitude. You can do nothing more at this point except encourage the troupe—and be on hand to lend support in case of the unexpected.

Notes for Cast and Crew

In my opinion, amateur producers, directors, and designers should not be expected to give opening night gifts or flowers—the cost is prohibitive, and cast allergies can make the presence of flowers backstage a bad idea. However, it is a great idea for every member of the company to receive an opening night note. To avoid writer's cramp, split up the job. The production team leaders can figure out in advance who will write to whom, making sure to cover everyone in the company. The producer and director should both write to the other production team members. Cards are okay, but simple handwritten notes are best—just a few words thanking each individual for his or her efforts and wishing him or her a wonderful opening. Distributed as people arrive for the performance, these notes can do a lot to convert opening-night jitters into positive energy.

Opening-Night Jitters

You will find those infamous opening-night nerves breaking out all around you. Most people will have nothing more than a case of "butterflies," but some may shake with fright. Extreme cases can feel downright ill. Reassure everyone that nerves are a good thing, a natural by-product of the mind and body getting ready for an important effort.

> **Backstage Whispers** _____
>
> The greatest professional performers suffer from opening-night nerves. When Al Jolson was billed as the "World's Greatest Entertainer," he used to keep buckets in both wings on premiere nights so he could upchuck between numbers. The one exception to this rule was Ethel Merman, who denied ever feeling jitters. She told curious colleagues, "Why should I be nervous? If anyone could do this job better than me, they'd be up here and I'd be out there."

People can manifest jitters in surprising ways, and not all of them are benign. Those who feel unprepared may "act out" in rude or even aggressive ways. If anyone engages in inappropriate behavior, your reaction must be sympathetic but firm. It is important to put an end to any nonsense without shattering nerves that are already rattled.

Setting Up

On opening day, the house manager should be on hand at least one and a half to two hours before curtain time to allow other staff access to the theatre and to be sure the following chores are handled:

- Check (and if necessary, adjust) the temperature in the lobby, backstage, and performance areas.

- Be sure all public areas (lobby, rest rooms, auditorium) are clean and ready for use.

- Check with the box office for any messages.

- Have all ushers, ticket takers, and box office and concessions staff on hand an hour before showtime.

> **Gremlins** _____
>
> It's a good idea to provide some public seating in the lobby. Early arrivals often include people who cannot stand for long periods of time. And there's no point in making your audience uncomfortable before they enter the auditorium!

- Assist concessions with change and handle any problems with setup.

For the house manager, cool efficiency is the goal. Being on time, unrushed, and upbeat sets a constructive tone for the rest of the house staff.

The box office should be set up and ready for business at least a full hour before curtain time. If problems pop up, do not waste time playing blame games—just implement solutions as best you can. Whatever transpires, the box office staff should treat everyone with courtesy. Never rush! If a long line develops, just inform the house manager. The curtain can be held for several minutes while sales are completed.

All cast and crews should have a specific preperformance check-in time. Be sure to include ample time for wardrobe and makeup. The PSM should have emergency contact info. If a leading cast member is unaccounted for at 30 minutes to official curtain time, prep the understudy.

Be sure everyone observes the rules for backstage etiquette listed in Chapter 24. Do not permit family and friends backstage before the performance. Once in costume, cast members must stay backstage. Do not permit darting out to see Grandma or peeking out around doors or curtains! Aside from wrecking backstage discipline, such behavior can ruin the theatrical illusion your company has spent so many months creating.

Superstitions and Traditions

On Broadway, the opening night of every musical begins with the stage manager's announcement, "On stage for the Gypsy Robe." In a ceremony that dates back several decades, the chorus member with the most Broadway credits wears a robe (which is decorated with artwork from other recent productions) and walks around the stage three times counterclockwise, giving all the cast and crew a chance to touch the garment. The robe is then worn into every dressing room, all in the hopes of bringing good luck to the production.

Every amateur group develops its own set of opening-night traditions and superstitions. Almost everyone knows the most popular ones:

- Never say "good luck" to an actor on opening night! Go with a more negative statement, like the classic "Break a leg!" Italians and opera performers use "*In bocca di lupo*" (literally, "In the wolf's mouth").

- No one is allowed to whistle anywhere backstage. Whistles were once used by stagehands to communicate cues, so a casual whistler could cause havoc. This once-practical rule has long since evolved into a superstition—as if whistling will bring down the wrath of heaven rather than a sandbag. Laugh at this tradition if you like—but respect it.

◆ Under no circumstances should anyone mention Shakespeare's tragedy *Macbeth*—unless it is the play being performed. Many of the greatest talents in theatrical history have met disaster in this difficult piece, giving it a reputation for causing bad luck. If pressed, one is permitted to refer to it as the "Scottish tragedy." In England, anyone saying "Macbeth" backstage is required to leave the room, dance about on one foot three times, knock, and then utter a profanity before he can be allowed to re-enter.

Silly as these superstitions may seem, they help people of the theatre bond, marking them as a special team and helping reduce any tension. It is quite all right to let your group develop its own traditions, as long as no harm is done to people or property. Some of the more unusual ones I have heard of include the following:

◆ The stage crew stepping out into the parking lot an hour before curtain time to smash "The Bad Luck Coconut" with 2×4s.

◆ The lighting crew sacrificing a burnt-out bulb in a small outdoor bonfire.

◆ The full cast and crew doing the "Hokey Pokey" onstage just before the audience is admitted.

While encouraging such rituals, you must discourage any practical jokes that could unnerve performers or disrupt the show. Make it clear ahead of time that any small-minded people taking out their opening-night nerves on others will face serious consequences—and follow through if anyone is foolish enough to then pursue such behavior. People who refuse to respect the rest of the team have no business being part of it.

Curtain Time

The house should open to the public about 30 minutes before the announced curtain time. If there are no reserved seats, it is okay to let people "save" one or two seats for absent companions, but ushers should overrule those who try to single-handedly commandeer an entire row.

The performance may be scheduled for 8 P.M., but that does not mean the curtain should go up at that exact time. At the official time, the house manager and PSM should confer on readiness. Hold the curtain if there is any delay in seating the audience. It is standard procedure at professional performances to give audiences a brief grace period, holding all curtains for a minimum of five minutes. In case of rain or snow, the wait is increased to 10 minutes—up to 30 for severe conditions.

However, short of a real emergency (see "Acts of God," later in this chapter), there is no reasonable excuse for holding a curtain beyond a quarter of an hour. Amateur performances are infamous for holding curtains up to an hour, usually as the result of sloppy planning. Don't let your group get into this appalling habit! The people in your audiences have lives (baby-sitters to pay, pets to walk, etc.), and it is not reasonable to hold up their schedules more than a few minutes.

The Speech

Just before opening the house to the public, the director should gather the full company onstage for a preperformance pep talk. This speech is a hallowed part of opening nights and can take various forms. I suggest keeping it brief, five minutes or less. A few sincere, upbeat words of affection and encouragement are all that is needed. It's too late to give notes, and this is not the time to thank specific people. Keep your comments aimed at the entire company, reinforcing the sense that this is a great moment to be enjoyed, rather than feared.

> **On Stage**
>
> On opening nights, director-choreographer Tommy Tune has his casts stand in a gigantic circle onstage, all holding hands to form a "circuit" of common energy—a great nondenominational approach now used by many amateur companies.

A great final touch can be to end by having everyone join hands for a moment of silence—or ending with a cheer like athletes before the big game. If it is appropriate to your group, a brief prayer is a great idea.

Once the speech is over, the director should leave the backstage area and join the audience. Now, like it or not, it is time to let go and let the company do what you've prepared it to do.

Preshow Announcements

The director and producer have no business making preperformance speeches to the audience. They have come to see a show, not to hear an oration. The stage manager or a member of the cast should make the brief preshow announcements that have become a tradition in recent years. Instead of trotting someone onstage, an invisible announcer speaking as the house lights dim takes far less time and effort.

I have attended amateur performances where the announcements droned on for a full five minutes or more. Yikes! Keep it brief. On Broadway, this process is handled in a minute or less, and your company should have no trouble doing it in the same amount of time. The only points that need to be covered are …

1. "Welcome to our show" (no need to tell them which show it is—those who don't know by now are past caring).

2. "The use of recording devices and cameras is prohibited. Flash devices can be dangerous to the performers."

3. "Please turn off all cell phones and other paging devices now."

4. "Please unwrap all candies now."

5. Announce any understudies who are appearing.

> **On Stage**
>
> On Broadway, *Spamalot* threatens that the armed knights onstage are liable to attack anyone whose cell phone disturbs the performance. This wins an early laugh and does a great job of getting folks to turn off those blasted phones!

Of course, the bit about candy wrappers and turning off cell phones is so ubiquitous that it has become a great opportunity for creative thinking. Perhaps something like: "Because our show is set in 1912, when cell phones and pagers did not exist, we ask you to turn yours off now to help us maintain period atmosphere."

"That's My Barney!" Syndrome

In *The Music Man*, swindling salesman Harold Hill convinces the people of River City, Iowa, that he can turn their school-age boys into a marching band. Fact is, Hill cannot read a note of music, but all summer long he has the kids humming the theme from Beethoven's *Minuet in G* ("Lah-di-dah-di-dah-di-dah-di-dah") as part of his phony "think system." In the final scene, Hill is revealed as a fraud and arrested. He faces the painful prospect of tar and feathers if the band cannot play. Handcuffed and expecting the worst, he waves a baton … and his ragtag bunch of untrained musicians makes a sound. It's way off key, but darned if it doesn't sound like the *Minuet in G!* From the throng of once-angry parents, a mother bursting with pride bellows, "That's my Barney!" Every mother and father joins in the acclaim. So what if it's not perfect? Their kids are playing Beethoven!

"That's My Barney!" syndrome is quite real. Families, friends, and neighbors come to amateur performances ready to praise. Many is the time I've seen producers and directors cringe at what they perceived as a disappointing performance, only to suffer a shock when a delighted audience leaps to its feet cheering. When this happens, the public is not being condescending or charitable—they are quite sincere!

In all the hoping and planning that goes into a show, it can be too easy to forget one thing: the very fact that amateurs have found the courage to get up in public and put on a performance is one heck of an accomplishment. If performers do not always live up to the director's personal vision, that's okay. So long as the auditorium does not burn down, it's a good bet that your opening-night audience is going to love the show. Of course, if your team has put together a genuinely entertaining effort, the praise will be all the higher.

When Murphy Comes to Call

Once the house opens, the producer and director can greet members of the audience and then take seats and see the show. Many theatre professionals have been known to pace in the back of the theatre, praying for a good audience reaction, but there is no need for you to subject yourself to such torture. You've trained your people well, covered all foreseeable contingencies, and know that your audience will be well cared for. If little things happen (and they often do), let your cast and crews show what they are made of. This is the time to let your well-built production team do its various jobs while you sit back (as best you can) and enjoy the fruits of your many months of labor.

Ah, but the unexpected just may rear its pretty little head, and in rare cases, the producer and director must be ready to tear off their opening-night togs to reveal the superhero leotards underneath. Okay, I'm kidding about the leotards, but you get the idea. The point is, when push comes to shove, they will still need you.

Acts of God

The most common problem on performance days is the weather. Sudden, unseasonable heat or cold waves are nothing more than nuisances, but severe storms can snarl traffic, flood parking lots, and make it too dangerous for ticket holders to reach your facility. The old saying that "the show *must* go on" is a lot of hogwash. If it is clear that conditions are impossible and people will have trouble making it to your show, you may have to cancel a performance. If the unthinkable happens and your area is struck with destructive weather or some other form of natural disaster, be realistic and put off your show until another date.

Facility emergencies can also delay or force cancellation of a performance. Burst pipes, power failures, fires—anything that creates unsafe conditions for the audience, cast, or crew cannot be overlooked. Something as simple as a failed furnace can make a performance space unusable, depending on the time of year.

On Stage

When a power failure struck Broadway in 1960, a performance of *The Sound of Music* went on as Mary Martin and the rest of the cast carried flashlights to illuminate their faces. Power was restored after half an hour, and the performance resumed with normal lighting, but Martin felt the audience was reluctant to switch from what had been such a unique theatrical experience.

In the House

I think it fair to say that 99.9 percent of theatregoers are out to have a good time—but that leftover fraction can be real doozies. The misbehavior of a few can drive other reasonable theatregoers into a rage. If the ushers and house manager politely discourage poor behavior, most offenders will cooperate. Seat latecomers during a scene change or comparable break in the action—never during intimate dialogue or solo ballad.

Real problems begin when someone with a grudge tries to disrupt a performance or a ticket holder is intoxicated. These obstreperous lunkheads can usually be escorted out without too much fuss, but be prepared to step in if things reach the crisis stage. Some will require cajoling, others the classic "bum's rush"—judge such situations as best you can. If your security person has some experience as a barroom bouncer, it may come in handy.

On Stage

Whenever a flashbulb went off in mid-performance, actress Katherine Hepburn would stop the show, plant herself front and center, and angrily demand, "Who flashed that bulb?" After pointing out that such behavior endangered the actors, Hepburn would refuse to resume the show until the offender was removed from the theatre. Instead of being annoyed, supportive audiences cheered on Hepburn every time.

Then there are those parents who must have a full photographic record of their little darling's performance. It is easy to overlook those who discreetly videotape a bit of action here and there, but flashbulbs pose a genuine threat to those onstage. I can tell you from personal experience that a flash from the audience can momentarily blind performers. Imagine being onstage and unable to see where you are going—it can be terrifying! If audience members refuse to curb their shutterbug activities, escort them from the premises.

We live in an age of terrorism, and it is not unheard of for nutcases to call in bomb threats to theatres just before showtime. Do not let such events rattle you or your team—they have happened for decades and are rarely anything more than annoying pranks. However, take no chances. If you receive a bomb threat, call in the authorities, and be sure they search the facility before trying to go on with a performance.

Behind the Scenes

Aside from the jittery nerves discussed earlier in this chapter, all sorts of dramas can develop backstage, unseen by audiences but all too real for those suffering souls who must get the show on. Actors get locked in dressing rooms, costumes fall apart— every amateur performer will have tales of behind-the-scenes nightmares. The producer and director should let the PSM, cast, and crews handle these problems and only step in if it is necessary.

On the Stage

Most amateur productions do not have a prompter during performances. Let your cast know they are on their own and must make the best of whatever happens. Even the most inexperienced performers can prove resourceful in a pinch. So take it for granted that lines will be flubbed and cues missed—and that the cast will handle those flubs with some adroit improvisations.

On Stage

Improvisation can be used to save the day. Actor Otis Skinner was in a play that called for him to pick up a gun off a table and shoot someone. He came onstage one night to find that the stage manager had forgotten to provide the gun. With no other likely weapons in sight, Skinner gave his victim a swift kick in the rear end and explained to the confused audience, "Luckily, the tip of me boot is poisoned!" To prevent such moments, actors would do well to double-check the placement of their props before curtain time.

Curtain Speeches

Audiences hate being forced to sit through prolonged curtain speeches, listening to an endless list of people receiving thanks for their efforts. However, such speeches are a hallowed theatrical tradition, and attention must be paid. If someone has to give a curtain speech, just be sure he only gives it one time! Some groups fall into the tedious habit of following every performance with a curtain speech, and I find that unthinkable. Limit your company's curtain speech to opening or closing night (an easy decision if you are giving just one public performance!), or better still, save any speeches for the cast party.

The post–curtain call thank yous should begin with a leading actor speaking on behalf of the cast, then introducing either the producer or director for a few words. And I mean a few! After a performance, emotions run high, and tongues can babble on without the guidance of a script, so I strongly advise that these remarks be written out ahead of time.

Postperformance Cleanup

Once the curtain comes down, everyone will be anxious to head off with family and friends to celebrate a job well done, but that job is not quite done yet! If you are giving only one performance in a particular space, your team may have to strike set immediately. (You will find this subject covered in detail in Chapter 26.) However, even if you are giving additional performances in the same space, your team needs to clean up every time.

The secret to a quick postshow cleanup lies in the old adage, "Many hands make light work":

◆ The entire front-of-house staff must take part in cleaning up the lobby and storing supplies.

◆ All ushers must lend a hand picking up abandoned programs and other litter in the audience area.

◆ Every member of the stage crew has to take part in re-setting the stage and backstage areas for the next performance.

◆ The entire cast must see to it that costumes, props, and makeup are stored away and that all dressing areas are left in decent condition.

Please note that dressing rooms can be a particular challenge. Crews accept cleanup as part of their jobs, but actors often expect their backstage spaces to take care of themselves. The director must make it clear that the costume and prop crews are not there to play housemaid! Each cast member is responsible for any costumes, accessories, and props he or she uses. These items must be returned to the appropriate crews, and any damage must be reported to the appropriate people.

After the cleanup, someone in a position of authority must be assigned to close the facility. All public and backstage areas must be checked and cleared of people. (It is astounding how many folks love to hang around after performances!) This includes checking that everyone has left the building before locking up—so it's a good idea to have a team of intrepid volunteers (working in pairs) to lend a hand with this process. The house manager should maintain a lost and found for any personal articles left behind by the audience.

The Least You Need to Know

- ◆ On opening night, present a note of thanks to every member of the cast and crew before showtime.

- ◆ Jitters are actually a good sign that people are on edge and ready to give their best.

- ◆ It is customary to begin a performance 5 to 15 minutes after the announced curtain time. Anything later than that can be a major inconvenience to the audience.

- ◆ Know and respect the traditions and superstitions connected with opening nights—they help a company bond.

- ◆ Handle unexpected problems as calmly as possible, and trust your audience! Remember that people are coming to enjoy your show.

- ◆ Follow every performance with a quick but thorough cleanup.

26

What's Next?: "After the Ball Is Over"

In This Chapter

- Getting through a multi-performance run
- Cleaning up after the last performance
- Throwing a cast party
- Holding a postmortem
- Considering the future

Did you think everything ended with the final curtain? Well, as a famous witch once put it, "Our little party is just beginning!" There are plenty of important tasks still ahead for the producer and director, from cleanup to cast parties ... to planning your next show.

Surviving a Run

After a successful opening, a "Hey, this is a piece of cake" attitude can set in. Folks who were hours early the first night may barely make it in on time for the third. Both cast and crew may become lax about safety precautions. This becomes more pronounced when a run goes beyond a single weekend. To survive a run unscathed, the PSM and house manager must show real determination, running complete safety checks before every performance and insisting on a proper cleanup afterward. When it comes to safety, there can be no slacking!

Because most amateur productions have no more than a handful of public performances, there is normally no problem keeping everyone motivated—the presence of audiences tends to provide plenty of focus! To guarantee that performances will not become ragged during multi-week runs, the producer and director can schedule a midweek pickup rehearsal. No orchestra is needed—just the cast (with piano, if it's a musical) running through the entire show or at the very least the most demanding scenes.

However, multiple performances can give some people more time to play practical jokes on their colleagues, to "break the monotony." While you cannot hope to outlaw such silliness altogether, make it clear to everyone in the company that pranks must never interfere with anyone's ability to give a good performance and must never, under any circumstances, disrupt a performance.

A case in point: on the closing night of a college production of *Man of La Mancha*, several ladies of the ensemble decided to spike a prop stew that the leading man had to taste—with a liberal dose of laxative. The lead was a great guy, well liked by the entire cast—the girls were just bored and looking for a "good laugh." That "laugh" could have spelled disaster for someone whose demanding role kept him onstage for all but a few brief scenes. As a supporting player, I had no qualms about warning Don Quixote as to what awaited him. He kept the infused stew well away from his lips, turning his head from the audience to mask his cautious "tasting." The jokesters were disappointed, but the audience was not.

A note on costumes: perspiration and makeup are facts of theatrical life. On Broadway, union rules require that all costumes be cleaned on a daily basis. While this may not be feasible or necessary for your production, the costumes crew should be sure all costumes are neatly stored after each performance and repaired or spot cleaned as needed. If your company is staging more than one weekend's worth of performances, clean all costumes before the run resumes.

During any break between performances, store all costumes and props in a secure space. If space is not available, the costume and prop teams should have plans to take items home for safekeeping.

Strike Set: Cleanup Time

The good news about strike set is that it takes far less time to take down and demolish a production than it does to put one together. The bad news is that the process can be a little sad, as people see months of hard work disappear into nothing more than memory. Strike set can also be something of a hassle, especially if it has to occur immediately after your final performance. In some cases, amateur groups can finagle a few days to clear everything away, but get it done before enthusiasm wanes. Be sure your PSM and the various crews will be on hand in full force to make the work fly.

Set Elements

With set elements, the stage crew has several options:

◆ If storage space is available, save reusable solid items (such as cubes, flats, doors, windows, and stairs).

◆ Dismantle oversized solid elements, and store the raw materials (lumber, plywood, etc.) for reuse.

◆ Roll and store backdrops (folding ruins most drop fabrics).

◆ Arrange for the safe and legal disposal of all nonreusable materials.

Too often, amateur productions do not give a thought to this process until it's too late to arrange for sufficient dumpsters or storage space. So the producer and PSM must plan ahead. Be certain to store or dispose of paint and other chemicals in accordance with any local regulations.

On Stage

There is no shame in reusing set elements. Paper Mill Playhouse in New Jersey is one of the most popular regional companies in the United States. They have a handsome set of faux marble pillars with gold trim that were designed for a 1996 production of *The Merry Widow*. They have reused them in various productions and leased them out to other companies for the better part of a decade. Amateur companies can also make a pretty penny leasing out durable props, such as the "Audrey 2" plant puppets used in *Little Shop of Horrors*.

Lighting and Sound Equipment

Lighting and sound equipment is valuable, so return it to the original owners or store it with great care. Because most of these items are so bulky, theft is rare, but it is amazing how easily they can be misplaced. Volunteers often move on in life, and their knowledge goes with them. I have worked on many amateur productions where the crew "discovered" forgotten equipment that had been languishing in a closet or crawl space since heaven knows when. Have crews document the contents of all storage areas, and be sure copies of the resulting lists can be accessed as needed—by the group, facility managers, administrators, etc.

Costumes and Props

Clean and return all rented or borrowed costumes and props, again in a timely manner. Few amateur companies have the space to store more than a few such items from year to year, but it would be a great mistake to toss it all away. If possible, encourage cast and crew to keep items constructed for the production. Do people really hold onto these things? Well, after more than three decades, props from my college shows still fill a shelf in my home office—including a silver tree branch from *Camelot* and a writing tablet I used as the padre in *Man of La Mancha.* These items will never mean much to anyone else, but I wouldn't trade them for the world.

Scripts and Scores

Collect, clean, and ship back any rented scripts and scores to the licensing company. No matter how often you ask the cast and musicians to erase all pencil marks, there is always some unfinished erasing to do. To simplify this mind- and thumb-numbing chore, I advise that the producer and PSM throw an erasing party. Order in a few pizzas, chill several liters of soda, provide a box of good-quality erasers, and call in some dependable volunteers. All erasing should be thorough but gentle—a challenge with scripts and scores that have probably been in use for years. Most licensing companies have very specific instructions for return shipping. Follow these guidelines, and get all materials returned within a few days of your final performance.

The Facility

At the end of strike set, be sure you leave the facility in clean, useable shape. If you rented the space, meet any final requirements spelled out in the lease agreement. Most landlords will be reasonable, but be ready to pay for the repair of visible damage to walls, floors, seats, etc. A school production should take the best possible care of the auditorium and classrooms. In some places, it is customary for productions to leave a gratuity for the facility's security and custodial staff.

Cast Parties

You may have been surprised to find nothing in the previous chapter about opening-night parties. Unless you are giving just one performance, I advise against having any celebration on opening night. Performers have been through a lot in the days leading up to a premier, and worn-out vocal chords that must endure more performances do not need the additional strain of a party. Spirits may run high, but encourage the cast to take it easy and save themselves for the next day.

I find it best to put off the cast party until closing night or, better still, until sometime after strike set. This helps reinforce everyone's understanding that the strike process is a crucial part of the production, not just an afterthought. Let the cast party be the true final gathering of the company, held after all the work is completed and everyone is ready to celebrate a job well done.

The style of your cast party depends on the size and age bracket of your group. Elementary school children can share snacks and sodas, teens will be more likely to enjoy a pizza party, and adults may want anything from a cookout to a cocktail party. If someone is willing to offer his home for this shindig, that's fine, but there is nothing wrong with using whatever common facility (classroom, cafeteria, etc.) is available. The camaraderie and general sense of satisfaction will make the party glow, so you can keep the decorations simple. Put up some photos of the production, and pick music that fits the group's taste. If divergent age groups make music a sore issue, then skip it altogether.

It is not unusual for the producer and/or director to say a few words—especially if they did not give a public curtain speech. Some amateur groups give tongue-in-cheek awards at cast parties—"Best Flub," "Most Likely to Win a Tony," etc. After all the months of shared effort, emotions will get the better of some people, so expect sentimental tears—including a few of your own.

> **Backstage Whispers**
>
> We all know that it is illegal to film, videotape, or otherwise record copyrighted works without the express written consent of the license holders. If one of these illegal tapes somehow falls into your hands, before destroying it, you might want to show it at the cast party. Most performers get a real kick out of seeing themselves in action.

Postmortem: What Worked and What Didn't

Soon after everything has been cleared away, it's customary for the leading members of the production team to hold an informal meeting to discuss what worked and what didn't. This is referred to as the "postmortem," and with good reason. Those who are wise enough to examine the corpse of a recently deceased production can learn a lot. This get-together should include the producer, director, business manager, publicity coordinator, PSM, and the designers—anyone who had a role in using resources or spending money.

Dollars and Cents: The Bottom Line

Begin the postmortem with a detailed financial report. Remember that budget we planned? This is the time for your educated guesswork to meet up with cold, hard reality. What were your final figures for income and expenses, and did they leave you in the red or showing a profit? Whether you are thrilled, annoyed, or just plain flabbergasted by the answers, be honest.

If your production lost money, it is not the end of the world—or of your theatre group. You must take time to figure out the real causes of this loss. Did your team miscalculate costs or expect too much income from ticket sales … or program ads? Certain problems may have been beyond anyone's control. The best-laid budget plans can be thrown off course by unexpected expenses, emergency repairs, etc. You may need nothing more than some additional fund-raising. Depending on the size of the deficit, anything from a bake sale to a generous sponsor may be the answer.

Of course, it's great to find that your production has made money, but don't let good results go to waste. Almost any budget is open to improvement, even one that works. For example:

- Were any of the budget estimates way off base?
- Should the production have spent more (or less) in any key areas?
- Did we make the most of auxiliary income sources (program ads, concessions)?

If you announced your production as a fund-raiser, be sure any resulting profits go to their intended cause. Funneling such finds in other directions, no matter how "well intended," is both immoral and illegal—and yes, people have been prosecuted for such shenanigans.

"What Have You Learned, Dorothy?"

Beyond any financial lessons, the complex process of putting on a show always has something to teach those involved. After four decades working in amateur theatre, I still find myself learning from every production I'm involved in. For first-timers, the opportunities for horizon expansion are vast.

You've learned a great deal about the people in your company, the facilities your group used, and the publicity methods you utilized. Would you do it all again exactly the same way? If not, that's great! It is impossible for anyone to take on such a massive project and get every detail right the first time—or any time, for that matter. Here are some basic questions worth tossing around:

- ◆ Did we miss any publicity or artistic opportunities?

- ◆ Would anything have improved everyone's overall experience?

- ◆ What went seriously right, *and* what went seriously wrong?

Encourage everyone at the postmortem to share their thoughts, but don't waste energy arguing or placing blame—which always seems to land on someone who is not present at the meeting. Once identified, weaknesses can become lessons learned, empowering any future productions the members of this team take part in. Speaking of future productions, this would be a great time to …

Start Planning Your Next Show

The title of this section may send some people into shock or at the very least fits of laughter. I can hear you now, saying, "Another show? Do you think I'm crazy enough to go through this again?" Frankly, yes! If you're crazy enough to put on one show, odds are that you're crazy enough to do it again. If putting on a musical has left you so exhausted that you cannot conceive of a "next time," that's natural. As weeks pass, you may find your perspective changing. You and your cast will enjoy a sweet taste of local celebrity as neighbors, store clerks, and total strangers take the time to say how great the show was. Your cast and crews will start showing the results of the new sense of accomplishment and healthy self-confidence their theatrical experience has given them. I've had former students tell me decades later how doing a successful school show changed their lives, even if they were "just" part of the ensemble.

The postmortem is as good a time as any for people to toss out some ideas about what sort of show would work next time, when the next time might be, and who would be likely to take part. We're not talking about solid plans—this is a non-committal brainstorming session. Here are some questions worth considering when discussing future productions:

 ◆ Did we have too much of anything—sets, tech issues, unsold concessions?

 ◆ Did any departments have a noticeable shortage or surplus of staff?

 ◆ Do we need to expand our talent pool?

 ◆ Do we need further audience development?

The last question is one every new company should pay special attention to. Most first timers will want to upgrade or expand future ticket sales programs. If your show was lucky enough to play to sold-out houses, your next production will need either a larger space or more performances—and yes, a more ambitious sales program to fill the additional seats.

Steps to Skip, Steps to Repeat

You now know what your abilities are and what your local talent pool is—no need to run through those detailed assessments again. Each production calls for most of the steps discussed in the course of this book:

 ◆ Making the decision—are you willing and able to take on this challenge again? What are your specific goals for this next production?

 ◆ People power—knowing your talent pool, you can make a better informed choice of material.

 ◆ Picking material—reserve performance rights anywhere from 6 to 12 months in advance.

 ◆ Facilities—always reconsider your rehearsal and performance space. Are better options available?

 ◆ Equipment—consider what upgrades can you afford in lighting, sound, etc.

 ◆ Finances—plan a solid budget, and do whatever fund-raising is needed.

 ◆ Production staff—know who will return and whom will you have to replace.

 ◆ Volunteers—no matter how well the last show went, you will need to build a new, complete team.

- ◆ Casting—run extensive auditions and avoid precasting. You can never guarantee who will be the best choice for a role or who will have "other plans."

- ◆ Publicity—plan well and reach a larger audience.

One of the unavoidable truths in amateur theatricals is that people move on—students graduate, colleagues change jobs, and neighbors find new homes. Just when you put together a "dream team," events can pull it apart and leave you starting from square one again. The survival of any amateur theatre group depends on its ability to rebound and regroup when valuable people leave the team. As long as your group can stay resilient, it can have a future.

Targeted Fund Raising

Most new theatre companies are short on equipment or would like to upgrade certain items. From lights to sound boards to stage rigging, these items tend to carry hefty price tags. Equipment is not just a purchase; it's an investment in your troupe's future, so it always makes sense to buy the best. Instead of moaning that money is tight, consider some targeted fund-raising. Holding fund-raising events may be appropriate, depending on the amount needed. Better yet, corporate and private sponsors are often interested in donations that cover the cost of specific items that will see long-term use. Knowing that the items will bear an engraved plaque announcing the donor—and that future programs will include thanks for this generosity—gives sponsors a special sense of satisfaction.

As with production proceeds, you must use targeted donations as promised. Be certain that every penny is spent as the donor expects. If an unexpected price reduction leaves you with any leftover money, contact the donor immediately and ask what he would prefer you do with the money. In most cases, you will be told to use the remaining funds as you see fit, but never take this generous courtesy for granted.

> **On Stage**
>
> Professional performing arts organizations have long understood the value of sponsors paying for long-term items. I have seen everything from theatre seats to spotlights to prosceniums marked with shiny "special thanks to" plaques. Many theatres, schools, and sports arenas bear the names of individuals or companies that paid for construction or renovations.

Thinking of Turning Pro?

The performing arts and sports have several factors in common, most notably that almost all professionals in both fields begin their careers as amateurs. Over the years,

I have received hundreds of e-mails from people with amateur theatre credentials who are thinking about going into the professional theatre. Because I made that transition myself, they want to know what it's like.

For starters, professional theatre is a very different place. The glamour and excitement are still there, but the basic environment changes when your hobby becomes your livelihood. Most of the idealism and volunteer spirit that make amateur shows so exciting are gone, replaced by the harsh realities of a workplace environment. Professional theatre has plenty of glamour, but it is as cutthroat as any corporate office and as unforgiving as Wall Street. The stereotypes immortalized in *All About Eve* barely begin to tell the truth. Survival belongs to the fittest, or should I say the most unrelenting. I have seen some gifted people succeed with their hearts and souls intact, but many others have lost large parts of themselves in the struggle to stay afloat.

I'm not trying to talk anyone out of a career in the performing arts, but it's important to enter this field with your eyes open to the truth. However talented or dedicated you are, plenty of others are entering the field with at least as much talent and dedication, if not more. Competition for all theatre-related jobs is fierce (people fight to be hired as Broadway ushers!), and many times you will wind up doing things you hate to get the bills paid. Current estimates are that less than 10 percent of Actor's Equity and Screen Actor's Guild members make their living by acting. Since the 1960s, most professional actors have relied on nonacting jobs—waitering, word processing, etc. It is no easier for the overwhelming majority of professional playwrights, songwriters, stage managers, designers, or techies. And while most people picture professional producers as working in glamorous Manhattan offices, most work from their apartments while searching for a hit.

> **Backstage Whispers**
>
> When a now-powerful British producer was first trying to establish himself, he had his mother answer their home phone, "Cameron MacIntosh Productions"—giving the impression that he had a secretary and a production office. Years later, MacIntosh's resolve was rewarded when he presented international mega-hits like *Cats* and *Les Misérables,* earning himself millions and a knighthood.

If you manage to break through, the rewards can be heady. Oh, the jealous congratulations one basks in when he lands a promising theatre job, or when his latest project wins raves and settles in for a long run! But as more than a few showtunes point out, luck can turn in the "business they call show." You know Sondheim's line about going from top billing Monday to touring in summer stock on Tuesday? I could introduce you to Broadway veterans who wound up bartending between shows, fondly wishing they had a gig in stock! As the old cliché goes, "It's a long, hard struggle to get to the middle."

My years in professional theatre were rich and thrilling times, minus the occasional breaks for tedious office temp jobs and restaurant management positions. Year in and year out, money was tight. Items that others saw as necessities, I had to dismiss as unaffordable luxuries. Vacations? What were those? And while I never starved, I did learn every budget-stretching, tummy-filling trick in the culinary book. (There really *are* a hundred ways to make pasta!) Some of my friends made it right to the top, where they found the struggle to stay there as demanding and relentless as the trip up.

In the end, my advice is this: if the dream lives in you, you just might achieve it, but you have to be ready to give it everything you've got—and I mean *everything*. You will have to slog away against incredible odds with no idea of how long the struggle may last. There are times when little things like your quality of life, personal relationships, etc. will have to take a backseat. Then, even if you do beat the overwhelming odds and wind up as part of a hit, you have to re-live the struggle *with every new project you work on!* If this sounds irresistible to you, then go for it.

When to Call It Quits

As I said back in Chapter 1, amateurs do things they love to do—if you stop loving it, why bother? As in every other field of human endeavor, people in amateur theatre can reach the end of the line. Perhaps a rocky production proves to be too much to bear. In other cases, the enchantment of putting on shows can simply lose its luster. If that day comes for you, be ready to recognize it and to take your life in other directions. Few things are sadder than working on a production because you feel obligated to. If others insist that they cannot do it without you ... well, that's their problem, not yours. When you find that your heart is no longer in amateur showbiz, stop.

The great thing is that you can always change your mind and turn a retirement into a sabbatical. Take all the time you want to get a degree, raise a family, or rev up a business. When you are ready, all sorts of amateur productions will be looking for you to pitch in. And if not, you can go ahead and start one of your own. As Olympia Dukakis says in *Moonstruck*, "It ain't over till it's over."

Exit Music: A Final Thought

It is my heartfelt hope that the advice in these pages has been useful to you. If you have read it all through and are still undecided about putting on a show, I offer you the words of Shakespeare: "Oh reason not the need!" In the final analysis, there is only one bona fide reason to put on an amateur production: do it because your soul demands it. Whatever you decide, break a leg!

The Least You Need to Know

◆ Safety check before each performance and pickup rehearsals between weekends can keep things humming during a long run.

◆ Be sure your strike set process is thorough, leaving no physical or administrative messes behind.

◆ Hold a cast party that is appropriate to the age and attitude of your company members.

◆ Hold a postmortem, where production team heads can discuss what worked and what did not.

◆ A professional career in theatre is a tremendous challenge! Before entering the field, be sure it is what you really want to do.

◆ Work in amateur theatre because your soul demands it. Lesser reasons simply won't do.

Appendix A

Glossary

amplifier   An electronic device that strengthens audio signals.

apron   The stage area in front of the curtain.

arena stage   A stage area where the audience sits on all four sides of the performance area, which may be any shape or size.

aside   A theatrical convention that allows actors to speak directly to the audience while remaining in character.

ASM   Assistant stage manager.

auditions   Formal tryouts for any performers seeking roles in a production; can involve reading, singing, dancing, and/or an interview.

back light   Light that comes from upstage (behind the actor), designed to put a performer's head and shoulders in bolder contrast to the background.

backdrop   A large cloth (usually canvas or muslin) painted to resemble a scenic background element.

backstage   The cast and crew areas surrounding the stage but unseen by the audience.

batten   A metal pipe suspended over a stage and used to hang lights and scenery.

beam   Horizontal light positioned over the audience area.

beat   A specific moment in a script or song; also a specific bit of stage business.

black-box theatre   A room where the playing area and audience seating can be rearranged to suit any production format.

blackout   A sudden dimming of the lights, usually marking the end of a scene. Quick comic scenes in revues are sometimes called blackout sketches.

blocking   The planned movement and placement of actors onstage.

blocking rehearsals   Rehearsals devoted to perfecting stage movement.

body mike   A small, battery-powered microphone that can be hidden in a costume or hairpiece.

book   The script of a musical; also called the libretto.

boom   Any vertical lighting position.

border   A horizontal curtain hung above the stage to mask lights and other equipment from the audience's view. Can be a plain drape or a painted set element.

border light   A strip of lights hung parallel to the proscenium and border curtains, often found in traditional auditoriums. Also called strip lights.

box set   Using flats to create a realistic three-walled room, with or without a ceiling; the audience is the "fourth wall."

breakaway glass   Imitation glass that smashes safely.

bump buttons   Lighting board controls that "bump" lights to full power.

business   Any nonverbal stage activity, such as pouring a drink, dialing a phone, etc.

C-clamp   C-shaped metal clamps used to secure lanterns to battens.

call   The announced time when cast and crew are expected for a meeting, rehearsal, or preperformance prep. Also refers to the signal given to take places for the start of a performance.

callboard   A bulletin board where notices for cast and crew are posted. Can be backstage or in a more accessible public area.

casting   The tricky process of fitting actors to the roles in a show.

catwalk   A narrow metal walkway suspended above the stage, allowing crews access to sets and technical equipment.

changing booth   A temporary booth in the wings where actors can make quick changes.

circuit plot   A map or list of all lighting power sources in a performance space.

"Clear, please!"   A request for actors to get out of the way when crews are handling scenery or equipment.

closed   An actor facing completely away from the audience.

cold   A reading or performing without prior rehearsal.

color filter   A colored plastic sheet used to add color to lighting instruments.

comedy   A play that mixes humor and pathos to celebrate human foibles, usually with a happy ending.

commedia dell'arte   The improvisatory theatre of the Italian Renaissance, featuring clownish characters and broad physical comedy.

continental seating   A seating arrangement with no center aisle.

control board   A panel that controls the dimmers for all lighting instruments; can be either computer operated or manual.

costume parade   The cast's walk across the stage wearing full costumes for the first time.

costume plot   A full list of all the costumes used in a production, broken down by scene and character.

counterweight flying system   Cables and counterweights used to "fly" scenery.

covering   The action of an actor who stands in front of another or distracts the audience during someone else's "moment."

cross (or crossing)   Moving from one place onstage to another.

crossfader   A lighting board control that fades all channels at once.

crossover   Any pass space outside of audience view that allows passage from one side wing to another.

cue   A signal to an actor or crewmember.

cue sheet   A detailed list for technical crews, listing all cues for effects and changes of light or scenery.

cue-to-cue rehearsal   A full cast rehearsal designed to perfect all technical cues, including all lighting and scene changes.

"Curtain!"   This exclamation by the director or stage manager requires the immediate closing of the house curtain.

curtain call   The bows performers take at the end of a performance.

curtain line   The final line of dialogue in an act; also the imaginary line where the house curtain meets the stage.

DAT   Digital audio tape.

dead hung   Any hanging lights or scenic elements that do not move during a performance; the opposite of flying.

dimmer   An electronic device that raises or dims lighting instruments. All dimmers are managed by a control board.

dolly   A small wooden frame or platform on castors, used to move heavy equipment or set elements.

domestic comedy   Comic plays set in a typical home, usually examining the quirks of family life.

domestic drama   A play that examines the everyday lives of middle- and lower-class people.

double casting   The casting of more than one actor in a role, allowing each to go on for alternate performances.

down (or downstage)   The part of the stage that is closest to the audience, sometimes incorrectly called the "front" of the stage.

dress parade   A rehearsal where actors wear their costumes under the stage lights for the first time for final approval by the director and designers. Should be done as far in advance of the dress rehearsal as possible.

dress rehearsals   Final rehearsals involving all elements of a production in a simulated performance.

dress the stage   Using the placement of actors and set elements to balance the stage picture.

dry tech   A practice session with no actors present, devoted primarily to perfecting the technical elements of a production.

ellipsoidal   A lighting instrument that uses an ellipsoidal reflector and one or more lenses to produce a sharp-edged light beam.

emotional memory   A key factor in Stanislavsky's acting method, wherein actors capture a character's emotion by recalling something that caused similar emotions in their own lives.

ensemble   The full company of actors in a production.

equalization (EQ)   Improving a sound by adjusting specific frequencies.

farce   A fast-paced comedy relying heavily on physical activity and visual effects for humor.

feeler   A mailing, posting, or verbal announcement that literally tries to "feel out" any interest in the community, asking people who want to be part of your project to either contact you or attend a preliminary meeting.

flat   A wooden frame covered with canvas, that can be painted to simulate walls or backgrounds in a stage set.

flow sheet   A wall chart posted backstage listing all entrances, exits, and the order of scenes.

fly space   The air space above a stage where scenery may "fly" up out of the audience's sight; also called the "flies."

focus   Directing an audience's attention to a particular performer, area, or object.

follow spot   A large, high-powered lighting unit that can be directed (manually or electronically) to follow a performer onstage.

footlights   A row of low-powered, stage floor–level lights surrounding the apron, designed to provide general illumination. Once common, they fell out of use after the mid-twentieth century.

found space   A performance space that was originally designed for another purpose, such as a classroom, church, empty basement, etc.

fresnel   A lighting instrument designed to provide general area light, sometimes called nonfocusable. These are named for Jacques Fresnel, inventor of a special lens used by lighthouse beacons.

front of house   The auditorium and lobby areas of a theatre.

gel   A small, colored sheet used to change the color of a stage light.

give notes   When a director gives verbal or written feedback to the cast and crew regarding a rehearsal or performance.

give stage   When one actor defers audience focus to another.

gobo   A metal cutout inserted in a stage light to create a pattern or image.

green room   A room or offstage area where performers await their cue to go onstage.

grid   The metal framework used to support lights and sets over the stage.

grip   A stagehand who assists in moving scenery.

ham   An actor who overplays or who upstages others. The phrase comes from a time when stingy actors used pork fat as a cheap makeup remover.

heroic drama   A period drama with a triumphant ending, usually in verse form. Example: *Cyrano de Bergerac*.

hold book   To prompt or cue lines.

house   The area where an audience sits; also refers to the audience itself.

house curtain   The main curtain covering the stage.

leko   An ellipsoidal reflector spotlight that can be focused.

levels   Any steps or platforms raised above the stage floor.

libretto   The script of a musical; also called the book.

light bridge   A long platform suspended above the performance area.

light plot   A written plan listing all elements of a production's lighting system and all lighting cues.

light trees   Freestanding metal poles used to hold banks of lights.

line rehearsals   Rehearsals devoted to perfecting dialogue delivery and reinforcing memorization.

lines   The words spoken by actors; also the ropes or steel wires used to raise or lower scenery.

load in   The moving of a production into a theatre.

load out   The packing up and moving out of a production.

masks   Dark curtains used to hide production elements that are not in use.

mixer   The main sound control board, this electronic device adjusts and blends incoming audio signals before passing them on to an amplifier.

motivation   The reasons behind a character's actions.

objective   Stanislavsky's word for a character's goal. An over-reaching life goal is called a "super objective" or "spine."

off book That golden state when a performer has fully memorized his or her material and no longer needs the script in hand.

offstage Anywhere the audience cannot see.

open An actor facing the audience.

pace The overall rate of a performance, affected by speed, clarity, and intensity.

paper tech A rehearsal where the director, stage manager, and technical designers talk through a show before going into tech rehearsals.

performance area The stage, platform, or floor space where a performance takes place; sometimes referred to as the acting area.

pit In traditional auditoriums, a lower area in front of the stage apron designed to accommodate an orchestra.

"Places!" The final mandatory call given to cast and crew three minutes before a performance begins.

platform stage A performance area raised above the audience level for improved visibility, usually placed at one end or side of a room.

polishing rehearsals Rehearsals devoted to improved pacing and tempo.

precasting Selecting actors for specific roles before auditions can begin.

preview A special performance allowing the cast and crew a taste of audience response before a production performs for the public. Admission is often by invitation only, or tickets are sold at a discount.

principals The leading characters in a play; also the leading performers in any show.

production concept The director's vision or understanding of a play. It keeps all the creative and technical aspects of a production moving in a common direction.

projection Actors making their voice, gestures, and intention understandable to all parts of the audience.

prompt To give lines or cues to performers and crew.

prompt book A copy of the script detailing all stage actions and cues; sometimes called the sacred book.

props (or properties) Items that actors carry for required stage business, such as purses, handkerchiefs, toys, etc.

proscenium The picture frame around a traditional stage.

proscenium stage A traditional theatre space with all the audience facing a picture-framed stage.

read-through A rehearsal when the cast gathers to literally read through a script with no stage action.

reprise Repeating all or part of a song that has already been heard.

rigging A system of ropes and cables around and above the performing area, used to hang lights and set elements.

royalties Fees paid to playwrights or songwriters for the performance of their work. These fees are usually collected by licensing companies.

run The number of performances for a production.

run-through A rehearsal of an entire act or play, designed to improve continuity and encourage a more cohesive overall performance.

satire A comic play that spoofs social mores and human behavior.

scrim A sheer, gauzelike material used for drops or flats, it can be a plain color or painted like a backdrop. When lit from the front, it appears opaque; when objects behind it are lit, it becomes see-through.

set piece Any scene piece that can stand by itself.

share stage When two or more actors share the stage focus equally.

sides Scripts that give only one character's lines plus minimal cues.

simultaneous staging Depicting action in two or more locations at the same time.

sound plot A written plan listing all equipment used in a production's sound system.

special effects Any technical effect using sound, light, etc. to enhance dramatic action.

SRO Standing room only; when all seats are sold out.

stadium stage A stage setting where banks of seats face each other on either side of a central performance space.

stage center The exact center section of the performance area.

stage directions Suggestions in the script for blocking and movement, usually based on the original professional staging.

stage left   The stage area to an actor's left when facing the audience.

stage right   The stage area to an actor's right when facing the audience.

stand by   A warning to prepare for a cue.

standby   An actor's designated understudy.

Stanislavsky method   A popular acting technique created by Russian director Constantin Stanislavsky, allowing actors to realistically depict a character's "inner truth."

static scene   A scene that lacks movement and drive, requiring immediate rethinking and restaging.

strike   To remove a prop or set from the stage.

strike set   The clearing away of sets and props at the end of a production.

subtext   Stanislavsky's word for the unspoken thoughts accompanying a character's dialogue and actions.

tableau   A group of actors frozen from movement onstage, creating a "living picture."

tag line   The final line of dialogue in a scene, or a major character's exit line.

take five   Traditional way of announcing a quick break in rehearsals. It is common to expand this to 10 or 15 minutes, as needed.

take stage   The direction an actor is given to take a more prominent position or otherwise attract audience focus.

tech rehearsal   Any practice session primarily aimed at perfecting the technical elements of a production.

tempo   The overall rate at which a scene is played, affected by the speed of speech, cues, pick-ups, etc.

theatre in-the-round   *See* arena stage.

thespian   An actor, named for the first Greek dramatist, Thespis.

throw away   Underplaying a line or action.

thrust stage   A stage area where the performance space literally thrusts into the midst of the audience and is surrounded on three sides by seating.

top   Kicking up the pace or volume to increase emotional impact.

tormentors   Flats or curtains placed on either side of the stage above the curtain line, hiding the wings from audience view.

tragedy   A play that focuses on suffering, unhappiness, and injustice, ranging from Shakespearean works like *Hamlet* and *King Lear* to more modern works like *Death of a Salesman*.

trap   A door in the stage floor that can be opened to allow special effects.

trip   To fold a piece of scenery to save space, as when a backdrop is folded to fit up in the flies.

turn in   The turning of an actor to face upstage (away from the audience).

turn out   The turning of an actor to face downstage (toward the audience).

typecasting   Casting an actor based on physical type or personal reputation rather than on ability.

tyro   A beginner or learner, particularly a first-time performer.

upstage   The part of the stage farthest away from the audience, "toward the back." Also refers to actors standing in this area, forcing others to turn their backs on the audience.

walk-through   A rehearsal where actors literally walk through their stage actions without rehearsing dialogue. Commonly used to reinforce blocking.

wet tech   A practice session with actors involved, devoted primarily to perfecting the technical elements of a production.

wings   The offstage areas immediately next to the stage but hidden from the audience.

work lights   The basic lighting used during stage crew work and early rehearsals.

working rehearsals   Rehearsals devoted to a deeper understanding of the material.

Suggested Reading and Web Resources

Musicals101.com

Musicals101.com is an encyclopedia of musical theatre and film, with many resources you may find useful. In particular, updates and articles related to this book can be found at www.musicals101.com/idiotsguide.htm. Readers of this book are welcome to e-mail me with questions or comments at jkb@musicals101.com.

Acting

Hagen, Uta. *Respect for Acting*. New York: John Wiley & Sons, 1973. One of the most universally admired books on acting ever published, this is a must-read for anyone with a serious interest in acting or working with actors. An acclaimed actress and longtime teacher of the "Method," Hagen offers many personal experiences from her legendary stage career. While there are many important books on acting, this is one of the most accessible, so it is of special value to those new to the craft.

Jones, Ellis. *Teach Yourself Acting*. London: Teach Yourself Books, 1998. A professional actor-director discusses basic techniques and gives plenty of useful advice for those considering acting as a career. Although written from a British perspective, most of this information applies on both sides of the Atlantic.

Shurtleff, Michael. *Audition: Everything an Actor Needs to Know to Get the Part.* New York: Bantam, 1980. Written by a casting director who worked on many legendary Broadway musicals, this is still a definitive book on how to audition for any form of theatre, with useful ideas for amateurs and aspiring professionals.

Box Office Management

Beck, Kirsten. *How to Run a Small Box Office.* New York: OOBA, 1980. This book contains everything you need to know about running a box office with professional efficiency, presented in 68 pages; includes advice, valuable forms, checklists, etc.

Copyright

U.S. Copyright Law (www.loc.gov/copyright/title17). If you wonder why copyright issues can be so complicated, take a look at the text of the current law as posted by the U.S. Copyright Office. You'll find instruction on registering for your own copyrights and far more.

Directing/Producing

Boland, Robert, and Paul Argenti. *Musical!: Directing School and Community Theatre.* Lanham, MD: Scarecrow Press, 1997. This book is a well-designed, practical guide.

Clurman, Harold. *On Directing.* New York: Macmillan, 1974. A veteran of the Group Theater, Broadway, and the "Method," Clurman offers a solid primer on the art of directing. This has been a standard text on the subject for more than three decades. If you are serious about directing at any level, grab a copy.

Cohen, Gary P. *The Community Theatre Handbook.* Portsmouth, NH: Heinemann, 2003. Here you will find practical advice any amateur theatre organization could profit from.

Davies, Gill. *Create Your Own Stage Production Company.* New York: Backstage Books, 2000. This is an intelligent guide aimed at those looking to start up amateur and professional theatre groups and is cross-referenced for British and American readers.

Filichia, Peter. *Let's Put on a Musical: How to Choose the Right Show for Your Theater.* New York: Backstage Books, 1993. Written by one of the most knowledgeable musical theatre buffs on the planet, this little book gives the cast and production requirements for more than 200 popular musicals, broken down into useful categories.

Green, Joann. *The Small Theater Guide*. Harvard: Harvard Common Press, 1981. If you're thinking of starting up a community theater or other nonprofit theater group, this will give you a sane and sensible idea of what you're getting yourself into.

Grippo, Charles. *The Stage Producer's Business and Legal Guide*. New York: Allworth Press, 2002. Amateur or pro will treasure this well-written guide to rights issues, financing, safety concerns, and more, all explained in clear terms by a veteran attorney-producer-playwright. Nothing can replace access to live legal advice, but if you're starting up a theatre company (or taking over an existing one), this may be the most grief-saving $20 you'll ever spend.

Harris, Paul. *Producing Your Own Showcase*. New York: Allworth Press, 2001. This is a great guide for anyone looking to "move to the next level" by staging a showcase production.

Hopkins, Bruce R. *Starting and Managing a Nonprofit Organization: A Legal Guide*. New York: John Wiley & Sons, 2001. This book is not addressed exclusively to theatrical groups, but is bursting with valuable guidance. I would call this the informational equivalent of a weeklong seminar for a fraction of the price.

Miller, Scott. *Deconstructing Harold Hill*. Portsmouth, NH: Heinemann Publishing, 1999. An experienced stage director takes an insightful, innovative look at understanding some of the most popular musicals. If you don't know how to approach classic shows, these books may provide the fresh energy you need. This volume covers *Camelot, Chicago, The King and I, March of the Falsettos, Music Man, Passion,* and *Ragtime*.

———. *From* Assassins *to* West Side Story. Portsmouth, NH: Heinemann Publishing, 1996. This insightful volume covers *Cabaret, Carousel, Company, Godspell, Gypsy, How to Succeed, Into the Woods, Jesus Christ Superstar, Man of La Mancha, Merrily, Les Misérables, My Fair Lady, Pippin, Sweeney Todd,* and *West Side Story*.

Novak, Elaine A., and Deborah Novak. *Staging Musical Theatre: A Complete Guide for Directors, Choreographers and Producers*. Cincinnati, OH: Betterway Books, 1996. Exhaustive, detailed, and informative, this is one of the best general guides on this subject.

Peithman, Stephen, and Neil Offen. *The Stage Directions Guide to Directing*. Portsmouth, NH: Heinemann Publishing, 1999. An unusually practical, no-nonsense guide, this work is based on articles from *Stage Directions* magazine.

———. *The Stage Directions Guide to Musical Theatre*. Portsmouth, NH: Heinemann Publishing, 2002. Another fine book based on articles from *Stage Directions* magazine, this is a concise, helpful book for budding directors or producers of amateur musical theatre. It includes guidance on picking the right show, securing rights, working with a budget, and more.

Ratliff, Gerald Lee, and Suzanne Trauth. *On Stage: Producing Musical Theatre*. New York: Rosen Publishing, 1988. Here is a collection of informative articles covering acting, producing, and directing.

Varley, Joy. *Places Please!: An Essential Manual for High School Theatre Directors*. Hanover, NH: Smith & Kraus, 2001. This book is a great resource, custom fit to the needs of high school directors. It's a blessing to "newbies" and experienced hands alike.

White, Matthew. *Staging a Musical*. New York: Theatre Arts Books, 1999. An experienced British director gives some solid advice, of interest to directors and producers.

Young, David. *How to Direct a Musical: Broadway Your Way*. New York and London: Routledge, 1995. This is a sensational guide for first-timers, with solid advice that even the most jaded veterans will find worthwhile. The author staged more than 100 amateur and professional productions before writing this book and brings valuable experience to every page.

Fund-Raising

Flanagan, Joan. *Successful Fundraising: A Complete Handbook for Volunteers and Professionals*. Chicago, IL: Contemporary Books, 1993. If your group decides to go in for some heavy-duty nonprofit fund-raising (grants, corporate donations, sponsorships, etc.), this is a great introduction to the subject.

The Foundation Center is a vital resource for any American nonprofit group interested in obtaining grants. Along with offices and library affiliates in various cities, this fantastic organization has a superb website (fdncenter.org) that offers an extensive online library of free tutorials and other valuable information.

Hamon, Norman H. *Fund Raising for the Rest of Us*. Norman, OK: Lughnasa Press, 1997. This overview of fund-raising techniques for small and emerging nonprofits has many ideas amateur theatre groups can make use of. Dig in!

Magazines/Webzines

Amateur Stage. A great resource for British amateur theatre groups, with news, reviews, and more. It's a pity we don't have an equivalent publication in the United States! For information, write to cvtheatre@aol.com.

American Theatre. Theatre Communications Group aims this primarily at pros, but amateurs can find plenty of interest. Sample articles and subscription information are available at www.tcg.org.

Stage Directions. This is a great magazine for amateur and professional theatre groups. You can get a sense of their content and subscribe by visiting their website: www. stage-directions.com.

UK Theatre Web (www.uktw.co.uk). A great place for UK amateur groups to find useful resources.

Makeup

Buchman, Herman. *Stage Makeup*. New York: Backstage Books, 1988. One of the most popular books on the subject, and for good reasons—practical and informative, this book is written by a veteran Broadway and TV makeup artist.

Thudium, Laura. *Stage Make-up: The Actor's Complete Step-by-Step Guide to Today's Techniques and Materials*. New York: Backstage Books, 1999. Full-color photos make this guide easy to follow.

Meditation Techniques

Gawain, Shakti. *Creative Visualization* (various editions). This is one of the most popular books on personal meditation, but includes techniques that can be adapted for pre-rehearsal use.

Silva, Jose, and Philip Miele. *The Silva Mind Control Method*. New York: Simon & Schuster, 1977. This book introduced millions to the power of meditation and offers various techniques you and your cast may find helpful.

Performance Rights: Individual Songs

ASCAP (www.ascap.com). The American Society of Composers and Publishers handles the rights to many classic show songs. Its site includes a great explanation of performance rights, the ACE database to help you determine song ownership, and contact info to help you obtain a blanket ASCAP license for revues, cabaret-style performances, etc.

BMI (www.bmi.com). Similar organization to ASCAP, this site handles song rights for many contemporary composers.

SESAC (www.sesac.com/home.asp). Another song rights organization, it is mostly used for nontheatrical music.

Performance Rights: Plays and Musicals

For a complete, updated alphabetical list of rights holders to all currently available musicals, go to www.musicals101.com/alphinde.htm.

Copyright for Producers (www.angelfire.com/or/Copyright4Producers). This website gives the basics on rights issues for American stage productions.

New Dramatists Guild (www.newdramatists.org). This organization can link you with playwrights interested in showcasing their new works.

StageAgent (www.stageagent.com). This site gives useful resource for performers and producers, with info on shows, role requirements, and rights availability.

Publicity

Mackowski, Chris. *The PR Bible for Community Theatres*. Portsmouth, NH: Heinemann, 2002. Designed for community theatres, this compact volume has great ideas for promoting any amateur performing arts group.

Smith, Jeanette. *The New Publicity Kit*. New York: John Wiley and Sons, 1995. From preparing press releases to planning a PR campaign, this is a great "how to" for those seeking press attention on limited budgets.

Stage Management

Dilker, Barbara. *Stage Management Forms and Formats: A Collection of Over 100 Forms Ready to Use*. Quite Specific Media, 1991. This is a great resource for production stage managers, especially first-timers. These forms can be photocopied as is or adapted to your production.

Ionazzi, Daniel. *The Stage Management Handbook*. White Hall, VA: Betterway Publications, 1992. Step-by-step instructions on how to be an effective PSM are given, with useful charts, checklists, and more.

Technical: Lights, Sets, Props, and Costumes

Campbell, Drew. *Technical Theater for Nontechnical People*. New York: Allworth Press, 1999. The bewildering technical aspects of scenery, lighting, sound, and stage management are explained in terms mere mortals can understand. A wonderful book!

Carter, Paul, and George Chiang. *The Backstage Handbook: An Illustrated Almanac of Technical Information*. New York: Broadway Press, 1994. A superb reference work, this book is used religiously by pros and amateurs alike. This is *the* text for devoted techies.

Glerum, Jay. *Stage Rigging Handbook*. Southern Illinois University Press, 1997. This great book helps high school or community theatre tech teams deal with rigging systems.

Grovier, Jacquie. *Create Your Own Stage Props*. Englewood Cliffs, NJ: Prentice Hall, 1984. From gravestones to grandfather clocks to battle swords—this is a practical, illustrated guide to making hundreds of common stage props.

Ionazzi, Daniel. *The Stagecraft Handbook*. Cincinnati, OH: Betterway Publications, 1996. A member of UCLA's Theater Department put together this detailed, illustrated guide to scenery construction. Practical how-to's make this useful for anyone with decent carpentry skills.

James, Thurston. *The Theater Props Handbook*. White Hall, VA: Betterway Publications, 1987. Here you will find step-by-step illustrations for standard stage props, appropriate for pros and amateurs.

Theatrical Suppliers

All Pro Sound (sound and lighting)
1-800-925-5776
www.allprosound.com

Altman Lighting (lighting)
1-800-425-8626
www.altmanltg.com

Charles H. Stewart Scenic Design (curtains, backdrops)
978-682-5757
www.charleshstewart.com

Columbus McKinnon (rigging)
1-800-888-0985
www.cmworks.com

Drama Book Shop (scripts, scores, theatre-related books)
1-800-322-0595
www.dramabookshop.com

Eartec (headsets)
1-800-399-5994
www.eartec.com

ETC (dimmers, control boards)
1-800-688-4116
www.etcconnect.com

Footlight Records (theatre-related recordings)
1-718-963-0750
www.footlight.com

Graftobian Theatrical Makeup
608-222-7849
www.graftobian.com

Kyrolan (stage makeup)
415-863-9684

Rubie's (costumes, accessories, props)
516-326-1500
www.rubies.com

Stage Lighting Store
631-285-1146
fullstageonline.com

Stageworks Lighting (lighting—purchase or rental)
1-800-334-8353
stageworks-lighting.com

Tools for Stagecraft (tools, rigging, tech books, etc.)
1-877-80-TOOLS (1-877-808-6657)
www.toolsforstagecraft.com

Tracy Theatre Originals (costumes, props, and drops)
1-800-926-8351
www.tracytheatreoriginals.com

Index

D

G

S

U-V

W-X-Y-Z

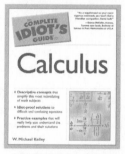